THE
MALTESE
TODAY

Vicki Herrieff

RINGPRESS

RINGPRESS

First Published 1996 by
Ringpress Books Ltd,
P.O. Box 8, Lydney, Gloucestershire GL15 6YD.

Discounts available for bulk orders
Contact the Special Sales Manager at
the above address. Telephone 01594 563800

ISBN 1 86054 080 5

Printed and bound in Singapore
by Kyodo Printing Co

CONTENTS

4

Ch. Snowgoose Kings Ransome JW (Ch. Snowgoose Hot Toddy – Ch. Snowgoose Exquisite Magic): Top UK Maltese 1987, Reserve Top winning Toy in the British Isles 1987, third top winning dog all breeds 1987, Best of Breed Crufts 1988. Owned and bred by Vicki Herrieff.

I dedicate this book to all my Maltese, those little rascals who have so enriched my life.

Acknowledgements

I am deeply grateful to all those friends at home and abroad who have so generously helped with this book. It would be impossible to say 'thank you' individually. However, I owe a special thanks to David, my patient husband, to Chris Ripsher for tirelessly helping with research, proof-reading, and all the line drawings, to Philippa Godfrey, B. Vet. Med., my 'one in a million' vet, to Dorothy McCabe, whose selfless caring for the breed knows no bounds, to Hartwig Drossard whose research and support has been so much appreciated, and to all those who sent photographs of their lovely dogs for us to enjoy.

Introduction

WHAT IS A MALTESE?

A Maltese is a spirited and courageous little dog, with a proud lineage stretching back to pre-Christian times – a dog that is quite unique, as a glance at the Breed's illustrious history will confirm. This is a gentle, kind breed, the loyal companion of Nobility throughout the ages. Long-lived, tough, with a big heart and very protective. What more could you ask for?

This bundle of fun is, first and foremost, a companion and has been so to mankind over the centuries, a task readily fulfilled to this very day. This is an eye-catching dog who commands your attention – standing less than ten inches in height to the shoulders, with dark sparkling eyes contrasting beautifully with the long silky pure white coat and jauntily plumed tail. The Maltese is an animated dog, with a sense of humour, always ready to enjoy a walk, yet just as happy to romp in a garden or lie quietly at an owner's side.

Here is a dog that offers enormous affection, content to be with the family whether they reside in a castle or a flat. It is a dog with a difference, referred to in the past as a 'comfort' dog, with properties for healing – a belief readily confirmed by some today. Alert, with acute hearing, the Maltese stands guard, warning of approaching strangers in no uncertain manner.

Photographs of the breed usually depict them in their most glamorous show pose, with every hair

The irresistible charm of Maltese puppies, illustrated by these pups of Villarose breeding.

The glamorous adult Maltese: Ch. Villarose Mischief Maker (Ch. Snowgoose Valient Lad – Snowgoose Calipso Magic of Villarose). Top Maltese Bitch 1988.

immaculately coiffured. Not for long! Disguised under that gorgeous flowing white mantle is a fun-loving clown. At home, the beautifully groomed and demure dog can, in a trice, turn into a ball of unlimited energy, demanding attention to race and play; but can then, just as quickly, settle down, snuggling closely into your body, quietly revelling in the pleasure of just being with you.

This is a breed that is trusting and slow to anger, a wonderful companion for the older, sensible child who would thoroughly enjoy the buoyant personality, but unsuitable for the very young who would, quite naturally, be drawn to the cuddly appearance, unaware that a small dog is vulnerable and at risk if dropped or if left on a high perch.

The Maltese does not have a twice-yearly moult. However, time must be set aside for regular daily grooming as this is essential, and a Maltese should not be chosen unless such careful attention can be guaranteed. This may sound daunting but, in reality, it is a relaxing and even therapeutic task, with a rewarding result.

If you are the right person for a Maltese you will never regret the decision to become an owner of this delightful Breed which, with the exception of presentation in the show ring today, has virtually remained unchanged over thousands of years.

My own life has been greatly enriched by owning many Maltese over the years since acquiring my first in the early 1960s. I would not have believed that such small dogs could be so captivating. My fascination with the breed started with my original little bitch who, by chance, introduced me to the heady world of 'show dogs' and on through many exciting adventures, including winning the Toy Group at Crufts, up to today. All my Maltese were, and many still are, my loving companions. My hope now is that some of the experiences and lessons learned along the way, and discussed in this book, will contribute to the pleasure of caring for your own, very special, Maltese.

Chapter One

THE HISTORY OF THE MALTESE

The little Maltese is one of the most beautiful of all the toy dogs, with a rich and exciting history, and devoted followers from all walks of life. Few breeds have enjoyed such affection and admiration over so long a period.

The Maltese is acknowledged as one of the oldest breeds of dog, clearly identifiable over hundreds of years. The beauty and lovely nature of these small dogs has been acclaimed from pre-Christian times by poets and artists alike. A model of a Maltese, presumed to be a child's toy going back as far as 8,000 BC, has been found in excavations, and it has been written that Charles Darwin placed the origin of the breed at 6000 BC; certainly there is an excellent likeness depicted on a Greek vase dated around 500 years before Christ.

ORIGINS

It would be easy to assume that, with many references occurring over this incredible length of time, the place of the little dog's origin would be well established, but this is not so. Early writings alluded to them as Melitaie Dogs: this is said to be the name given to them by the Romans and Greeks and derived from the Island of Melita, an earlier name for Malta itself, yet Strabo (AD25) writes: "There is a town in Sicily called Melita, whence are exported many beautiful dogs, called Canes Melitei". However, there is no doubt that, at that time, Malta was a thriving trading post and celebrated as a highly civilised country.

There is a thought-provoking reference in the first edition of Virginia Leitch's excellent book *The Maltese Dog* which reads: "Greek and Roman history is not an ancient one. The Greeks were barbarians at the time ancient civilisations were flourishing in Egypt, and it was not until 1600 BC that Cretan civilisation spread to the Greek peninsula."

Sculpture dating back to 2000-1500 BC, on display in an Egyptian Museum. It bears a distinct resemblance to the Maltese.

In fact there are many examples of very early Egyptian artefacts depicting dogs, some of which appear to be Maltese. So could the place of origin be in fact the East? It is known that there was an active commercial lifeline from this part of the world into Europe, and there are several accounts of ancient Egyptian scrolls depicting Maltese in everyday life. Effigies of long-haired dogs with flowing ears and curving tails have also occasionally been unearthed during Egyptian diggings. George Jennison wrote in *Animals for Show and Pleasure in Ancient Rome*: "Small pet-dogs which were common in Imperial Italy, were probably often of the Maltese kind, which for centuries had been popular in Egypt and Greece." Mrs Hunter, owner of the famous Gissing Maltese, was convinced there were grounds for believing that the Maltese originated in the Gobi Desert. It was her belief that the ancestors of the dogs of today lived in a hot climate. She believed their extreme love of heat and hot sun must be something bred in them for countless generations. She once said: "The sun, of which we never have sufficient in this country, is the greatest friend and benefactor to these little 'dogs of Ra'."

GIFTS AND BARTER

China saw the introduction of the Melitaie dogs during the first century and it appears the Maltese was a well-travelled fellow, used as barter for the exotic Chinese silk, so sought after by the nobility of Greece and Rome at a time when "a pound of silk was estimated not inferior to a pound of gold" (*The Jewels of Women* by Miss M. Iveria published by the British Maltese Club).

It would be easy to imagine how the Maltese travelled from country to country via the silk routes from Asia. Small, exotic dogs, particularly white ones, were often given as diplomatic gifts to royalty, along with rare fabrics and jewels, displaying the esteem in which these little souls were held.

In his book *The Dog,* published in 1872, the author Indstone writes: "The Maltese has probably been a domestic pet for more centuries than any other specimen of the dog family. There is little doubt that he was a favourite with the ladies of ancient Greece, and imported by their nation as one of the luxuries of the rich; and I myself have seen a very good model of the head of one of these little animals carved upon a knife or dagger handle by no 'prentice hand, and of the date of the Grecian Empire."

At the time of publication, it was Indstone's opinion that you would be hard pressed to find a Maltese in Malta. He draws attention to the fact that the specimen engraved to illustrate the work of Stonehenge, the pen-name of the writer J.H. Walsh, was derived from dogs imported from Manilla. In fact Indstone had, on several occasions, himself seen average examples of the breed but these had come from the West Indies. One commentator jested: "Indeed they are quite as uncommon in Malta as an honest gondolier."

Indstone relates the following delightful cameo: "Maltese, as they are called, are frequently brought to the shore for sale, or held up to passengers by the owners of shore boats, but they are simply long-haired little wretches, washed, starched, and combed out with all the "Buy a dawg, marm?" dexterity of Regent Street or St. Martin's Lane."

Even the London of today pays tribute to the little dogs of Malta – and in a very special but accessible place, the grounds of The Tower of London no less. If you have the opportunity, seek out the White Tower where, at its base, you will find a splendid Bronze Gun, probably Flemish, and dated 1607, the carriage being English and dated 1827. This gun was brought to England from Malta some time after 1800. It is lavishly decorated with floral scrolls, fruit and cupids, together with the Arms of Malta. The spokes of the truck are formed of the Maltese cross and sword. But what is so interesting is that sitting between the wheels you will discover a very fair representative of the Maltese breed. The associated literature reads: "The Bed is formed of the Dog, peculiar to

*The little dog from
Malta on the
cannon at the
Tower of London.*

the Island (called by) the Name (of) Bichou and mentioned as such in Roman History." Although it is a caricature of a dog, there is no doubt it is of the Maltese family.

Dr G. Stables writes in his book *Ladies Dogs as Companions* (1905): "White is the emblem of purity, and, I might add, of goodness and virtue. Pure white animals are usually remarkable for gentleness, affection and docility, nor is bravery and courage incompatible with these virtues." There is also a delightful reference in Virginia Leitch's first edition of *The Maltese Dog,* explaining that some Chinese books refer to these small dogs as being known by the name of Pai, describing them as "very small short-legged and short headed" type of dogs, which belong under the table!

There are two very fine, preserved, Maltese on display in the Zoological Museum, in Tring, Hertfordshire, and it is interesting to note that, according to the information displayed beneath the dogs, 'Maltese contributed to the ancestral breeding of the Pekingese in China.' Unfortunately neither dog is identified by name, but they are simply referred to as 'Male. Prize Winner 1901' and 'Bitch, Presented by Miss E. Wells'. Sadly I know no more than this.

There was a thriving trade between China, the Philippines, and the western trading world from the fifth century onwards in which, no doubt, the Maltese played its part, for not only were these dogs the prized possessions of the ladies of the Imperial Court of Rome but nobility in Europe came to enjoy their companionship – they were sometimes referred to as 'comforters', or 'shock dogs'. Mary Queen of Scots received her Maltese from France, where it was said some of the best dogs were to be found at that time, and many references declare that it was possibly this very dog that was discovered under her skirts after she was beheaded, and that would certainly be possible with this affectionate breed.

THE ENGLISH CONNECTION

Queen Victoria was renowned for her love of dogs and owned a Maltese by the name of Chico, but the story goes that in 1841 a Captain Lukey brought over two more from the Philippines as a gift for Her Majesty. The journey had taken several months by sea and when they arrived in Scotland their matted appearance made it impossible for them to be presented. However Psyche and Cupid, as they were named, were established with Captain Lukey's brother, who was a Mastiff breeder, and ultimately these two dogs proved worthy foundation stock for the future breeders in England,

Maltese with a Blue Bow: J.F. Maggs, English, 19th century (1863).

Maltese on a Table: English school, 19th century.

Pictures: The Metropolitan Museum of Art.

so all was not lost. C.G.E. Wimhurst, in referring to the Maltese in his book *The Complete Book of Toy Dogs* (1965), states that although the breed arrived in England during the reign of King Henry VIII, he feels we are entitled to assume that this was its second introduction, and he expands his hypothesis that: "as the breed was already popular in Rome when Caesar invaded Britain, the officers of the legions would have brought their wives with them and it is hardly likely that they left their little pet dogs in Rome. Although these dogs would possibly have bred and existed in fairly large numbers, not all would have been taken back to Rome by the families. Those that remained would have been considered useless by the indigenous population, in fact as 'eaters of good food', and they would have died out almost immediately or come to a natural end."

Fortunately, however, the breed began to set down firm roots in England in the early 1800s, as portrayed in English art. In 1839 the Duchess of Kent, Queen Victoria's mother, commissioned Sir Edwin Landseer to paint the portrait of her little dog 'Quiz' in which he was depicted snuggled up against the massive head of her Newfoundland. Later, around 1851, the Duchess once more commissioned a pastel portrait of her Maltese 'Lambkin', and copies of this delightful work are reproduced for sale to this day, illustrating clearly just how little the breed had changed since those times.1859 saw the first dog show established and here Miss Gibbs of Morden exhibited her tiny bitch, also named Psyche, a descendant of the two imported by Captain Lukey in 1841. By all accounts this was a truly delightful little creature, described by the writer who went under the pseudonym of Stonehenge in the following terms: "At twenty months she is pure white, weighs three and three-quarter pounds, measures in length of hair across shoulder fifteen inches, and when in her gambols presents in appearance a ball of animated floss silk, her tail falling on her back like spun glass."

TERRIER, SPANIEL, OR JUST A MALTESE?

Following the lineage of dogs at that time can be a little confusing, for many carried identical names to those of their forebears and sometimes even those of dogs from different kennels, with nothing to distinguish one from another. This unsatisfactory situation continued until the establishment of the Kennel Club in the British Isles in 1873, when priority was given to setting up the Stud Book. It took time, but gradually the breed gained in popularity and Maltese were exhibited at the early English Dog shows under the heading of Terriers. Although there was a debate at that time as to whether the Maltese should be classified as a Terrier or a Spaniel, there was a general feeling that the name Terrier was appropriate, as the little Maltese was a game little fellow and quite capable of despatching a rat or two.

Between 1860 and 1870 Robert Manderville of London swept the board at shows held in Birmingham, Islington and Crystal Palace with his dogs Fido and Lilly. Fido was a six and a half pound dog standing quite tall at eleven inches in height. J.S. Turner, in *The Kennel Encyclopaedia*, published in 1904, wrote that he well remembered the dogs exhibited by Mr Manderville, Bill Tupper and later, Lady Giffard. Apparently, at that time, there were also woolly-haired and curly-coated types which were called Cubans by the fancy. The ignorant, however, often erroneously called them Maltese. Mr Turner was of the opinion that, owing to the limited number of Maltese, it was difficult to avoid in-breeding: therefore, to expand the gene pool, he considered outcrossing might be tried with the Clysdale or Yorkshire. He felt the resuscitation of "so pretty a toy dog" should be left in the hands of the recently formed Maltese Club, as "great care would have to be taken to keep accurate records of any out-crossed made." Fortunately the then Maltese Club considered such radical action unnecessary. It is interesting to note that this club decided that dogs of any weight could be shown, with a preference for the most desirable weight to be from four pounds to ten pounds.

In 1862 Mr Macdonald gained the prize of £1 (quite a tidy sum in those days) for his Maltese dog 'Prince'. He had been entered in the extra class for "any known breeds of foreign dogs of small size, not used in field sports". The following year, 1863, he gained the same prize for the same dog, then described as a Maltese.

There were no actual classes for Maltese until the year 1864, when they were established in Birmingham. Mr Manderville triumphed, winning first and second with his two dogs – both named 'Fido'! It was Dr Stables' opinion, expressed in his book *Ladies Dogs as Companions,* in 1905, that all credit was due to Mr Manderville on two counts: "First he greatly improved, indeed perfected this beautiful breed of dog in England and secondly he bred Fido, a dog he considered contributed so much to the breed." I feel I must include his epitaph to the dog he so obviously deeply admired. It reads as follows: "He is dead and gone long ago, is Fido, but some of my readers may remember the doggie. In his glass case, and surrounded by the many cups he had won, he was quite a show in himself, and looked all a little prince; and Fido, you know, was the father of Mopsey, the Birmingham and Crystal Palace Champion. Of course I mean the old Mopsey; he too has gone to the 'land o' the leal'. Lovely as an Arab's dream of paradise was old Mopsey, hardly five pounds in weight; but what a wealth of snowy coat! His hair was from nine to ten inches in length, and he died at the goodly age of eight years. Died, but he has left a worthy successor in Mopsey the younger."

In the superb book *British Dogs*, Hugh Dalxiel tells us that the celebrated Fido entered the ring for the last time at the Crystal Palace Show in 1878. Dalxiel was the judge, and he placed Fido second to Lady Giffard's Hugh, and before Lord Clyde, a decision which Mr Manderville apparently 'expressly endorsed'. He explained that "Hugh and Lord Clyde are brothers, being out of Madge, who is by Manderville's Fido; and their sire, Prince, is by his Old Fido; and indeed most of the Maltese of any note that are shown are, more or less purely, of Manderville's strain." He goes on to say "On the show bench the late Lady Giffard's exquisite little pets, Hugh, Lord Clyde, Rob Roy, Pixie, Mopsey III, Blanche etc., each more charming than the other, usually proved invincible wherever they were shown."

There is a well-known engraving depicting Lady Giffard's Hugh, giving his Kennel Club Stud

Stuffed Maltese owned by the Duchess of Wellington and presented to the Weybridge Museum, Surrey, England, where it is on display.

Two stuffed Maltese on exhibition at the Zoological Museum in Tring, Hertfordshire, England. The inscription reads: "Male. Prize winner 1901 and Bitch. Presented by Miss E. Wells".

Book number as 6736. Hugh's sire was Mr Jacob's Prince, and his dam Lady Giffard's Madge. Apparently this excellent sketch was made when the little dog was between four and five years of age, and considered at his best.

If you can beg, borrow or buy any of the books mentioned, do, for they are superb reading. These little snippets are just to whet your appetite.

Mr Jacobs certainly played his part in producing good dogs too. Using Manderville's Old Fido, he retained a bitch from whom he bred Lord Clyde and Hughie, and later sold both these dogs to Lady Giffard. Lord Clyde was shown first, then Hughie entered the ring around 1872 and in the years up until 1885 Hughie won on twenty-three occasions and was considered the ideal type, weighing, as he did, just four pounds ten ounces. Lady Giffard later returned the compliment to Mr Jacobs by selling him Pixey who, it is written, went on to win the very first Challenge Certificate offered by the Kennel Club, in 1897.

There is a beautifully preserved little Maltese in the Weybridge Museum, Surrey, who was owned by Elizabeth, the Dowager Duchess of Wellington, widow of the second Duke, who resided in Hersham, Surrey, from 1887 until her death in 1904. It was there that this little dog met an untimely end by being run over by her coachman – while he was riding his bicycle!

The Duchess was an honoured and much loved 'great lady' in Hersham. Among her interests was dog breeding and she had a great many Maltese Toy dogs. Sadly the little dog under the glass dome is, yet again, not named, but the inscription draws attention to the fact that it is fully-grown, not a puppy. It certainly looks tiny, measuring twenty-eight centimetres long and sixteen centimetres high, reclining on a velvet cushion.

In 1902 the Maltese were still labouring under the Terrier title when classes were introduced for "Maltese Terriers other than white, not to exceed eight and a half pounds in weight." However, as mentioned before, in 1904 the first special club was formed and named The Maltese Club of London, thus establishing the breed in its own right, neither terrier nor spaniel, just Maltese.

ANECDOTES FROM THE 1800s

Before moving on to more modern times I would like to include extracts from some writings, not just for amusement, but to illustrate how the breed was perceived in the 1800s and early 1900s. The deep affection with which it was regarded is illustrated in the fact that several lovely animals have been stuffed, mounted and donated to so many Museums. The American Museum of Natural History has several excellent examples of Maltese from the 1800s onwards.

Captain Thomas Brown describes the breed as follows in his book *Sketches and Anecdotes of Dogs* written in 1829: "The Maltese. He is extremely affectionate to his owner, but generally peevish and ill-tempered to strangers." Captain Brown goes on to recount: "Lieut-General Sir John Oswald brought home a Maltese Dog named Adrian, which always remained in the room of the housekeeper at Dunnikier. Lady Oswald's maid, who came home some time after the dog, used it very ill; in consequence of which it took a great dislike to her, and voluntarily leaving the house, took up its abode in the farm, about a quarter of a mile distant. This female-servant remained in the family for eighteen months, during the whole of which time the dog never once showed his face at the house; but the very day on which she went away (a Sunday) he returned to Dunnikier and has never since left it. It would be difficult to account for that instinct which told Adrian that the object of his dislike had taken her departure."

Indstone in *The Dog* (1872) comments: "As though aware of their beauty, Maltese pets are most remarkable for cleanliness and freedom from all taint or smell, but they require washing and combing. Soap is apt to detract from the gloss of the coat, and it should be seldom if ever used. Eggs beaten up in chilled water are generally preferred, as they add to instead of decreasing the lustre of the coat."

In *The Kennel Encyclopaedia,* 1904, J.S.Turner declares: "The Maltese is a very quick and intelligent little companion, and is a beau ideal of what a toy dog should be. The coat must never be neglected. In washing great care must be used in the selection of a soap and the best for this purpose is pure white Castle soap. It is best to make a weak lye and to thoroughly saturate the coat without rubbing at all, by simply sponging down, taking parts of the coat in detail; afterwards use the whites of eggs and a small quantity of Borax beaten up and dissolved in about twice the bulk of water, thoroughly filling the coat with this; lastly, rinse the coat thoroughly with tepid water, either filtered rain water or distilled water is best. Hard water which contains lime is deleterious to the silkiness of the coat. Unless the dog is really dirty, soap is not required at all and the white of egg alone may be used."

The Complete Book of the Dog by Robert Leighton (1927) makes reference to the Maltese: "The diet is important, balancing the proportions of meat and vegetable. Too much meat is prone to heat the blood, while too little induces eczema. Scraps of bread and green vegetables well mixed with gravy and finely minced lean meat form the best dietary for the principal meal of the day, and plenty of exercise is necessary. Coddling is to be avoided. Owners who keep their canine pets in jewel caskets have only themselves to blame if the little things fail to exhibit the intelligence which comes of unrestrained enjoyment of free life. It is well to preserve the beauty of the silky white robe, but not at the sacrifice of its owner's physical comfort and freedom. The best way to keep a Maltese is to give it plenty of open air exercise, to feed it judiciously, and to let the coat be subjected to as little grooming and washing as will serve merely to preserve it from tangle and from dirt. If it is intended for exhibition, there will be plenty of time to get the hair in condition a fortnight or so before the show."

It is evident from the above that great care was being given to the breed in those days.

POST-WAR REHABILITATION

On now to the intervention of the First World War, 1914-1918. Dog shows ceased, and most kennels closed following a Kennel Club decree that no pedigree dogs were to be bred. As a consequence The Maltese Club of London ultimately disbanded and most of the breeding dogs were lost.

In order to re-establish the breed once hostilities ceased, Miss May Van Oppen (later to become Mrs Roberts) set about the daunting task of locating the breed on the Continent, having first discovered that there was not a single Maltese to be had in Malta itself.

Eventually while in Holland and Germany, she found and purchased four bitches who were duly mated and produced their offspring in quarantine. This nucleus of dogs was joined, at a later date, by four more puppies from abroad, so with these, together with the handful of remaining English dogs, once more she and other dedicated people reinstated the breed.

1922 saw six registrations at the KC but by 1932 these had risen to sixty-six. (Five hundred and twenty-eight were registered with the English KC in 1994.) Mrs Robert's own celebrated home-bred dog Ch. Harlingen Snowman went on to win fourteen CCs, a record for males, only to be surpassed by Mrs Muriel Lewins' Ch. Ellwin Sue Ella, who became the breed CC record holder in 1973, holding this position until 1994 when my own Ch. Snowgoose First Love claimed the title.

So it was that the Harlingen prefix was to be the foundation of those early eminent kennels such as the Miss Neames' Invicta and Miss Betty Worthington's famous Fawkhams, and we are privileged to have Betty Worthington as the Maltese Club's President this very day, ensuring all is in good order.It was in 1927 that the Maltese were granted their own sets of Challenge Certificates, four in all, and what an exciting first show that must have been. The bitch CC was

A group of early Harlingen Maltese (left to right): Ch. Harlingen White Flame, Ch. Harlingen Moonbeam and Ch. Harlingen Mystic Moon.

*Harlingen
Sensation.*

*Ch. Abbyat Royal Rascle of
Snowgoose: Top winning Maltese
1991. Breeder: Carol Hemsley,
owner: Vicki Herrieff.
Maltese enthusiasts kept the
breed going during the Second
World War, so that the breed was
able to re-establish itself once
hostilities ceased.*

won by White Madie owned by Mrs Card. 'Madie' went on to become a Champion, as did the dog CC winner, Harlingen White Flame, owned by Mrs Roberts. How appropriate it was that a dog bred by the lady who re-established the Maltese, should win this day.

1934 saw the formation of the present-day Maltese Club following the concerted efforts of May Roberts and the Miss Neames. Their dogs became sought after worldwide, forming the base of many successful overseas kennels.

In 1939 the Second World War brought everything to a standstill once more, with shows suspended for nine years, but despite the loss of one kennel during the bombing, the little Maltese survived through thick and thin, trooping to the shelters whenever the siren sounded.

It was a struggle to maintain classes in the immediate post-war period; however, those steadfast prefixes of Harlingen, Invicta and Fawkham ensured that all would not be lost. Other keen enthusiasts were attracted to join them, and soon the breed was going from strength to strength, being granted its first all Maltese Open Show by the KC in 1965. The Club's President, Miss Worthington, had the honour of officiating and found her Best in Show in Mrs White's Ch. Vicbrita Delight. No fewer than sixty-six dogs were entered that day.

The following year, 1966, the KC gave the club its final accolade by granting them their very own set of CCs. The Dog CC was awarded to Mrs Kirk's Immacula Top O the Poll, with the top honour of Best of Breed being awarded to Mrs Darcy's Triogen Toppet, bred by Mr and Mrs Hogg. The quality of today's Maltese is such that they not only win many Groups at Championship level, but can be seen proudly standing on that Best in Show podium at All Breed General Championship shows, where over sixteen thousand dogs have been on exhibition at the one event.

THE MALTESE IN AMERICA

Just as in England, records of the early Maltese in the United States are virtually non-existent, and the only information available comes from old show catalogues, where the Maltese were included in the Miscellaneous Class. Records can be found of these dogs being exhibited in 1877 so, clearly, they were in existence before this.

The first official registrations in the American Stud Book were in 1888: one was Snips, whelped February 1886, pedigree unknown, and the other was Topsey, apparently an imported bitch, whelped May 4th 1885, also pedigree unknown. The next registration was Bebe, whelped March 4th 1900, which included the information that the sire was named Toto and the dam was called Contessa. Around this time the American Museum of Natural History in New York received three excellent examples of mounted specimens of mature Maltese, donated by thoughtful owners, two of which were presented in 1896.

Slowly the registrations increased. In 1912 approximately twenty-seven Maltese were born and documented, and some very dedicated people had been attracted to the breed.

It is interesting to note that during the 1914-1918 hostilities, when the British Maltese suffered such a dramatic setback, the American stock was building steadily and just under two hundred were born and registered during this period, providing a healthy foundation for those that followed.

Agnes Rossman's prefix Arr was establishing itself about this time, later to become renowned

BIS BISS Ch. C & M's Tootsey's Lollypop: One of the many top-quality Maltese in the USA today.

for quality small dogs that were greatly sought after during the following years. She bred Sir Toby of Arr who was purchased by Eleanor Bancroft, the owner of the highly successful kennel Hale Farm, and this dog became a very influential stud.

These prefixes, allied to some fine kennels, built the breed up but it was not to be long lasting, for there was a gradual decline of registrations until they reached the very low ebb of four dogs bred in 1937, four again in 1938 and one litter of four in 1939, all from Miss Bancroft.

However, the Maltese weathered this decline, thanks to the dedication of a small band of breeders, which included the celebrated Dr and Mrs VinChenzo Calvaresi, owners of the Villa Malta Kennels that, in the 1940s, were based on Hale Farm stock, and to Mrs Virginia Leitch, of Jon Vir fame, whose first dog was Ch. Toby of Villa Malta. The situation gradually improved, helped along by the publicity surrounding Dr. Calvaresi's superb teams of Maltese dogs in the ring during the 1950s.

Virginia Leitch later achieved her ultimate goal and produced some beautiful, small Maltese of exquisite quality by using a retired Arr stud while, at the same time, reviving the Arr bloodline into the bargain.

Fresh blood was then introduced both from England and the Continent, thus strengthening the existing kennels. The following years saw many excellent dogs gracing the ring carrying prefixes that will long be remembered in the history of the breed.

Today, the United States is blessed with healthy Maltese clubs throughout the country, whose members breed and present their dogs to the highest level. This success can be seen at any one of the Maltese Specials held annually, and was demonstrated admirably by the handsome dog Ch. Sand Island Small Kraft Lite, who went through to win the Toy Group at Westminster in 1992.

THE MALTESE IN GERMANY

As is the case with many countries, it is difficult to pin-point exactly when the Maltese arrived in Germany as they were bred without pedigrees of any kind, but it is thought they arrived around 1860, or perhaps a little earlier. Certainly the latter part of the 1800s saw the breed appearing at shows. Being aware of the growing interest in dogs generally, the "Verein zur Veredelung der Hunderacen" (Club for improvement of dog-breeds) decided to name three exhibitions at which lst or 2nd prizes (or places) would entitle a dog to be registered in the stud book. At the first exhibition in 1879, 63 dogs from 27 breeds were entered, amongst them one Maltese. 29 dogs were judged worthy of the first place and 34 worthy of the second. I have no information as to which category the Maltese achieved. Out of these 63 dogs, 28 were actually registered two years later in the Deutsches Hunde-Stamm Buch. Maltese were now being offered for sale to the general public, the price for a "nice couple", in Germany, then being three to four hundred Marks.

In 1881, at the "II Deutsches Hunde-Stamm-Buch", two classes were offered specifically for

Ch. Pillowtalks Peg O' My Heart (Am. Ch. Dodd's Good 'N' Plenty – Chalet Bubblicious). Bred and owned by Monika Moser.

German Ch. Nico von Herzogstein
(H'Lover-Boy von Herzogstein – Comtesse
Chu-Chu von Herzogstein). Owned and bred
by Karin Finkbeiner.

German Ch. Miss Elana von Herzogstein.
Bred and owned by Karin Finkbeiner.
Photo: Kehm.

'Maltheser und Haveneser' and attracted four dogs. Then the following year, three dogs called 'Muff', 'Martha' and 'Netty' were being exhibited in this category at the same show. 1882 also saw the great five-day International Dog Show in Hanover. Here five Maltese were entered, with 'Lilly' winning first prize and 'Tessy' the second prize, and the three remaining exhibits, 'Lily', 'Thor' and 'Pitschel', all receiving "Praise Mention".

It was not until 1900 that the first Stud Book was established, but from this point on, the breeding of dogs was being taken very seriously and in 1902 the Lapdog Club of Berlin was founded, followed two years later with the first issue of a Standard for the Maltese breed, and in 1910 by the publication of the first Toy Dog Breed Register, which was later expanded.

Around 1925 Mrs May Roberts (nee Miss Van Oppen) who was so extremely influential in the Breed, was busying herself blending her recently-imported German bloodlines with her English dogs in order to re-establish the breed in the UK. She mated Harlingen Dolly (Imp), whose parentage was Hans v Rosenberg x Mira v Malesfelsen (and grandparents Puschu x Lotte), to King Billie, sired by The Artful Dodger x Snowstorm. This successful pairing produced Ch. Harlingen Snowman, whose birth on February 17th, 1926 provided the foundation so urgently required. 'Snowman' proved himself to be not only an excellent sire, but an outstanding exhibit, winning over 70 first prizes and 14 Certificates in Great Britain.

Maltese in Germany were increasing slowly but steadily at this time, and around the year 1922 articles on the breed began to appear in magazines and newspapers. The registrations improved steadily over the intervening years, only to fall back considerably in 1939, then decline dramatically during the War. Peace saw the registrations begin to re-establish themselves and climb once more. It took time, but the breed itself returned to favour. In 1948 the VDK (Verband Deutsche Kleinhundezuchter) was founded, taking charge of the Maltese. This club is continuing to go from strength to strength towards its 50th anniversary in 1998, and the past few years have seen stock imported from Britain and America help to strengthen the indigenous dogs. Today enthusiastic breeders have built the Maltese up once more, by fostering a healthy interchange of bloodlines throughout the Continent.

Chapter Two

SELECTING YOUR MALTESE PUPPY

Every family has a different lifestyle, and every breed of dog has different requirements. Let us assume that you have investigated thoroughly the whole matter of bringing a dog into your home, and reached agreement within your immediate circle that the Maltese is the breed for you.

DOG OR BITCH?
In this breed both are very affectionate, so there is not a lot to choose between them as far as temperament is concerned. When I analyse my own feelings, I seem to have had a particular bond with my boys. On the other hand, my girls snuggle down beside my husband in his chair – so perhaps it is just the attraction of opposites. In the end it is very much a matter of personal preference.

If you are not very familiar with the world of dogs you may be asked, when enquiring about a puppy, what exactly you are looking for. You might think that a strange question, because your answer is that you want a Maltese. But there is more to the question than you may at first think. There are dogs to fulfil different functions even within the one breed, and it is necessary to

Ch. Mannsown Special Delivery (Ellwin Royal Encore of Mannsown – Mannsown Wanda Woman), Best of Breed Crufts 1989 and 1990. Owned and bred by Jean and Fred Mann. If you plan to show your Maltese, your puppy must be of a specific quality.

ascertain whether you wish to show your dog, which would mean the puppy would have to be of a specific quality, and would be in a different price range, or to breed your dog, in which case he or she would have to be of sufficient quality or size to justify this; or whether you really only wanted a family companion, and this would possibly be a puppy that did not quite meet all the requirements for the show ring, but would, nevertheless, be a pure-bred lovely Maltese.

In this chapter, we will assume you are seeking a companion, so having chosen a Maltese with a pedigree, no doubt you will feel a certain pride in the fact that many years of dedication on the part of breeders, and a lot of care, has gone into ensuring that the dog has kept true to kind, both in temperament and appearance.

If your preference is for a bitch, remember she will come into season, and be out of bounds to other dogs, for a period of three weeks, twice a year, and this could prove inconvenient, as you no doubt would wish to avoid an accidental, ill-assorted or unwanted litter; but it is not an insoluble problem.

WHEN TO NEUTER

If it is your intention to have your Maltese as a family pet, then you should consider the question of neutering. With a bitch this operation is carried out when she has fully matured, which is usually around eighteen months of age, or following her second season. Then you should wait a further twelve weeks after this season and book her in with your veterinarian, as this is the best time to carry out the operation to avoid any hormone imbalance. It is an old wives' tale to say a bitch should have just one litter in her lifetime. It would be of no benefit to her whatsoever. On the contrary, producing puppies can be very traumatic, and even life-threatening, for your little Maltese, who may be totally unsuitable for the task. Believe me, what she has not had, she certainly will not miss; so, if you don't want to breed from her, just enjoy her for what she is – a lovely companion.

There is not the same worry with boy dogs, although I do remember that, years ago, a lady telephoned me to ask if she could "bring her Oscar to visit my bitches". She felt he was missing out on life as "he seemed so keen on the ladies". She had the impression that Oscar could have just one quick liaison and would then be content. Having pointed out I was not running a 'house of ill repute', I assured her that, if she pursued this line of thought, Oscar would be far from content in the future; in fact he could become a positive nuisance!

There are only a very few instances when the neutering of males is necessary and it is usually for health or social reasons, in which event your vet will advise you about the best course of action to take. In fact, the surgery involved in neutering males is relatively straightforward, and there are no detrimental side-effects. If you have had behavioural problems with your dog, neutering could be of some benefit.

FINDING YOUR PUPPY

Now we have to consider how to go about finding your companion Maltese. Most countries have a Kennel Club who will be only too happy to give you the names of Maltese Club secretaries, and, possibly, of breeders. Also there are many weekly and monthly publications covering all aspects of the dog scene, and these usually contain various references to the breed you have in mind.

Another very good method, and one I would strongly recommend, is to look out for a dog show that is scheduling Maltese classes and visit it. Again, your Kennel Club would be able to supply you with dates and locations. There you will be able to see and meet breeders and make your interest known to them. Just one word of advice: when you arrive and locate the Maltese benches you will notice that preparation for showing requires a lot of work and concentration, so interruption may not be welcome at this time. Wait until after judging has been completed before approaching an exhibitor, who will then be able to give you undivided attention.

However, no matter which course of action you decide to follow in finding your puppy, remember you are bringing a new life into your family. This is a truly exciting prospect, but a very serious undertaking, so do not rush into impulse buying, no matter how pressured, or tempted, you are.

CARING BREEDERS

If you are offered a puppy and the conversation develops into a 'hard sell', be cautious, because this does not sound like a person who cares about their dog's future destiny, and you could find you have been tempted into a very expensive mistake, both emotionally and financially.

Caring breeders will want to know something about you and your family, and will want to ensure that you are offering the right home for their puppy. The breeders' knowledge and understanding of their own stock is invaluable, for every puppy has a different temperament. Most youngsters are very outgoing and would fit in anywhere but, occasionally, there is a sensitive one, who requires a quieter household, and the responsible breeder will seek to marry the right puppy with the right home.

VISITING THE LITTER

Let us assume you have learned where a litter is available and you have made arrangements to visit. If this is to be a family affair, remember that children can sometimes be over-enthusiastic on seeing these beautiful fluffy babies and, in their excitement, they may pressure you into a situation you may not wish to pursue. Try, therefore, not to let them get their hopes too high beforehand. If they are old enough, have a quiet word before setting out, and explain that you are only going to look. Thus, if you do decide on a puppy, the unexpected turn of events will be wonderful to them.

It may seem obvious to say that any puppies you are offered should always be in wholesome surroundings and be perfectly clean in themselves, but sometimes the excitement of the moment

NZ Ch. Villarose Sweet Sensation (as a puppy), winner of 52 CCs, with her sister, Villarose Hot Chocolate. Bred by Chris Ripsher. When you are choosing a puppy, the mother and other close relatives will give you some idea of how your pup will turn out.

Villarose Hot Chocolate and Villarose Toffee Apple bred by Chris Ripsher. The puppies should look clean and healthy, with bright, sparkling eyes.

may cause you to overlook this side of buying. Smelly, grubby surroundings may indicate slap-dash rearing, and, clearly, a poorly-reared puppy could mean you are buying ongoing problems.

Maltese have very small litters, so it is possible that only the one puppy will be available, who will come in, all of a waggle, looking bright and bold, bustling about investigating anything that looks interesting. You should expect to see lovely dark eyes sparkling at you, with no sign of discharge (some do tear-stain the hair under the eye, but this is not the same as a discharge). The nose should be healthy-looking, neither runny nor dry, and, as the Maltese is a white dog, it is easy to check that the coat and skin are lovely and clean, with no evidence of an earlier upset tummy or infestation of any kind. If you do happen to be offered the pick from several puppies, always choose the outgoing one.

Ideally, you should also be able to see the mother, sometimes the father, and possibly one or two other relatives. I always introduce as many dogs as possible, pointing out the mother, the grandfather, a cousin, and so on. It is lovely to see Maltese of all ages being cuddled by the family of a prospective buyer – a family which then leaves knowing the Maltese they want has come from a caring background

PAPERWORK

As with most things in life, a certain amount of paperwork is involved when purchasing a puppy. At the very least, you must be handed a signed pedigree, together with the certificate covering any vaccinations already given. Although you will have been told what your puppy is eating, and the frequency of meals, you should also receive a fact sheet detailing this clearly, as well as a few helpful suggestions on grooming and general care. Ask if the puppy has been wormed and, if the answer is affirmative, note the date and enquire when best to give the next treatment.

The receipt for the puppy is most important. This should show the date of birth, the dam, the sire and, most important of all, any special arrangements that may have been discussed and agreed, for example, about breeding and showing.

Buying directly from the breeder has so many advantages: you see the surroundings in which the

Northward's Good Time Girl, aged eight months. When you take on a puppy, you are responsible for its well-being for its entire life.

puppy has been reared; you should be introduced to the dam and possibly other relatives; you stand a better chance of buying the right puppy for your circumstances because the breeder knows all the little characteristics of her stock; you will be given a complete background, and told when the dog was last wormed and if paper training has been completed. Most breeders will give you a few days' supply of the food the puppy is accustomed to, which will give you time gradually to change to whatever food is most convenient to you.

You will have the comfort of knowing the breeder is concerned for the welfare of the puppy, and will be there to advise and guide you through the early days.

ADVANCE PREPARATIONS

Acquiring a new puppy is very like bringing home a new baby and you have to have a certain amount of equipment ready in advance. Your basic items would be a bed, some nice soft bedding, a brush and comb, two bowls, one for food and one for water, and some paper, in case the weather is not suitable for the puppy to be put out to be clean. The more organised you are in the beginning, the smoother the introduction of this new arrival will be for all concerned.

CARRIERS AND PENS

A most useful piece of equipment is a travelling or carrying box. There are several types. One of the two most popular designs is the open wire-grilled carrying basket, which is excellent for travelling or for restraining a dog but more limited in general use, particularly if the opening is at the top, although it is easier to install and remove a dog from this type of carrier.

The second type is totally enclosed, with a wire grill door at one end and air-holes along the side. Should you choose this more solid style it can, if required, double as a small kennel; some are even suitable for travelling on an aircraft. Such boxes come in a variety of sizes and you should select one that is large enough to accommodate an adult Maltese, so it will come in very useful later on.

Before the first outing in the closed-in carrier, take time to convince the puppy that this is his own safe hideaway. Introduce the cosy interior by feeding the puppy into it with the door left open, over a period of time, leaving the box where the puppy can go in and out at will. If you are giving the treat of a biscuit, toss it to the back of the box. The puppy will quickly learn that this is a safe haven and will not be alarmed later on when being transported in it.

Another useful item is a puppy pen, or large puppy crate. There are times when you may wish to restrict a little one, and later on an adult, either for your convenience or for the dog's safety. It is also useful if you are staying in hotels, as is the travelling box, but the pen gives more room. These can be bought in sections and therefore made as large or as small as you wish. There are those who may prefer to use a crate, of which there are many different types and sizes, some of which fold flat for storage when not in use.

Again, make any area of restraint comfortable and interesting. You will find both the carrier and the pen are invaluable, not only when staying away from home, but also for restricting a dog who is unwell in any way, or recovering from an operation, from moving about too much.

TOYS

Should you ever have to leave a dog alone, whether in a pen or loose, you may find it useful to retain a collection of special toys for use only on such occasions. These fresh playthings help to distract for a while. Maltese are not over-destructive. They should have plenty of toys and playthings to amuse them, particularly the very soft vinyl toys that squeak without too much effort, but keep an eye on the actual squeakers as they can be chewed out and swallowed. I have serious reservations about the long hide 'chews', for I have known them become entwined in the hair as they tend to become very sticky after use.

Bones will keep a puppy amused for hours, but only certain types are acceptable. Small cooked or brittle bones are totally unsuitable, as are those from poultry. Make sure your dog cannot chew pieces off. I ask my butcher to saw (not chop) a marrow bone into manageable pieces and use the centre sections for the dogs. My dogs prefer to have this raw, but be warned – this does result in their faces becoming horribly greasy, so I save it as a treat just before I intend bathing them. It is possible to boil this section of the bone and remove the soft centre, but it is not half the fun, or as nutritious, for the puppy.

Soft toys are tremendous fun. I frequent jumble sales and purchase the outgrown baby toys. These are not only washable, but the eyes and noses are safe and cannot easily be pulled out. They are also very light and even very small puppies can toss them about. Lightweight balls are also avidly played with. These should not be too small, yet light enough to be knocked and bounced around with ease. Avoid the soft sponge type as these can be pulled to pieces and choked on. You will find there is a wide variety of excellent toys available for dogs nowadays, and some of the most unexpected household items can amuse. The only materials to fear are foil, and thin plastic, such as the bags which might contain your shopping, as this can suffocate.

BEDS AND BEDDING

There are many different types of dog beds on the market, ranging from soft, fur-fabric lined ones that you can put in the washing machine, to firm plastic, or similar material, beds which can be wiped clean and filled with soft bedding. I worry about the wicker-type traditional dog bed, as I have seen these chewed, leaving spiky pieces jutting out, which is not only highly dangerous but ruinous to a dog's coat.

You can now buy excellent special bedding for animals which allows any accidental wettings to go straight through to paper beneath, thus keeping your Maltese dry and snug. This material, which can be bought at any pet shop, washes beautifully and dries very quickly.

FOOD DISHES
Turning now to dishes for food and water: the water bowl should be reasonably heavy and flat, to prevent it being tipped over. There is a very good special type that is virtually impossible to turn over, which is very useful if you have, as I have had, a puppy who simply loves paddling. It is amazing just how far a small puppy can spread an equally small bowl of water. The food dish should not be too large to start with, and must be unbreakable, as many little ones simply love to pick up their dinner dish and toss it around. All dog dishes should be washed separately from the household utensils, and you should keep a brush solely for use with them.

PAPER TRAINING
We are not all in the lucky position of being able to guarantee fine weather for long periods, so house training can sometimes pose a problem. In any case, it is very useful for your puppy to be paper-trained, as this saves problems when the weather is bad or when you travel. Try to use white paper, as the ink from the print on some newspaper can stain a Maltese coat but, of course, it can be used in an emergency. It is possible to buy white paper; sometimes butchers will sell you a pack already cut into large squares. If not, seek out a company which prints newspapers, who may sell you the end of rolls or put you in touch with a company that deals with waste paper and they may sell you the end rolls, which you can then cut up for yourself.

GROOMING EQUIPMENT
As it is essential to begin grooming from day one, a few basic items of equipment are required. You will need two combs, one being a wide-toothed metal comb for the body hair, and the other a fine one, or nit comb, as it is sometimes called, for round the eyes. You will also need a pin-brush, for brushing the body hair. It is important to ensure that the pins are set in soft rubber so that when you pass your thumb through them, they are very flexible. Test that the ends of the pins are rounded and will not scratch. A good quality bristle-brush is another necessity. Scissors will be required for trimming the hair on the feet, and nail clippers too. I prefer the guillotine type. A box of cotton buds and some cotton wool should be at hand, together with a small bowl for warm water. You will also need paper tissues and cornflour for attending to the face hair. One final item is a plastic spray-bottle containing water, as you should never groom a dry coat. Keep your grooming equipment together in one place, or container, for convenience.

COLLECTING YOUR PUPPY
Plan ahead when it comes to collecting your new puppy. Make arrangements for a friend or relative to accompany you or, better still, get someone to drive you, so you can give your whole attention to the puppy, for this is a very stressful experience for the little thing, with new noises, new smells, and nothing familiar. The puppy may not have travelled far in a car before, and might well be sick, so take towels and tissues, just to be on the safe side.

If this is the first experience of being in a car, a very young puppy will travel much more happily on the passenger's lap, rather than being confined in a crate or box. Needless to say, you should never drive with a puppy loose on the seat beside you, or on your lap. If you are unaccompanied, then of course, the puppy must be crated.

Chapter Three

CARING FOR YOUR PUPPY

Now you have arrived home with your new Maltese puppy. Again, I am assuming you have not had a puppy before. Here I would add a personal preference: try to collect the puppy as early in the day as possible, in order to allow time for the new surroundings to become familiar before bedtime.

You will already have established the puppy's bed in a warm, draught-free corner of the kitchen, and set a bowl of water close at hand. Also, you will have chosen a quiet place to lay the paper on which, hopefully, the puppy will be clean.

HOUSE TRAINING

The breeder will have told you whether the puppy is, in fact, paper trained or not, so, immediately upon arrival, introduce either the special place where you have chosen to put the paper, or go into your garden, which you will have securely fenced. This last is a must, as a mischievous Maltese can escape through an amazingly small hole.

I well remember hearing of one elderly lady who, having changed into her night-dress in preparation for bed, popped her new puppy out in the garden last thing, but when she later called him to come in, he did not appear. She had to go into the garden in her night attire, and try to coax her rebellious puppy back, as he slipped in and out through a crumbling fence at such a speed she could not catch him. It is vitally important to have any outside area made safe, both to prevent an

The Maltese puppy has a lot to get used to when it arrives in its new home. This is Charity, aged eight weeks. Owned by Sabine Reitberger in Germany.

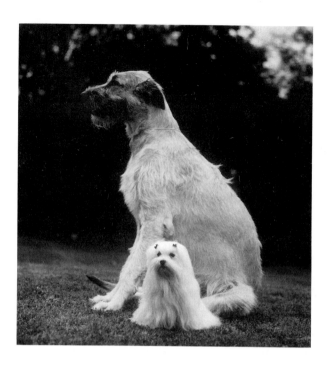

Ch. Snowgoose Valient Lad with his giant-sized friend. Maltese will fit in with all members of the family, providing you supervise introductions.

Photo: Sally Anne Thompson.

inquisitive puppy wandering off, and to stop unwelcome visitors coming in. Even if your puppy has been spotlessly clean in the breeder's home, everything will now be so new and exciting. The puppy will bustle about investigating every nook and cranny, becoming familiar with the new home, so you must expect the odd accident or two. If you have some precious carpets or objects, it would be wise to confine the puppy to just a few rooms while your routine is being learned, and where there is no risk of something being spoiled or distress of any kind being caused.

Young puppies need to relieve themselves quite frequently, so, if you realise the pup is just about to squat away from the designated place, just say firmly "No", whisk the offender up quickly into your arms, and then, as you place the puppy on the paper say "paper". Then give lots of warm praise when the task has been completed. Or if the puppy has been accustomed to using the garden, shoo the little one out, but again praise warmly when all has finished. Never scold unless you actually witness soiling in an undesirable place, as a small puppy will not associate a past mishap with the present moment.

Dogs are creatures of habit. Therefore, if you follow the feeding regime set out by the breeder, which would probably be four small meals a day, reducing down to two after six months, then it is a good idea to encourage the puppy to urinate and defecate, in an undisturbed atmosphere, immediately after every meal. As with little children, some puppies learn faster than others and some are naturally clean. If you happen to have one of the slower learners, patience is the word. Do not expect miracles. Most dogs will relieve themselves upon waking, then again after meals, and of course, last thing at night, but some little ones may also wet when excitement overwhelms them. This can happen when puppies have yet to gain confidence, but, as time goes on, they nearly always grow out of it.

Even if you have a secure garden, as I have said, paper training is very useful on so many occasions, especially if you enjoy your dog accompanying you when travelling.

INTRODUCING THE FAMILY

Naturally the family will all want to pet and cuddle the new acquisition but, at this confusing time, do everything in moderation and ensure the puppy has ample time to become familiar with the new surroundings, or, if tired, is allowed to climb into bed and sleep, undisturbed by eager fingers.

If your family includes children or animals, introduce them gradually and quietly. Get the children to sit on the floor and encourage the puppy to climb onto their laps rather than allowing them to scoop the puppy up in the air for a cuddle.

A dog's bed is a sanctuary, and this should be respected at all times. If told right from the start, children readily understand that the puppy, when asleep in bed, is not to be disturbed, and is 'out of bounds' to them.

If there is already an older-established dog, allow the two to meet in a quiet atmosphere, preferably with only adults present. Sometimes the relationship between the two is excellent right from the beginning and you will find they hit it off straightaway, dashing about, revelling in each other's company. Occasionally, however, the original dog feels displaced and, if this is the case, it is important to reassure that dog and not make too much fuss of the puppy when the two of them are together. Keep those extra cuddles for when you and the puppy are on your own. Try to not over-react if the established dog mildly shows disapproval of a pestering infant. The two will have to establish their 'pecking order' at some time, but keep the established dog's usual routine, ensuring that the puppy is not too demanding initially.

INTRODUCING FRIENDS AND RELATIVES

So, having allowed your little Maltese a day or so to accept the strange surroundings, now is the time for showing off to friends and relatives. In the interest of the new arrival's safety, a little tact may be required here to ensure that those who are not familiar with tiny, wriggly creatures do hold on to their charges very firmly, to avoid a sudden unexpected jump from their arms. You also must make sure they do not ultimately leave the puppy stranded on a high perch from which there could be a leap to disaster.

Children really are very sensible if shown from the start that it is much more fun to sit on the floor to play with a baby Maltese, quite apart from the fact that this is safer for all concerned. Small animals are very quick in their movements and may leap from a child's arms without warning. The little running legs of active children are wonderfully exciting to dogs generally – a tiny puppy could easily be stepped on, or tripped over, and badly hurt.

FEEDING

Start as you mean to go on and keep to regular meal times. Small, regular meals are the ideal. After allowing a reasonable time for the puppy to eat, remove the dish, even if it has not been completely cleared. This may seem drastic, but the puppy will quickly realise that food left is food lost, and after a while will look forward to regular mealtimes. If you leave food down to be picked at as and when the mood requires, you will only encourage a finicky eater. Fresh water should be left down at all times.

There are so many prepared products of good quality on the market nowadays that it has taken all the hard work and worry out of keeping your dog in good order. Diets are available to suit every type and age of dog, and many owners like the convenience of these and find their dogs do well on them.

Maltese do not eat huge amounts of food, yet, because it is an active breed, they usually have good appetites. Initially, you will follow the food and schedule given by the breeder but you may then change on to a different variety. If so, this should be done gradually by replacing a small portion of the original food with the new on the first feed, then increasing the ratio of original to new in the subsequent meals. I feed a reasonably low-protein, all-in-one, meal that is moistened with warm vegetable stock. This then has extra protein added, in the form of meat or fish, according to each dog's needs; more for the active dogs and less for the oldies. In this way I can also give variety. All my dogs have dry hard food to crunch every day, even those oldies with almost non-existent teeth, and they love it.

If your puppy has an upset tummy but does not look ill, this may be due to too much protein in the form of tinned food or meat, and, sometimes, milk can have this effect too. Changing a diet is a question of trial and error. Many Maltese love fresh fruit, and I have a friend whose little bitch brings hazel nuts in from the garden and cracks them open herself to get at the centres. One of mine had a craving for oranges, and another would sacrifice everything for spaghetti, and as for grapes – well, I would only get one in every six for myself!

VACCINATIONS

If your puppy has not already been vaccinated, contact your veterinary practitioner. Discuss the best time to give the first vaccination, and arrange an appointment. At the same time, give the vet the last worming date and take advice about how best to continue the treatment.

Even before the first vaccination you can take your little Maltese on short journeys in your car, just as long as you do not put the puppy on the ground where other dogs have been, or allow any contact with any other dogs, as they may not have been vaccinated or protected in any way themselves.

A word of advice here on visiting a vet with a puppy yet to be vaccinated. Keep the puppy on your lap and do not handle or fondle other dogs in the waiting room. Avoid any form of contact. Puppies always attract attention, but explain to anyone wishing to stroke your baby that no protection has yet been administered and therefore you would prefer they did not touch: they will understand. When the time comes, if vaccination is by injection, hold the puppy in your arms, thus giving feelings of security and comfort, especially if you vigorously caress the opposite end to where the needle is being inserted, while all the time distracting the puppy with reassuring words. Then gently massage the site of the injection. A further reason for holding, rather than placing a puppy on the table is that, should you later wish to show your Maltese, being placed on an alien table and having a strange person leaning over – i.e. the judge – will not conjure up any bad memories of injections.

There are two different methods of vaccination: either a course of injections, or homoeopathy, which is medication by mouth. It is a good idea to familiarise yourself with the advantages and disadvantages of the two methods prior to making a firm arrangement.

BASIC TRAINING

A dog is a dog – no matter if it is a Great Dane or a Maltese, and all dogs respond well to training. In fact, if you start gentle training from the day your puppy arrives, this will lead to a happy, rich relationship for the two of you. It is very easy to fall into the trap of thinking the dog is too young, or just a puppy – and that you cannot be firm with such a little thing. One day that little thing will grow into a big thing and it can become a battle of wills, because Maltese are very intelligent, and know how to twist you round their little paws!

I suppose Maltese respond well because they simply love being talked to and, if they can please you by performing some trick they have devised, this is bliss to them.

I have one little bitch who, if scolded, will immediately rush off to find a toy, then rush back and offer it to me. It has not been unknown for her to drag in a soft toy almost as big as herself,

Maltese will respond to training, as can be seen with this group of Snowgoose Maltese, pictured with David Herrieff.

reducing every one to laughter and making us completely forget her misdemeanour. They really are thinkers and very clever at outwitting you. The art of any training is eventually to get your dog to listen to you and respond, and this is a matter of keeping everything simple and consistent.

A dog that readily responds will be a happy dog because a certain level of understanding has been achieved with the owner. I think this can be illustrated with the simple key word 'stay'. This, of course, would be for the slightly more mature puppy. This key word can be taught by making a game of placing the dinner on the floor as usual, then encouraging the puppy to sit for just a moment or two before being released from the command. Gradually you extend the period of waiting. If the puppy stands up, you quietly put the puppy back into position, repeating the order to 'stay'. You can reinforce the word 'stay' by changing the game, e.g. by using toys or, perhaps, when waiting to have the lead attached, so that the word 'stay' is associated with sitting still until told to move. Always say the dog's name first though: "Benji – stay".

Now, just imagine this same dog being walked along a busy road and suddenly accidentally slipping the lead. All those games may be a lifesaver then. It started as a game, but really you were training the dog to listen and respond.

Maltese react very well to the intonations in your voice. They are very sensitive, and the repetition of certain key words such as 'No', 'Down', 'Come' etc., together with the tone of your voice, will contribute to the dog's understanding of any situation. Nevertheless, Maltese are also masters in the art of taking liberties – so be prepared.

The very fact that Maltese love being talked to is a great asset in training. However, not only the tone of your voice but your body language and facial expressions will influence their response as well. From the very beginning, do reward good behaviour with happy, encouraging words and discourage misdemeanours with firm 'punchy' key words, ensuring you change the tone accordingly. Supposing a situation requires the command 'NO', say just that, prefacing it with the dog's name. Give the key word in a firm but punchy voice – 'NO'. If you use a long sentence such as "Now don't be a naughty boy, don't do that", your Maltese will take advantage of not understanding a word you said.

As time goes on, the key words will have significance for your dog and, if included in a sentence in the correct way, will have the desired effect. Keep commands short and firm – "Benji, No – get down". The moment he obeys, give plenty of "Good boy" praise in a softer voice.

A fluffy white puppy tugging at a trouser leg may be cute, but would not be viewed that way when, as an adult, the dog grabs the back of a visitor's leg. This slip from grace would not be the dog's fault. It would be yours for not discouraging this habit initially. Be gentle, be firm and be consistent right from the beginning, and you and your companion will be welcomed everywhere.

If all this is beyond you and you seek outside help, I would only recommend general training classes provided these are confined to smaller dogs and well supervised. A badly organised class of mixed puppies from large and small breeds can be a recipe for disaster. All are there to train their unruly dogs and it would not be fair to condemn, say, the owner of a bouncy boxer, if their charge jumped all over your puppy in its excitement, leaving you with an extra problem to overcome in rebuilding your puppy's confidence. Well-organised training classes for small dogs can be of great benefit. Failing this, there are many good specialist books on training available, whilst common sense and love should keep you on the right lines.

Once your puppy matures and you have achieved this responding rapport with your Maltese, you can have enormous fun going on to Obedience and Agility training. I have had the pleasure of watching Maltese taken to a very high level in Obedience Competitions in the United States – and loving every moment.

GROOMING YOUR PUPPY

There are several differing methods of grooming a Maltese but, as we are concentrating on your first puppy here, I will discuss the method of grooming a mature dog in a later chapter.

Your puppy may already be accustomed to being groomed, and, in this case, you are ahead of the game and very lucky. However, let me assume that your little one has had a minimum of grooming previously and that you are not exactly overconfident yourself.

Make the whole procedure fun, yet at the same time endeavour to be firm. Settle yourself in a comfortable chair with your box of equipment beside you. Place a large towel or piece of cloth across your legs and sit the puppy upon it. Now, some puppies sit quietly, enjoying every moment. Others just cannot keep still for one second, so if you have one of these, hold on firmly.

Place your whole hand on the puppy's back with your fingers pointing towards the head. Place your other hand directly underneath, between the puppy's front legs, cupping the bottom of the ribcage in your palm. Then turn the puppy onto its back, place between your legs and hold there with your hand on the ribs. At first the puppy may wriggle, and even turn right over again, but be firm and replace, at the same time gently reassure with lots of tickling and stroking. Keep your hand on the chest until you feel the puppy is reasonably quiet – and be prepared, as more wriggles may occur at any time.

Take your pinbrush with your free hand and brush the inside of the legs, under the chin and down the throat – in fact anything you can see, lifting the fingers, or even the whole of the other hand, as the puppy relaxes. When finished, take the wide-toothed comb and go through the hair again, paying particular attention to the area where the body hair rubs against the leg hair.

If your puppy is relaxed you can brush and comb the individual legs. If the puppy squirms into an upright position, just very gently place your hands as before and resume the original position. Do this as many times as it takes to get the puppy to stay reasonably still. Some puppies learn very quickly, others may take several grooming sessions before behaving themselves. Initially some dogs find this an unnatural position, and you must be firm in giving confidence and making it acceptable.

There are two areas where care is needed. First the lower part of the forefoot, where there may be a hidden claw here called the dewclaw. This is set apart from the four front claws on each fore-

This Maltese was sold without grooming instructions, and her coat became totally matted. With help, her owner learned to groom and care for Pepper, and eventually she grew a healthy coat to the ground.

A sensible option is to keep your Maltese in a pet trim. Brie, owned by Laurie Barnett, lives in New York.

legs and sit slightly higher up the leg on the inside. Some breeders remove these, but many leave them in place In a coated breed such as ours, it is wise to note exactly where this single nail is situated and take care not to catch it in the comb when grooming. The second area that requires special care is the tail. The bones within the tail can be slender and easily trapped between the teeth of some wide-toothed combs.

When you come across a tangle, tease it apart with your fingers, *never* just drag the comb through it. If you use the comb or your fingers to separate the knot, hold the hair with your fingers between the tangle and the puppy's body and tease the hairs apart a few at a time very carefully. If you are rough and hurt the puppy you will have a battle on your hands the next time you produce your grooming equipment.

Once the tummy hair has been combed through you can place the puppy on one side and brush from the spine down towards the feet, starting at the tail and continuing right up to the neck, but leaving the head for the time being. Side one done, you can turn the puppy over and repeat the procedure for side two. Alternatively, let the puppy sit on your lap facing away from you, and groom from the spine downwards. Do not just brush the top surface but go right down to the skin, opening the coat as you work.

Remember to check that the hair under the tail is totally tangle-free. This area must be examined every day to ensure that fine hairs have not dried across the anus after the puppy passed the last motion, thus preventing further stools from being released. If neglected, this can result in very serious problems and, in extreme cases, even death.

Finish the puppy off by going through the whole coat with the wide-toothed comb, making a parting down the centre of the back and smoothing the hair down on either side. It probably will not stay that way for long in the beginning, but do persevere.

Leave the head until last. With the wide-toothed comb carefully go through the hair on the top of the head, side cheeks and muzzle etc. Make sure not to go close to the eyes. A good idea is to place your free hand over the eyes when using the wide-toothed comb. The fine-toothed comb should be employed for anything near the eyes. Soften any crusty 'sleep' that may be round the

Abbyat Cinnamon Candy (Ch. Snowgoose Firebird – Snowgoose Nugget) and Abbyat Moondust (Ch. Tennessa's Dancing Flurry of Snowgoose – Abbyat Mint Julip): Bred and owned by Carol Hemsley. If you plan to keep your Maltese in full coat, you should accustom your puppy to grooming procedures at an early age.

eyes with cotton wool dampened with warm water, then remove any debris with the fine-toothed comb. Dry damp hair thoroughly with a section of the paper roll or a tissue. Then, taking a pinch of the cornflour, work this into the hair beneath the eye from which you removed the 'sleep', or any other area that looks a little stained, taking care not to get any in the eye itself.

EYE STAIN
Staining on a pure white face often gives rise to great anxiety on the part of owners, who may then refer the matter to their vet and subject the puppy to various tests, but I urge caution in seeking hasty, dramatic solutions. When a puppy under the age of twelve months is stained, it is invariably associated with the discomfort of cutting two sets of teeth, first the milk, then the permanent ones, with the last molars still coming through around a year old, causing tears throughout this time. Once the teeth have settled down you may be pleasantly surprised to find the tears slacken off, and the staining slowly improves, so be patient. Although stain can be unsightly, it is only cosmetic, and does not actually hurt the puppy. Further reasons for staining are discussed in the chapter on grooming the show dog. To keep your puppy's face reasonably clean, do maintain dry hair. Apply a tissue four or five times a day if necessary at first. Pinch the damp hair under the eye with the tissue between your finger and thumb, then rub until dry. Lastly, saturate the hair in cornflour. This should help to keep your puppy's face reasonably clean.

EARS
The very first time you groom your Maltese, inspect inside the ears – they should be clean and pink. Some puppies may have hair actually within the ear itself; if so, this should be removed to allow air to circulate inside. It might sound a bit off-putting but, if you hold the ear flap up with one hand, you will find you can take hold of the inside hair between the finger and thumb of the free hand. Take a few hairs (a little antiseptic powder on the fingers gives a better grip) and, with a quick movement, whip them out – believe me, it does not hurt the puppy as long as you only

remove a few each time. If the puppy moves at all it will be because of the unaccustomed feeling. An alternative is to use long tweezers, but a puppy can move quickly with unfortunate results, so it might be better to get the puppy used to having the hair removed with fingers before using tweezers. Continue until all the hair has been removed and you achieve a nice clean inside. Wipe away any wax that is visible with the baby-bud – but *do not* probe deeply. If there are deep, dark deposits, leave these for the vet to remove. Normal ear wax (if any) should be light to medium brown in colour. Inspect ears regularly. An unpleasant smell, or a dark deposit, requires professional attention. When you have been grooming your puppy on a regular basis for a short while, introduce tooth cleaning. You can start by gently rubbing your little finger round the puppy's gums at every grooming session, slowly progressing to using a cotton bud, or wrapping gauze round your finger. Once the puppy accepts this, it will become part of the grooming routine and you can progress to a baby toothbrush, or a special toothbrush, and toothpaste for dogs from your vet, to keep gums and teeth in good condition.

NAILS
Puppies grow long curved nails when they are young, but your breeder will probably have trimmed these prior to parting with your Maltese. Sometimes, however, they may be overlooked, or grow long once more soon after you receive the puppy.

Familiarise yourself with the nails well before intending to cut them. Ideally wait until the puppy is asleep on your lap, and you are in a good light. You will see that the nail has a pink inner line (called the quick) running from the paw outwards. From the end of the quick the nail tapers off into a grey, pointed, sometimes slightly hooked, end (it is, of course more difficult to see this inner line if the nail is black). The pink quick is a vein, so make quite sure you are not close to it when you clip the grey tip off. The non-pink part is painless, exactly the same as clipping the white part of your own nails. However, it would be painful if you catch the pink part, so take care. The nails are softer, and therefore easier to cut, immediately after a bath.

Inspect the nails as a regular part of your daily grooming. If you leave them to grow too long, especially if they are hooked, they can catch in clothes, ruin stockings and even catch in carpets. More important, such nails could damage your Maltese. Of course, do not forget the dewclaw (unless previously removed) which, you will remember, is situated a little above the paw on the inside. It has been known for this nail to be overlooked, and left just to grow and grow, until it breaks off painfully. If your Maltese has long hair under the feet between the pads, just trim this back to the level of the pad itself, to avoid collecting rubbish etc. that can matt the hair together – for example, chewing gum, tar from the road in the heat of summer, or snow in the winter, any of which can collect into balls underneath the pads.

Grooming is essential for the well-being of your dog and very therapeutic for the human companion. It has been proven that stroking and brushing can bring down an owner's blood pressure significantly – that is, if it is a well trained dog, otherwise it might do the opposite!

BATHING
Several different factors dictate when you should bath your Maltese; much depends on individual lifestyles. The coat itself does produce a certain amount of natural oil, yet it is not greasy. Really it is quite a dry coat, so dirt from country walks will usually brush out. Unfortunately dirt collected from roads heavily used by cars carries a certain amount of its own sticky grime, and will cling. Needless to say, a house dog will stay cleaner longer.

So, according to each individual situation, some dogs have to be bathed once a week, and others less frequently. For my part, because I live in the country, all my Maltese (other than show dogs) are bathed once a month. Use a good rich shampoo, followed by an equally good conditioner, these, together with regular grooming, will make your Maltese a joy to live with.

Now, down to the practical aspect of bathing. I find it less backbreaking to bath my Maltese in a sink, but some people favour the shower base, or the bath. Whichever you choose, you will achieve the best results with the aid of a flexible hose and shower head.

First set out the items you will require, and place them where you can reach them easily: two different types of shampoo, a baby or puppy shampoo for the head, and a good rich shampoo for the rest of the body. This shampoo can be Coconut or Almond oil or something similar. Use a quality conditioner to finish and have a small face-cloth handy, in case of need, because some dogs object to having water on their faces. Next, three large towels: one to have on your lap where you will be drying the puppy, and another with which to remove the puppy from the bath and squeeze out excess water; the third may be required when you have dried half of the puppy.

Finally, a hair drier. I really do think the purchase of a free-standing drier would be a labour-saving investment, as you will, hopefully, be bathing your Maltese for many years to come, and it is so much easier and quicker with this type than with the hand-held machines.

The initial step is to groom your Maltese, making sure all the tangles are out, because if you start bathing with tangles in the coat, it will consolidate the mat even further.

Then, stand your tangle-free Maltese where you intend to do the bathing. A little rubber mat under the puppy's feet can help inspire confidence. Wet the hair thoroughly, squeezing it right through the coat, then work the rich shampoo into the body hair. Again, squeeze the shampoo through the hair. Try not to rub, or you could mat the coat. Make sure the legs and the underneath are not forgotten. Now put the baby/puppy shampoo on the head and again work it in. Ordinary shampoo would hurt the puppy if it found its way into the eyes. Rinse off and repeat, then finish with the conditioner on the body hair. Finally, rinse this off. Always rinse thoroughly.

Gently squeeze the excess water out of the coat with your hands, pick the puppy up in the towel and again squeeze the remaining water out. Place the puppy face upwards, back downwards, on the towel that is across your lap and direct the drier.

DRYING

As we are assuming this is the first time you have done this, you will not know how your Maltese will react to the drier. It may be perfectly all right, but on the other hand it may not, so do not direct warm air directly on to the puppy at first. Having tested that it is not too hot, play it a little distance from the puppy's rear end and watch the reaction, gradually moving it closer until it is directly on the rear part of the body.

Using your comb or pin brush, start opening the hair up under the warm air, drying inside the hind legs, then the tummy and the front legs, continuing up to the chin, but not on to the face at this stage. Replace the damp towel on your lap with a dry one and turn the puppy over.

Dry from the rear first, brushing, or combing the coat from the spine down towards the feet all the time and gradually moving up towards the head. Dry the head last. Make it a pleasure and give constant praise, but again be firm. You will reap the reward when, as an adult, your dog lies quietly on your lap, totally relaxed, as you do the drying and grooming.

TOPKNOTS

As your puppy Maltese matures into a young adult the coat will be getting longer and longer, and you probably will find it easier to groom on a table, upon which you have placed either a rubber mat or a thick cover for comfort. The hair on the top of the head will have begun to flop into the dog's eyes, so this is the time to gather it into a topknot. Puppy Maltese usually have the hair taken

As the coat grows, you will need to start tying the hair in a topknot.

into just one small bunch on top of the head. Wrap a soft paper or piece of gauze around the base of the bunch and secure with a light latex band or similar restraint. Ease out the hair between the head and the band to prevent discomfort. As the hair grows longer you can have the pleasure of varying the style, using any one of those which are described fully in the chapter on grooming your show dog.

There are a couple of ways of grooming: You can train your Maltese to stand quietly whilst you go through the body hair, then sit to have chest and head attended to, finally lying down with the chin flat and the head directly towards you to complete the finishing touches to the face and arrange the topknot. An alternative is to train the dog to lie flat first on one side and then on the other to groom the body hair etc., then flat on the tummy to complete the head. The earlier you can train your puppy to put the head flat on the table the better. Gently, but firmly put your hand at the back of the youngster's head and press it down until the chin lies flat on the table, saying "Down". All this may sound straightforward, but at first you will probably find your young Maltese does not stay as quietly as you would like. It may take a lot of patience on your part, while wishing at this point that you had three pairs of hands; but persevere and insist that your puppy stays head down, even if it means re-doing the whole thing several times.

Once you have mastered the topknot you will have the pleasure of varying the styles. As the body hair grows longer it must be parted in a straight line down the middle of the back and brushed smoothly down each side. Again, this parting can be made with either the comb or a small knitting needle, and finished by combing the hair smoothly into place. Depending on the type of coat your Maltese has – for they all differ slightly – it must be groomed thoroughly at least every other day, to prevent tangles building up. Also, I recommend that you 'top and tail' every day, by which I mean clean the face and check the hair under the tail to ensure it is all perfectly clean and problem-free.

The whole of this chapter is intended for first-time owners, who are learning to look after their companion Maltese themselves. How good you will feel when those admiring comments are the result of all your care and attention!

Chapter Four

THE SHOW MALTESE

Dog showing is a wonderfully versatile pastime that can be enjoyed either in a modest way, with just the one family dog, or taken to breathtaking heights. It is a very social sport enjoyed by people exhibiting their Maltese in many countries throughout the world, and those of us who participate have the one interest in common – the love of this very special breed. Once you become actively involved it is possible, given time, not only to enjoy the company of fellow enthusiasts in your own country, but also the company of those abroad.

As this is your first prospective show dog you will experience exciting anticipation as you watch your Maltese develop. You will also have the fun of training, or joining up with others at ringcraft classes, where you can practise the intricacies of handling and exhibiting. There will be decisions to make, such as which show to go to, and which class, or classes, to enter. If you have success, there will be the pleasure you feel upon receiving your award, and the enjoyment of reminiscing over a memorable day. Nevertheless, it has to be said that dog-showing also makes demands on your emotions. In the first instance your potential show dog may not attain all the qualities required for top competition. Then again, if all goes well and you find yourself proudly exhibiting alongside your fellow competitors, thoroughly convinced you have the best exhibit there, this opinion may not be shared by the judge on that particular day, with the inevitable disappointment but take heart, for there is always another show!

By choosing a Maltese you will, in fact, have selected one of the most difficult dogs to exhibit, for an enormous amount of work is necessary when putting this particular breed into the ring. Naturally, all your hopes and aspirations are high, and therefore it follows that disappointments can be equally painful. Whoever wrote that 'Competition does not create character, it exposes it' might well have been a Maltese exhibitor, because showing can be a roller-coaster of emotional highs and lows, thrills and disappointments, but at the end of the day you and your dog still have each other. Your dog is just as special and just as precious; nothing has changed in that respect.

ACQUIRING A SHOW DOG
There are many differing routes when embarking on dog showing for a hobby. Some hopeful competitors prefer to purchase a puppy and take a chance that ultimately the dog meets the standard set out for the breed. Then there are those who try to ensure their dog is showable by buying a more mature youngster, whose potential is already promising. Others might buy an adult or, occasionally, a proven show dog, in the hope of succeeding.

Do not be in too great a hurry. Read as much about the breed as possible, especially the breed standard. It may take several months to find the right dog, but be patient and, in the meantime, go to as many Championship shows as possible, simply to study the Maltese in the ring.

Ch. Snowgoose Firebird (Nivatus Mr. Chips – Snowgoose Quincey): Dog CC Crufts 1986, Best of Breed Crufts 1987. Bred and owned by Vicki Herrieff. Co-owner/handler: Chris Ripsher.
The Maltese is one of the most difficult dogs to show as so much work is needed to prepare a dog for the ring

Even though a breed has a standard to which all exhibits try to adhere as closely as possible, when you visit several shows scheduling Maltese classes you will become aware that there are subtle variations within that standard, which differentiate one show dog from another, and often one show kennel from another. This is what makes the whole dog world so interesting.

At first glance there appears to be a ring full of identical small white dogs, but it is not so. As your eye becomes accustomed to the breed, the differences will become more apparent and, eventually, you will find some dogs more personally appealing than others. So, find out the kennel or kennels from which they originate and enquire whether they might have what you are looking for in the near future. Buying a very young puppy, then watching the growth and development of the dog, is one way of familiarising yourself with a breed, and it does have some advantages. Socialising is no problem, as the normal hubbub of family life, with its variety of outings and the comings and goings of friends and children, is excellent in accustoming the puppy to accepting the majority of situations, but, as I mentioned earlier, there is always the chance that a young puppy may not mature into a suitable show dog.

For example, although everything may be proceeding well, a major hurdle has to be overcome at around six months of age, as up until then it is not possible to be one hundred per cent certain that the second teeth will be perfect. You have to wait until the milk teeth have been replaced by the puppy's permanent set. The baby teeth might be reluctant to come out, and it is quite possible to see two sets of teeth in residence at the same time. Individual baby teeth can pose a problem as well, for if they are particularly stubborn and stay in place, they can push the permanent teeth out of alignment, thus totally spoiling an otherwise good mouth.

Anyone wishing to take up showing seriously, would be unwise to buy a young dog and live in hope, as so many things can alter as the puppy matures. No reputable breeder will guarantee that one so young will make the ring, no matter how illustrious the parentage, although there are those less scrupulous who would have you believe they are blessed with this insight.

Sometimes the phrase 'show potential' is used by the breeder, but this means the puppy looks as if all the required qualities are present at that point in time. It does not promise that these qualities will remain at the same level into maturity; Maltese can alter considerably as they develop and disappointment is still a risk to be considered. You will probably have to wait until something suitable becomes available and, of course, you must expect to pay appropriately more for an older dog that has been 'run on' and is a show prospect. Nevertheless, if you see the type of dog you like, aim for that one, although you will not necessarily get one quickly. Those who are too impatient are often doomed to disappointment if their hasty purchase does not fulfill their hopes.

If at all possible, it is wiser to buy a dog around six to seven months of age, for, although there is probably still some growing yet to come, you will be better able to appraise the dog's movement and structure and assess coat quality. Also the second, permanent teeth should be through by then and you will have the opportunity to check that the bite is correct. This is also a good time to confirm that pigmentation is fully developed, and that, if the dog is male, he is entire, which means that both testicles have descended into the scrotum, as well as checking that every other aspect required of an aspiring show Maltese is in order, not forgetting, of course temperament. Remember that no dog is perfect, but as long as you like what you see at this point, the future looks promising.

A good breeder, knowing your intention is to show, will certainly also wish to ensure that you have a suitable youngster with promise, for they will be only too aware that this dog is going to represent their kennel. If you are offered such a dog you will also have a responsibility to the breeder, which is to care for and, ultimately, exhibit your Maltese to the very best of your ability. Then everybody will be happy.

SHOW TRAINING

A puppy which is purchased at around seven months of age will almost certainly have received some sort of basic training from the breeder. At the very least, the dog would have been groomed on a regular basis, and therefore have been taught to stand quietly. On the other hand, if you have raised your potential show dog from a puppy yourself, then this side of life is down to you. Hopefully, you will have achieved a happy relationship with your puppy long before you even consider serious training, as it is a mistake to be too intensive in the early days, especially with a youngster.

LEARNING THE STAND

Training should start in a very simple manner. When you have finished grooming, encourage the puppy to stand quietly, head up, tail over, all four feet placed firmly on the table. Tickle your Maltese under the chin for a few moments while saying "Stand". Do not keep this up for too long at first, talk all the while, then make a big fuss of the puppy to show that it is time to relax and that you are pleased.

When the time comes to enter the show ring, your Maltese will be placed on many different types of tables, and in strange surroundings, to be examined by the judge, so practise this short 'stand' on a variety of surfaces, such as work tops and tables of different materials, giving reassurance all the time that it is safe and the puppy is doing well.

Once the dog understands what you want, get your Maltese to stand quietly, head up, tail over, while you make an examination. Place the legs correctly, look in the mouth and eyes. Make a big fuss every time the dog accepts your attentions. If you over-do training, so that it becomes boring or leads to strong resistance, all your good work will go to waste. Inevitably there will be days when things do not run smoothly and, when this happens, you should ask for something very simple to be done that you know your dog is capable of carrying out correctly. Once this is completed, give lots of praise again, and call it a day. Always finish by praising, even if the work is not perfect. Practising standing on the floor is sometimes made a little easier by using a large mirror placed flat against a wall. Stand your puppy in front of it and go through your routine. This will help you become aware of how others see your dog. When using the mirror, make allowances for your puppy's natural curiosity, as the reflection may be mistaken for another dog – not a self-image, and this will result in a loss of concentration. Again, when friends or relatives visit, make a game of this standing and encourage them to look in the dog's mouth, or just handle the dog generally. This will then accustom the dog to accept confidently the attentions of a stranger. While you stand and set your puppy up, ask these friends to pretend to be the judge and encourage them to attract the dog's attention. In this way the dog will learn to look at the judge when it eventually sets foot in the ring. Use the mirror to stack your puppy on the floor. Kneel down and stand the puppy in front of you. At first, your potential show dog may try and climb into your lap thinking 'this is a good game'. However, gently but firmly set your Maltese up, guiding the head away from you towards the mirror, saying "Stand". Brush or comb the coat a couple of times and put the dog back into position if there is any inclination to play. Do not spend too long doing any one exercise, and finish while all is going well.

LEAD TRAINING

Many Maltese take to lead training quite naturally and trot alongside you as if this is something they have been doing all their lives. More often than not, though, this first outing is met with some sort of resistance and it may take patience to overcome any anxieties on the puppy's part.

A reluctant puppy may be helped if a lightweight collar is placed round the neck and left on for a short while, without a lead attached, just to get accustomed to the feel of it. Choose a buckle-type collar that can be fastened loosely, but not so loose that it can be pulled over the head or allow a paw to be trapped underneath if the puppy tries to remove it. The slide type of collar is not a good idea, as it could prove dangerous if the puppy is very energetic in endeavouring to despatch this strange contraption. Leave the collar on all the while the puppy is reasonably happy, but at any sign of distress, remove it, then replace it for short periods over several days and the puppy will quite quickly settle down to accept it.

I start training with the light, flat show leads and find the puppy initially often hardly realises they are attached at all. There are several different types of these leads, and you will probably acquire quite a collection before you find which type best suits you and your dog. The most popular seem to be those that have the lead and collar all in one, with a sliding loop that expands or contracts the collar section to suit the different size dogs. These are thought not to detract from the dog when in the ring. Then there is the style which also has the collar and lead all in one, but with a slightly thicker section for round the neck. Some people feel these give greater control. Finally there is a wide selection of very light, attractive, collars and leads available, any one of which would be suitable. The biggest selections are to be found on the stalls at major shows – in fact this applies to the majority of dog equipment.

A word of warning, though. The thin, lightweight show leads with the sliding loop are not suitable for exercising in public places, as it is possible for a dog to run backwards and slip out of them if alarmed or over-excited. So, by all means use this type at a show or at home, but remember to put a proper collar on before venturing anywhere else.

Be prepared for a hectic first outing on a lead, when your puppy may dash and leap all over the place, especially if you are out in the garden and on the grass. Go with this at first, let the puppy take you round, talking encouragingly, and gradually persuading the puppy to follow you once the first burst of energy has subsided. Do not worry, just take your time and allow the puppy ample space to settle – which will happen eventually, believe me. Keep the dog on your lefthand side, as this will be required in the ring, and make the training pleasurable. There will always be the rebel puppy who puts the brakes on or leaps about at the end of the lead and you despair of ever achieving a straight line, but do not give way to anger and *never* drag a puppy along. As with all your previous training, try and finish with your Maltese doing something well and being rewarded – you may even resort to bribes.

Having a favourite tidbit as a reward makes training easier, especially in the early days. Remember though, if you are using food as a bait, this will leave a lovely fragrant odour on your fingers, and your dog will naturally be excited every time your hand approaches, in anticipation of further treats, so it is worthwhile giving thought to what you use. Should you find this does present a problem, gently but firmly say "No" or "Leave" as your hand approaches without a bait.

If you have a particularly rebellious youngster, put the show lead on, holding one end loosely, and encourage the dog to walk beside you, following a tempting offering held above and in front of the dog's head. The dog will gradually learn to move alongside you, head up, aware of the lead, yet more aware of the tidbit. Give a reward quite frequently, talking at the same time and always using the same words where appropriate, "Steady" "Forward" "Turn" "No" and so on; it all helps your Maltese to understand what you want. Gradually reward less and less with the tidbit while carrying out the movement, but continue to praise. Offer the treat when the walk has been finished reasonably well.

When you feel your puppy is moving steadily on the lead, try going in a triangle as if you were walking for the judge. Finally, get your puppy to stand as still as possible, head up, looking 'four square'. If this does not work at first, keep changing your position until the puppy does stand for a moment, then give congratulations, the reward of a tidbit and finish. Eventually the dog will complete the walk and stand looking up at you as a matter of course, but it will take time and patience. If you lose your cool, all will be lost.

LEARNING THE TURN

One of the most important moves to practise is the turn when the judge asks you to make a triangle. Have your dog on your lefthand side, and walk away in a straight line. Now, when it comes to the corners, you don't want to break the rhythm of your dog's movement, so try and make these turns as smooth as possible. You may also be asked by the judge to walk away and then come straight back. Some exhibitors change the hand holding the lead when arriving at the turn, so the dog goes away on the handler's left and returns on the handler's righthand side. Another method is for the handler to walk round the dog in order to return. Whichever way you choose, practise it well so that corner-turning is as smooth as possible.

Go through the whole routine regularly, but not so often that it becomes boring. Your dog is unlikely to get everything right every time and if, for any reason, you feel things are not going well, cease all training and baiting for a few days.

Eventually you will offer fewer and fewer baits, until you only reward at the very end of each specific practice, otherwise you may find your dog is looking for food at every approach of your hand. The essence of training is to get your dog to listen to you and concentrate on what the two of you are doing, despite any distractions around you. Shows can be noisy places with other fascinating breeds in adjacent rings. It is a whole new strange life to get used to. Your puppy will be expected to behave reasonably well when surrounded by other dogs regardless of age. All the training will come into its own now, and your dog will thoroughly enjoy doing things well and pleasing you into the bargain.

SHOWING ON A LOOSE LEAD

One of the most hotly debated subjects is whether a dog should be shown on a loose lead or not.

Nobody likes to see a dog 'strung up' as, unwittingly, this could denote the dog has a problem with front movement. On the other hand, a dog must be very well trained before you can allow the lead to hang loosely, if this is your preferred method of handling, otherwise there is a tendency to wander all over the place, making it very difficult for a judge to assess movement, and you could rightly be placed down as a result. However, there is a happy medium, which is to take the lead up sufficiently for the handler to 'feel' the dog, or convey messages, yet to retain a certain amount of slackness in order to let the dog show freely. Personally, I like to be in contact with my charges, and do believe they respond better. Finding the right pace at which to walk a dog is not always easy. If you have a Maltese that likes moving slowly you have to find a way to encourage a more lively pace. Conversely, if you have ones that are too full of themselves (as all mine seem to be), this may prove difficult also. Ultimately, you have to find the best pace at which you and your dog can move smoothly together, a pace that will show off all the Maltese virtues.

SOCIALISING

If socialising a puppy proves to be a problem, training classes run by canine societies can be very beneficial. These classes are designed specifically to train novice dogs for the show ring. Initially, make enquiries and find out what is available for the smaller breeds. But I must repeat a word of caution: I strongly urge you to visit beforehand to see if the class is well-run and appropriate for you and your puppy. A badly organised group could prove disastrous. Should a class for small breeds not be available then training at home can be just as good, as long as you socialise your puppy by getting friends and relatives involved in handling, and as many dogs as possible are introduced. The more your puppy has associated with other breeds before the first show the better, as these encounters are then less likely to be overwhelming. Dogs are always happier when mixing with their own kind, so try and enter your puppy in a breed class at the first show and this will add to the enjoyment of the day for both of you.

GETTING USED TO THE CAR

Your puppy may be a bad traveller and could be car sick, so must become accustomed to it as early as possible. Nothing is worse than arriving at a show with your newly-bathed Maltese requiring urgent attention. It is quite a good idea in the beginning to simply sit in the vehicle with the puppy while it is stationary at home. Settle down in the rear seat and play – you could put the radio on to make things even more friendly. Keep the first journeys very short, gradually lengthening them. Do this a few times and your puppy will regard the car as a pleasant place. Just before travelling, try giving a drink of glucose in water, as a precautionary measure. If this proves ineffectual and the puppy is actually sick, next time try giving half a teaspoonful of Milk of Magnesia or a similar type of tummy settler, the sort that is suitable for children, just prior to leaving. Travel sickness tablets are very good, but can have a sleepy effect, so you would have to practise how much to give and how long it takes to wear off. You do not want your dog half asleep in the ring. Make sure you know exactly how well your dog travels long before attending your first show together.

THE GOVERNING BODIES

Today, many countries are fortunate in having their own Governing Body watching over the world of dogs. The Kennel Club in England is proud to have been the first to be established in 1873 and is now known simply as the KC. Soon after, in 1884 the American Kennel Club came into being and is referred to as the AKC. Canada then joined the ranks, four years later, in 1888. The success of these earlier societies encouraged a number of the European countries to merge and, in 1911, form the Federation Cynologique Internationale to watch over the interests of dogs in the affiliated countries. This is known as the FCI. The next large grouping was in the Scandinavian countries, who joined together under the umbrella of the Scandinavian Kennel Union, the SKU, in 1953. Associations blossomed in many countries, all with the same goal in mind. 1886 saw New Zealand join the ranks, but her neighbour, Australia, established its governing body much later, in 1949.

The systems of judging and the types of classes in each country are so varied that it is sometimes difficult to equate one with another. Should you hope one day to either visit shows or even judge abroad, it is wise first to thoroughly understand exactly what the procedure is in any particular part of the world and, if you are officiating, make sure you know exactly what will be expected of you.

The composition of the groupings of the breeds can differ from country to country, although, without exception, the Maltese is classified as a Toy everywhere. Nevertheless, there are slight variations in the requirements for the breed as set out by the individual governing bodies for each country. Therefore these should also be studied carefully.

DOG SHOWS IN THE US

Enthusiasts on the American continent, do not have the benefit of quite so many different types of shows as in the UK. There is the Match for pedigree dogs run by the breed societies or all-breed clubs. The Match is an event where dogs meet in pairs to be judged. The winner will go forward to the next and subsequent rounds until, ultimately, a Best in Match is achieved. This event generates much fun and socialising and is ideal for the newcomer, but Championship points are not awarded. They are excellent shows at which the novice can learn all about exhibiting.

To gain the title of Champion in America a dog must gain 15 points under three different judges. Points are awarded on a scale of 1 to 5 according to the number of entries. To become a Champion a dog must win at least two major point shows under different judges. These major shows award a minimum of 3 points. The unbeaten Maltese compete against each other in what is called the Winners class (one for dogs and one for bitches), and the winning dog and the winning bitch both receive points towards their crowns. These two now challenge the winners of the 'Champions', or BOB class, and from these dogs the Best of Winners, the Best of Breed and Best Opposite Sex are selected. If it is an All Breed show the Best of Breed will go forward to compete for Best in Group and possibly Best in Show.

The first type of 'pointed' show is the General Championship show in which Maltese have classes, and where you can accumulate points towards your Champions crown. These shows are many and varied. Some are quite small but the more prestigious attract around 3,000 dogs of

Ready to go into the ring: Am. Ch. Fantasyland Vital Sun Isle (Ch. Fantasyland Vital – Sun Isle Sadi). Owned by Carole Bladwin and Liz Flewellen.

The late Dee Shepherd: One of the USA's greatest professional handlers. A good handler will bring out the very best in a dog.

differing breeds, and if you are prepared to travel vast distances, it is possible to attend four in any one weekend, year round, but that would be for the true campaigner. The number of Maltese entered would range from a modest number up to 60 or more, with the shows scheduling four classes for each sex, plus the 'Champions' class (mixed dog and bitch).

Next you have the Specialty Shows, and what splendid affairs these are, with Maltese coming from far and wide, making them the ideal show for the enthusiast to visit. In 1990 the AMA held their 25th Anniversary Specialty, which I was privileged to attend. Day One saw a fine entry of l03 for the Sweepstake classes. These are for youngsters aged 6 to l8 months of age, 4 classes each for dogs and bitches, but without points. Day Two scheduled the Regular point-winning classes with 174 dogs entered and the two successful Best of Winners joined a breathtaking Best of Breed class boasting an entry of 38 Champions!

In the US there are those who may wish to own a pedigree Maltese and would love to win a Champions crown, but perhaps lack either the time or the ability to present, or even the confidence to handle the dog themselves. Fortunately they have the opportunity to employ the help of one of the many professional handlers, who will then take the Maltese into their own care, to condition, prepare and ultimately present the dog in the ring. These handlers are true experts at their job who travel the whole country with their team of charges, which may include several different breeds. The dogs at the end of their successful careers are returned to their owners, who may then bask in the warmth of their dogs' achievements. If you intend showing your own dog yourself, you could not do better than study these dedicated professionals in the ring and do your best to emulate them. There are excellent professional handlers in the UK as well, but compared with the numbers in the US they are few and far between.

DOG SHOWS IN THE UK

I do not think we realise just how lucky we are in the UK to have so many different types of shows available. There is plenty of opportunity for the novice exhibitor, and novice dog, to practise the art of showing, then gradually to move on through to the 'big time', starting with the Match, run on similar lines to the ones in the US. Another enjoyable event is the Exemption Show, so named because it is exempt from some of the regulations which apply to other shows, although it is still licensed by the Kennel Club. Exemption shows are often fund-raising events, or run in conjunction with local functions such as Agricultural shows, and they offer several classes for pedigree dogs, and several novelty classes, all of which are entered on the ground, on the day. These shows are great fun and ideal for the novice dog or dog handler, because Champions, or dogs that have obtained any award that counts towards the title of Champion, are not eligible for entry.

Two other events which will be of interest to a novice are Sanction shows, which are small shows at which Champions or dogs with high honours are not eligible, and Limited shows. These are limited to members of a Society and, again, are restricted to those who have yet to achieve top awards. Open shows are a stage further on. These events are very popular and can vary in size from quite small to very large indeed, extending over more than one day. They are open to all, including Champions and will schedule breed classes, as well as variety classes for those breeds not separately classified. Although a win at an Open show does not contribute towards the title of Champion, it is a very valuable training ground and one where lovely trophies and rosettes are usually on offer. A dog who is unbeaten in a breed class, may then challenge all the other unbeaten dogs in that breed for Best of Breed. The majority of Open shows are run on the group system and a dog who is awarded this title of BOB is then eligible to represent that breed in the appropriate group, the winner of which will then go forward for Best in Show.

Unbeaten puppies can challenge each other for Best Puppy and, in some cases, there is a Best Puppy in Show award. An unbeaten dog in the variety classes may challenge all the other unbeaten dogs in that section and go forward to the group representing all those dogs without classes of their own. There are slight differences with each show but they all follow a similar pattern.

Championship shows are open to all, with the exception of Crufts. To enter Crufts a dog must be either a Champion, have won a Challenge Certificate or Reserve Challenge Certificate, or have been awarded a Stud book number. Alternatively a dog may qualify in certain classes at one of the Championship shows held during the previous year. The qualification required is decided by the KC and is reviewed from time to time.

The majority of classes scheduled at Championship shows offer Kennel Club CCs, one for the best dog and one for the best bitch in the breed. To be awarded the title Champion, an exhibit must win three CCs under three different judges. However, a dog cannot be crowned Champion under the age of twelve months, no matter how many CCs are won up to that age. A qualifying CC will only be approved when won after a dog is over twelve months of age.

This might sound reasonably easy, but in order to win a CC a successful candidate must beat every other Maltese, including every other Champion in their sex, entered on that day. Not an easy task, because those Champions present could all be in fine form, together with several other promising challengers who already possess one or two Challenge Certificates, to say nothing of the dogs who have won several Reserve Challenge Certificates. Somehow your hopeful representative must first win a class, or classes, and remain unbeaten in order to challenge every other unbeaten dog of the same sex that day, which can include some powerful title-holders. A daunting task indeed.

A Res.CC does not contribute in any way towards the title of Champion. It is a certificate stating that, in the judge's opinion, this dog is worthy of being awarded a CC should the CC winner that day have the award withdrawn for any reason. However many RCCs you win, they will not give you that final accolade. You do, however, have the satisfaction of knowing yours is considered a quality dog by certain judges.

You may carry your CCs over from one year to the next and I have known Maltese owners patiently trying to attain those elusive 3 CCs over a period of several years. However, many, especially bitches, have to retire with just one or two to their credit plus a hatfull of RCCs.

To illustrate how difficult it can be, in 1993 the Maltese in England, Scotland and Wales were given a total of 20 sets of CCs (20 chances that year to try and win the coveted CC), yet only two males won through the established Champions to gain their own Champion's 'crowns', and in 1994 the established Champions were even harder to beat and only one new male won his 'crown'.

As I said earlier, we are very fortunate in the UK to have so many different types of shows to choose from. A dog who is not quite up to Championship Show standard can still have great success and be highly acclaimed at the various Open shows, with the dog's name and perhaps a photograph appearing in the dog journals. Then again, if your Maltese does not attain that standard, there are still the 'fun' shows at which you can have a thoroughly enjoyable day in the company of both novice and more experienced owners.

Maltese in England are usually owner-handled, with most being breeder/owner-handled, as the majority of kennels are very small, consisting of a handful of carefully bred dogs that have a litter from time to time. In the majority of cases it is really a 'hobby', yet one approached in a professional way and taken to an extremely high standard.

In the past, exhibitors in the UK were able to use one of the wide selection of coat sprays available to enhance their Maltese just prior to entering the ring, but today an exhibitor must adhere to the KC regulation which states: 'No substance which alters the natural colour, texture or body of the coat may be used in the preparation of a dog for exhibition either before or at the show. Any other substance (other than water) which may be used in the preparation of a dog for exhibition must not be allowed to remain in the coat of a dog at the time of exhibition.' To highlight this rule the KC make spot checks, testing dogs at random as they leave the ring.

I well remember the very first time a Maltese was checked. Three small samples of hair were taken from three different sections of the dog. Each of these samples was then divided into three portions; one of each sample was retained by the exhibitor, the same by the KC, and the last three sent off for testing. Thankfully the samples were found to be totally satisfactory and the owner was duly informed a few days later. However, this dramatic intervention certainly brought everyone's attention to the regulation, in no uncertain manner.

EUROPEAN DOG SHOWS

There are really only two types of shows on the Continent: the fun shows, which comprise small gatherings, usually put on by the clubs – again, they are good training grounds for all concerned; then there are the Championship shows, and these range from the smaller National gatherings to the major International shows such as the World Show and the Winners Show. Dogs are not eligible to be entered at these Championship Shows under the age of 9 months.

Judging on the Continent is a protracted affair, as each dog entered is graded and receives a written critique while at the judges' table. These critiques pronounce a dog as excellent, very good, good or moderate.

Int. Ch. Carmidanick Al Pacino (Ch. Mannsown Remote Control – Carmidanick Hot Gossip). Imported from the UK and became the top winning Maltese in Austria 1991 and 1992. Bred by Carol Tredinnick, owned by Christine Ruf.

Photo: Pet Pictures.

There are two awards to which a dog may aspire:, the CAC (Certificat d'Aptitude au Championnat) which is awarded at National Championship shows, and the CACIB (Certificat d'Aptitude au Championnat International de Beaute) which is awarded at International Championship Shows. Both these awards are given to the dog which has been placed highest and has been graded Excellent. The dog has also to be considered worthy of this high placing by the Judge.

To give one example: to achieve the title of Champion in the Netherlands (some other European countries may differ slightly), a dog must win four CACs at three different shows (the Club Show and the 'Winner Show' count as two) under three different judges, and the last CAC must be gained after the dog has reached 27 months of age. The CACIB is awarded by the FCI and has to be won from either the Open or Champion class, and a dog must gain 4 CACIBs under three different judges in three different countries, one of the countries being the one where the dog is registered. As the Open class is only for dogs of 15 months and over, and there must be at least one year between gaining the first and the last CACIB, this ensures a dog is more than 27 months old before gaining an International title. Presentation in the European and Scandinavian countries has progressed by leaps and bounds during these past few years. The quality of the homebred dogs has also risen noticeably in the hands of some very dedicated breeders, who have blended the bloodlines from various countries to attain top-quality Maltese, claiming high honours at some of the major shows. As in the UK the majority of Maltese on the Continent are owner-handled, or owner/breeder-handled. The method of making dogs into Champions differs in each country in one way or another, with many, like Australia, Canada and New Zealand embracing the points system but with their own individual variations, each a tried and tested method of acknowledging a quality animal.

Chapter Five

THE BREED STANDARDS

Every country has a standard for the Maltese, and although these all relate to one breed, you will see they vary considerably in their composition. The American edition paints quite a descriptive picture, the British is much shorter and more concise, while that provided by the FCI for those exhibiting on the Continent is very detailed and extremely precise. No doubt individual Continental countries précis the FCI requirements into a convenient form, but the sum total of all three of these standards, to a greater or lesser degree, is the same dog.

THE BRITISH STANDARD

GENERAL APPEARANCE: Smart, white coated dog, with proud head carriage.

CHARACTERISTICS: Lively intelligent, alert.

TEMPERAMENT: Sweet tempered.

HEAD AND SKULL: From stop to centre of skull (centre between forepart of ears) and stop to tip of nose, equally balanced. Stop well defined. Nose black. Muzzle broad, well filled under eye. Not snipey.

EYES: Oval, not bulging, dark brown, black eye rims with dark haloes.

EARS: Long, well feathered, hanging close to head; hair to mingle with coat at shoulders.

MOUTH: Jaws strong, with perfect, regular and complete scissor bite, i.e. the upper teeth closely over-lapping the lower and set square to the jaws. Teeth even.

NECK: Medium length.
FOREQUARTERS: Legs short and straight. Shoulders well sloped.

BODY: Well balanced, essentially short and cobby. Good spring of rib, back level from withers to tail.

HINDQUARTERS: Legs short, well angulated.

Ch. Snowgoose First Love (Ch. Villarose Chocolate Charmer – Snowgoose Paper Moon): Breed CC record holder in the UK. Owned and bred by Vicki Herrieff, co-owner/handler Sarah Jackson.

Photo: Robert Killick.

FEET: Round, pads black.

TAIL: Feathered, carried well arched over back.

GAIT/MOVEMENT: Free, without extended weaving.

COAT: Good length, not impeding action, straight, of silky texture, never woolly. Never crimped and without woolly undercoat.

COLOUR: Pure white, but slight lemon markings permissible.

SIZE: Not exceeding 25.5 cm. (10 ins) from ground to withers.

FAULTS: Any departure from the foregoing points should be considered a fault and the seriousness with which the fault should be regarded should be in exact proportion to its degree.

NOTE: Male animals should have two apparently normal testicles fully descended into the scrotum.

Reproduced by kind permission of the English Kennel Club.

THE AMERICAN STANDARD

GENERAL APPEARANCE
The Maltese is a toy dog covered from head to foot with a mantle of long, silky, white hair. He is gentle-mannered and affectionate, eager and sprightly in action, and, despite his size, possessed of the vigor needed for the satisfactory companion.

HEAD
The size of the dog. The skull is slightly rounded on top, the stop moderate. The drop ears are rather low set and heavily feathered with long hair that hangs close to the head. Eyes are set not too far apart; they are very dark and round, their black rims enhancing the gentle yet alert expression. The muzzle is of medium length, fine and tapered but not snipey. The nose is black. The teeth meet in an even, edge-to-edge bite, or in a scissors bite.

NECK
Sufficient length of neck is desirable as promoting a high carriage of the head.

BODY
Compact, the height from the withers to the ground equalling the length from the withers to the root of the tail. Shoulder blades are sloping, the elbows well knit and held close to the body. The back is level in topline, the ribs well sprung. The chest is fairly deep, the loins taut, strong and just slightly tucked up underneath.

TAIL
A long-haired plume carried gracefully over the back, its tip lying to the side over the quarter.

LEGS AND FEET
Legs are fine-boned and nicely feathered. Fore legs are straight, their pastern joints well knit and devoid of appreciable bend. Hind legs are strong and moderately angulated at stifles and hocks. The feet are small and round, with toe pads black. Straggly hairs on the feet may be trimmed to give a neater appearance.

Am. Ch. Sand Island Small Kraft Lite (Am. Ch. Keoli's Small Kraft Warning – Am. Ch. Melody Lane Lite N' Lively Luv): Top winning Maltese of all time in the USA.

Booth Photography.

COAT AND COLOR

The coat is single, that is, without undercoat. It hangs long, flat and silky over the sides of the body almost, if not quite, to the ground. The long head hair may be tied up in a topknot or it may be left hanging. Any suggestion of kinkiness, curliness, or woolly texture is objectionable. Color, pure white. Light tan or lemon on the ears is permissible, but not desirable.

SIZE

Weight under 7 pounds, with from 4 to 6 pounds preferred. Over-all quality is to be favoured over size.

GAIT

The Maltese moves with a jaunty, smooth, flowing gait. Viewed from the side, he gives an impression of rapid movement, size considered. In the stride, the forelegs reach straight and free from the shoulders, with elbows close. Hind legs to move in a straight line. Cowhocks or any suggestion of hind leg toeing in or out are faults.

TEMPERAMENT

For all his diminutive size, the Maltese seems to be without fear. His trust and affectionate responsiveness are very appealing. He is among the gentlest mannered of all little dogs, yet he is lively and playful as well as vigorous.

Approved March 10, 1964.
Reproduced by kind permission of the American Kennel Club.

FEDERATION CYNOLOGIQUE INTERNATIONALE (F.C.I.) STANDARD

GENERAL CHARACTERISTICS

The Maltese is scientifically classified in the braccoid group, miniature type (according to the classification of Pierre Megnin); a non-sporting dog of extremely old origin. Italian and probably Maltese (Cf. Pliny, Strabo and Columella, all of whom called it Canis Melitensis). The general conformation is that of a small dog, whose trunk exceeds in length the height at the withers. The body should give the overall impression of being narrow and long. The Maltese is an elegant dog with head, trunk, tail and legs covered (on all sides) with silky, very white, highly glossy hair long enough to be almost excessive. The Maltese is intelligent, of vivacious personality and devoted to his master. The rich, pure white coat makes a most highly preferred companion.

WEIGHT AND SIZE

Weight: 6½ to 9 lbs.
Height : males 8¼ to 10 inches; females 7¾ to 9 inches. The upper limit may be increased by ⅖ inch in dogs of exceptional beauty.

HEAD
Mesocephalic; its total length is 6/11 of the height at the withers. The length of the muzzle is 1/3 of the total length of the head, i.e. 37/10. The naso-cephalic index is therefore 37.46 and should never be above 40 or below 35. The width of the skull should never be more than 3/5 of the total length of the head, giving a total cephalic index of 60.06. The directions of the upper longitudinal axes of the skull and of the muzzle are parallel.

NOSE
On the same line with the nasal bridge; seen in profile, the forepart of the nose is on the vertical. It should be large compared with the volume of the head, wet and cool with the nostrils well open. It is round and absolutely black. No other colour is permissible.

NASAL BRIDGE
Straight. For the length of the nasal-cephalic index, see above. Its width, measured at the midpoint, should be 72% of its length, or 26% of the total length of the head. The nasal bridge has extremely long hair, which mingles with the hair of the beard.

LIPS AND MUZZLE
The upper lip, seen from in front, has the shape of a semicircle with an extremely long chord. The lips do not appear high as seen from in front and in profile; therefore the commissure is not visible. The edges of the lips must absolutely be black. The edges of the upper lip, moreover, meet the edge of the lower lip over the entire length; this means that the lower profile of the muzzle is supplied by the mandible. The medial furrow is pronounced. The muzzle should be in height 77% of its length; the sides are parallel, but the forepart of the muzzle is not perfectly flat and square since its sides join the sides of the muzzle itself in a gentle curve. The sub-orbital region should be well chiselled. The lips and the entire muzzle are covered with extremely long hair similar to that found on the ears.

JAWS
Light in appearance and of normal development; the upper and lower teeth meet in a scissors bite. The edges of the lower jaw are straight throughout their entire length. The lower jaw itself is normal, that is, neither prominent nor receding. The teeth are white and irregular, 42 in number and completely developed. The stop is very pronounced, because the profile of the apophyses of the nasal bones and upper jaw rises towards the frontal bone with an accentuated slope. The sinuses are well developed. The angle of the stop is 90 degrees.

SKULL
The length should exceed the length of the muzzle by 3/11 of the total length of the head. Its width is almost equal to its length. The average difference between length and width of the skull is about 1/10 inch. Its shape is very slightly ovoid, the occipital protuberance is very slightly marked. The back part of the forehead should be flat. The height of the sinuses and the supra-orbital ridges accentuate the stop. The medial furrow is almost non-existent. For the direction of the upper longitudinal axis of the skull, see above. The parietals are somewhat convex.

EYES
The expression is vivacious and intelligent. The eyes should be well open and rather larger

than normal. The shape tends to be round. The eyelids are close-fitting. The eyes are slightly protruding and should never be deep-set. They are set well up on the forehead. Seen from in front, the eyes should show no haw. The colour is deep ochre, the pigmentation of the eyelids is black, identical to that of the nose.

EARS
Triangular and flat. Their length is slightly more than 1/3 of the height at the withers. In a dog measuring from 81/2 to 93/4 inches at the withers, the length of the ears is 3 to 31/2 inches. The base is broad and the ears are set on high, considerably above the zygomatic arch. They hang close to the sides of the head, as close as the abundant hair permits. Although set on very high, the ears have little erectile power because of the weight of the hair. They are entirely covered with long thick and non-wavy hair reaching at least to the shoulders and, preferably, beyond. They are further covered by hair falling from the crest of the skull.

NECK
In spite of the abundant hair, the forward and upper lines of the nape should be clearly visible. The length of the neck is approximately equal to half of the height at the withers, that is, approximately the same length as the head, and with a circumference equal to or greater than the height at the withers, when the neck is normally feathered. The throat and jaws should not have loose skin, meaning that there is no dewlap. The neck is carried erect, giving the impression that the head is thrown back.

FOREQUARTERS
SHOULDERS
Should be 1/3 as long as the height at the withers; its inclination to the horizontal varies from 60-65 degrees. In a dog 83/4 inches high at the withers, the scapula is about 3 inches long. The shoulders should be free in their movement, and their direction in relation to the centre plane of the body is slightly inclined at the point, which means that the scapulae tend to a vertical position.

UPPER ARM
Well joined to the trunk in its upper two-thirds. The inclination to the horizontal is about 70 degrees, and its longitudinal direction is almost parallel to the center plane of the body. Its length, greater than that of the scapula, is 40-45% of the height at the height of the withers.

FOREARM
Straight and vertical, lean, well-boned, with few muscles; the bone is quite strong considering the size of the dog. The length of the forearm is less than that of the humerus (33% of the height at the withers), and the height of the entire foreleg to the elbow is 50-54% of the height at the withers, which means that in a dog measuring 83/4inches at the withers, the height of the foreleg at the elbow is about 43/4inches, that is, slightly more than half the height at the withers. The elbows should lie in a plane parallel to the center plane of the body. This means that they should not be close to the ribs, thus eliminating the armpit, nor should they be turned outward. The forearm, from the elbow to the lower end of the pastern, is covered all around with long hair, which in general is flocked, forming a fringe on the backside of the foreleg.

WRISTS
Follow the vertical line of the forearm. They are very mobile, should not be knotty, and covered with thin skin. The wrist is covered on all sides by long, thick hair.

PASTERNS
Follow the vertical of the forearm and, like the wrists, should be lean and covered with fine hair. The pasterns are short and straight and covered, like the forearms and the wrists, with long, thick hair in every part.

FEET
Round, with closed toes, well arched, covered with long, thick hair, there is also long, thick hair between the toes. The pads are black, and the nails are black or at least dark.

BODY
The length of the trunk, measured from the point of the shoulder (external scapula-humeral angle) to the point of the buttock (posterior point of the ischium), exceeds on the average the height at the withers by 3 inches, or more precisely, for every inch of height at the withers there corresponds 1.38 inch of length in the trunk.

RIB CAGE
Roomy, reaching beyond elbow level, with moderately sprung ribs. The sternum region is long, its outline being a semi-circle of very large radius which ascends slightly towards the belly. The circumference of the rib cage should be 2/3 more than the height at the withers, and its diameter should be 36-38% of the height at the withers. The depth of the thorax should be 65% of the height at the withers, or at least half the length of the trunk, and it is better if it exceeds it. In a dog 9 inches high at the withers, the rib cage should have the following dimensions: circumference (behind the elbows), 14 1/2 inches; depth, 6 inches; height, 4 1/2 inches; diameter, 3 1/3 inches.

BACK
The withers are slightly raised above the back line, which is straight. The back line goes from the withers to the root of the tail. The length of the back is about 65% of the height at the withers; that is, in a dog 9 inches high at the withers, the back is close to 6 inches long.

LOINS
Perfectly joined with the back line, the loins continue its outline. The muscles are well developed. The length is 1/3 of the height at the withers, and the width is the same.

BELLY AND FLANKS
The belly is rather low, ascending very little from sternum to flank. The flanks should be almost equal in length to the loins. The hollow of the flanks should not be pronounced.

CROUP
Continues the straight back line. It is broad, and its width should be 1/3 of the height at the withers, its length about 3/4 inches greater than its width in a dog measuring 9 inches at the withers. The inclination to the horizontal, from the haunch to the root of the tail, is always less than 10 degrees.

SEXUAL ORGANS
The testicles should be perfectly developed.

TAIL
Set on level with the croup, it is very thick at the root and fine at the tip. In a dog measuring 9 inches at the withers, the tail should measure 5 1/2 inches. The tail is correctly carried in a single large curve, with the tip touching the croup between the haunches. A tail curved over to one side is tolerated. The tail is covered with very long, abundant hair, which falls entirely on one side of the body, that is, on the flank and thigh, rather like the branches of a weeping willow. The hair on the tail should be long enough to reach the hocks.

HINDQUARTERS
THIGHS
The thighs are covered with hard muscle; the back edges are arched. The length of the thighs is 39% of the height at the withers. The direction of the thighs is somewhat sloped downward and forward and, in respect to the vertical, it should be parallel to the center plane of the body. In a dog measuring 9 inches at the withers, the width of the thighs is about 1 1/4 inches less than its length. They are covered with long hair which forms a fringe at the back edge.

LEGS
Extremely well boned for a dog of this size; the furrow between the bone and the back tendon is not pronounced. The legs are slightly longer than the thighs; their inclination to the horizontal is 55 degrees. The legs are covered on all sides by long hair which is generally flocked and fringed on the back surface.

HOCKS
The distance from the soles to the points of the hocks is a little more than 1/3 of the height at the withers. The forward angulation is 140 degrees. Seen from behind, the line from the point of the hock to the ground should be on the vertical and on the prolongation of the buttock line.

METATARSUS
The length depends on the height at the withers; it should lie on the vertical, as seen both in profile and from behind. It is covered all around by long hair, generally flocked, which forms a limited fringe on the backside.

FEET
Round like the forefeet and otherwise similar.

COAT
HAIR
Dense, glossy, heavy, very long; its texture is silky. The hair is straight throughout its length. The average length of the hair on the body should be a little less than 8 3/4 inches, that is, the longest hair should be equal to or slightly more than the height at the withers. Such long hair should cover the entire body-trunk, forequarters, tail, neck, ears, skull and muzzle. Besides being glossy, long and white, the thick mass of hair on the Maltese should fall heavily to the ground, like a solid mantle fitting close to the trunk, and the hair should be without flocks or

tufts (except on the forelegs from the elbows to the feet and on the hind legs from the stifle to the feet, where tufted hair is permitted). The entire mass of hair should be superlatively glossy. The coat should reveal only the principal curves and projections of the body. There is no undercoat.

COLOR
Pure white; a pale ivory shade is permitted. Very limited pale orange tints are tolerated, but they constitute a fault. Decided markings, even if very small, are not acceptable.

SKIN
Close-fitting to the body at all points. The head (skull and muzzle) should have no wrinkles; there should be no dewlap. The skin is in part or over the whole body pigmented with dark spots; when the hair is parted, the skin color, especially on the back, should be of a more or less intense wine red. The pigment of the lips, nose and eyelids should be black. The pads must be black; the nails also should be black or at least dark.

GAIT
The trotting gait consists of short, very rapid steps, giving somewhat the impression of rolling. The gait should in no way resemble that of the Pekinese.

FAULTS
General Characteristics: Undistinguished overall appearance; heavy appearance; dull or coarse coat; lack of symmetry

Height at the withers: over or above standard.

Head: Upper longitudinal cranial-facial axes divergent or convergent; naso-cephalic index above 40 or below 35, disqualification.

Nose: Lower than the line of the bridge, protruding over the vertical line of the forepart of the muzzle; nostrils not well open; small nose; deficient pigmentation; traces of depigmentation on the nostrils; total depigmentation, disqualification; any color besides black, disqualification).

Nasal Bridge: Short; narrow; converging sidelines; arched, hollowed. If decidedly arched, disqualification.

Lips and Muzzle: Short or excessively long muzzle; lips too large, to the point where they cover the lower jaw; deficient in development; forward convergence of the sides of the muzzle, that is, pointed muzzle; forepart of the muzzle not broad; conjunction of two halves of upper lip form an inverted V; lack of chiseling in the sub-orbital region.

Jaws: Undershot: If this condition harms the appearance of the muzzle, disqualification.

Overshot: If for insufficient length of underjaw, disqualification. If caused by crooked teeth, fault; sides of lower jaw curved; teeth irregular or not full complement; horizontal erosion of teeth.

Skull: Small, short, too narrow at the parietals; spheroid (very serious fault); Skull not flat; supra-orbital ridges flattened; sinuses insufficiently developed; occipital protuberance excessively pronounced; medial furrow pronounced; stop insufficiently accentuated or receding; convergence or divergence of the upper cranial-facial longitudinal axes.

Eyes: Small or too prominent; light eyes, wall eyes, disqualification; slanting, almond eyes; ectropion,; entropion; eyes too close; cross eyes; partial depigmentation of the eyelids; total depigmentation is a very serious fault; total bilateral depigmentation is a disqualification.

Ears: Thick, too short; narrow base; rigidity caused by excessive thickness; curling; short hair.

Neck: Massive and short; insufficient arching; lack of definition in nape; dewlap; hair too short.

Shoulder: Lacking in freedom of movement; straight.

Upper Arm: Too sloping or too straight; short.

Forearm: Spongy bone; arching at outside of radial (very serious fault); deviation from vertical; elbows in or out; short hair.

Wrists: Evident hypertrophy of the wrist bones; short hair.

Pasterns: Out of vertical; spongy; short hair.

Feet: Oblong; splayed; broad; crushed; carried inward or outward, that is, not vertical; bad arrangement of pads; deficiency of pigmentation in nails and pads; lack of hair between toes and on toes.

Body: Longitudinal diameter greater than the required length or shorter.

Chest: Manubrium of the sternum not pronounced.

Rib Cage: Deficient in height, depth and circumference; too narrow; decidedly carinated; xiphoid appendage curved inward.

Ribs: Insufficiently sprung.

Back: Short; breaking of the backline at the eleventh vertebra; saddleback (lordosis); roach back (kyphosis).

Loins: Narrow, too long, arched.

Belly and Flanks: Belly insufficiently or excessively drawn up; flanks excessively hollowed.

Croup: Narrow, sloping.

Sexual Organs: Monorchidism or cryptorchidism, disqualification; incomplete development of one or both testicles, disqualification.

Tail: Too long or too short; lack of tail or rudimentary tail, either congenital or acquired, disqualification; tail set on low; not thick at the root; not curved over the back (carried horizontally or hanging; a very serious fault); tail carried curved on one side of trunk; tail curled; lack of feathering, short hair.

Thighs: Carried away from stifle region; insufficiently feathered.

Legs: Insufficiently sloped; lack of hair.

Hocks: Too high; angulation too open or too closed because of forward deviation of metatarsus; out of vertical.

Metatarsus: Too long; out of vertical; dew-claws; lack of hair.

Feet: Similar to fore feet.

Coat: Hair not dense, dull, not long; woolly texture; mass of hair soft and fluffy, light; hair tufted or flocked; mass of hair not close fitting to trunk; curly hair, disqualification; wavy hair (serious fault).

Color: Any color besides white, disqualification, with the exception of pale ivory; pale orange tint; well defined markings, even if very small, disqualification.

Skin: Wrinkles on the head; dewlap; traces of depigmentation on the nose and eyelids; total depigmentation of the nose, disqualification; depigmentation of the edges of both eyelids of both eyes, disqualification) depigmentation of the vulva and vent; lack of pigmentation in the nails and pads; total depigmentation of the pads (very serious fault).

Gait: Ambling (very serious fault); Pekingese gait, disqualification.

DISQUALIFICATIONS
Height at the withers: In males, over 10$1/4$ inches or more than $3/4$ inch less than the minimum; in females, more than 10 inches or more than $3/4$ inch less than the standard.
Head: Accentuated divergence or convergence of the upper cranial-facial longitudinal axes; naso-cephalic index over 40 or under 35.
Nose: Total depigmentation; any color besides black.
Nasal Bridge: Definite arch.
Jaws: Overshot condition if caused by shortness of the lower jaw; accentuated undershot condition if it harms the appearance of the muzzle.
Eyes: Walleyes; total bilateral depigmentation of the eyelids; bilaterally crossed eyes.
Body: Longitudinal diameter $3/4$ inch over the maximum standard for height at the withers.
Sexual Organs: Monorchidism, cryptorchidism; incomplete development of one or both testicles.
Tail: Lack of or rudimentary, whether congenital or acquired.
Coat: Any besides white, with the exception of pale ivory; definite markings, even if very small.
Skin: Total depigmentation of the nose; depigmentation of the edges of both eyelids on both eyes.
Gait: Pekingese gait.

N.B: In judging in a show, when any part of the body involving type is rated zero, the dog is disqualified, even if the other parts are excellent.

SCALE OF POINTS

General appearance	20
Skull and Muzzle	20
Eyes and Eyelids	10
Ears	10
Shoulders	5
Rib Cage	10
Loins and Croup	5
Legs and Feet	10
Tail	20
Coat and Color	40
	150

Reproduced by kind permission of the FCI.

ASSESSING A SHOW MALTESE.
A correctly made adult Maltese is very eye-catching with four extremely important visual components – a balanced body shape, a lovely white silken coat, a beautiful head and flowing movement. The buoyant, affectionate temperament may not be quite as visual, but is of equal importance.

The overall appearance should be that of a compact, smart dog who looks animated on the move yet travels smoothly, with head high and tail well over. The body is sturdy, but in no way coarse, with a nicely rounded rib beneath a silky, straight, pure-white coat.

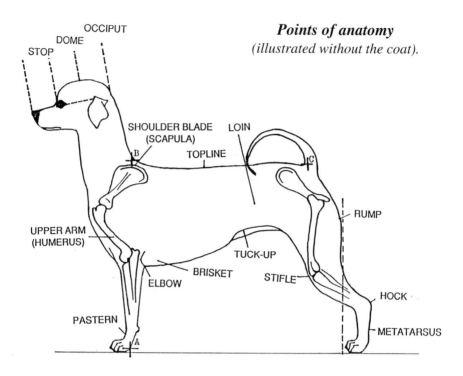

OCCIPUT
DOME
STOP

Points of anatomy
(illustrated without the coat).

SHOULDER BLADE (SCAPULA)
LOIN
TOPLINE
UPPER ARM (HUMERUS)
RUMP
TUCK-UP
BRISKET
STIFLE
ELBOW
HOCK
PASTERN
METATARSUS

The head should be evenly balanced, with a neat black nose. The muzzle sufficiently broad to house a perfect scissor bite, the stop moderate. The eyes should be of decent size. They should be dark, with a black 'mascara' eye line and haloes. The ears are set reasonably low on the skull. The neck must be of sufficient length to enable the head to be carried high. The fore-limbs must be straight, the hind limbs angulated, and the pads black. The topline should be level. The rib should be well sprung, and the dog should not have a long loin. The tailset is high and the plume arched over the back. The temperament should be outgoing and alert. This is a dog that should move with style and, finally, should be sweet-natured.

So, how does this compare with your Maltese? Do remember that the perfect dog has yet to be born. No dog has everything we desire.

Your very first show Maltese will, naturally, be to you the most beautiful creature of all, and this will always be so. But also be realistic and get to know your dog literally inside out. In that way you will understand more clearly what judging is all about.

It is a good idea to place a large mirror flat against a wall and stand your dog in front of it, but a little distance away, then you can appreciate the perception of others.

Walk up and down and see how your dog looks on the move.

The very best time to examine the shape of your dog is in the bath when wet. Make a point of really familiarizing yourself with this dog's particular body structure, while remembering that a poorly-made frame affects every other aspect of your dog. Acknowledge any shortcomings. Write down in a book exactly how you see your dog. Balance is the name of the game, not too much or too little of any one thing.

WHAT IS A BALANCED DOG?

Well, it is one that is in proportion throughout. You can have a well-balanced small dog and a well-balanced larger dog. It is not size that matters, it is how the whole blends together within the standard.

So look at the head first. From nose to stop and from stop to centre of the skull (between the fore-part of the ears) should be of equal distance, with the stop well-defined. In other words, it should be moderately deep, and certainly not sloping backwards, which would give the head an elongated shape and is often accompanied with an unsightly dropped fore-face (the muzzle sloping downwards). Yet the stop should not be over deep, as you do not want an excessively high crown, which could be construed as 'apple headed'.

A narrow, tapering head is incorrect. What is required is a muzzle well-filled under the eyes and sufficiently broad to accommodate the correct number of uncluttered, even teeth i.e. 42 in an adult (28 in a puppy) in a scissor bite, not undershot, not overshot nor wry. The muzzle should taper slightly, but certainly not be snipey, and the softly curved skull must be sufficiently broad to balance. The nose is black.

Eyes are tremendously important as they can be so expressive. A Maltese should have lovely dark, softly expressive eyes. They should be of decent size, not too small, for this would give a mean expression, yet certainly not bulging, giving a 'pop-eyed' appearance, which would be totally uncharacteristic.

Think of a triangle, with one point representing the dog's nose and the other two points the eyes, the distance between them being equal. This would be balanced. The eyes should have a 'mascara' line completely encircling the edge of the eyelid, and the skin surrounding the eye itself should be pigmented to create haloes. Weather can have a great influence here and, during the cold winter months, haloes vanish on some dogs, thankfully to reappear once the warm weather returns.

The ears are set slightly low on the skull, rather than high up on top of the head. If they were in this latter position it would suggest a Terrier type head, which would be very untypical. Nevertheless, young puppies sometimes carry their ears a little high while teething, but these settle down later on. The hair on the ears mingles with the coat hair as it grows longer.

A graceful neck of reasonable length can, when set on good shoulders, give a Maltese a wonderfully elegant head carriage; however, a short neck, particularly on a well-coated dog, gives the appearance of the head sitting directly on the shoulders and the undesirable overall effect is that of a 'stuffy' dog. Quite apart from appearances, a Maltese is not very high off the ground and a judge requires to see the forward movement – not easy when a low-carried, well-furnished head is filling the space.

The shoulder blade has considerable influence on both the dog's head-carriage and front movement. The ideal shoulder blade should slant at 45 degrees to the ground, forming an approximate 90 degree angle with the humerus at the shoulder joint. Good angulation contributes to an effortless stride and smooth forward action, while a correct layback will give a lovely smooth, continuous line down the back of the neck into the withers and along the spine. An incorrect layback will give an abrupt angle of neck to back.

Bad angulation will affect the muscle structure too, narrowing the width across the front of the chest and giving the appearance of less substance. Remember, you can have substance in the smaller dog. This does not mean coarseness, but is the lovely rounded feeling your hands find under the coat. A dog receiving inadequate exercise lacks muscle tone and condition which can prejudice any prize-winning chances in the ring.

A Maltese is not an Afghan, requiring long legs for racing; or a Dachshund needing short stubby legs for digging. The legs of a Maltese must be in direct proportion to the dog as a whole.

*Incorrect: Short upright neck,
giving a stuffy appearance.*

Correct: Level topline.

Incorrect: roached back.

*Incorrect: The topline is
sloping to the withers.*

When next bathing your Maltese take note of the shape of the fore limbs. They should be straight, with no bowing on the upper arm, and the elbows should lie snugly alongside the ribcage and not stand proudly away. In fact, if the rib shape is correct, you should only just be able to slide your finger between it and the elbow. The length of the upper arm also influences your dog's movement. Pass down to the pasterns and note whether or not they turn out: they should be forward pointing.

As a whole the Maltese should be compact and cobby because an animal with comparatively short legs must be cobby in body to be well balanced.

Obviously, the ribcage is important, for it has to accommodate life's essential organs. Almost every breed acknowledges that a dog must have a good spring of rib, for it has to house the inner working parts. You must have 'heartroom', since a Maltese is lively and active, with vitality as part of the overall attraction. A well-sprung, not barrel or shallow, rib also gives a certain width to the back, apart from lots of room inside. It therefore follows that a flat rib is highly undesirable. A good rib should be accompanied by a reasonable width of chest (or brisket) and, if you run your hand down the front of the dog, you will find a decent spacing between the legs. Too narrow or too shallow a chest will mean the forelegs will move too close; a barrel chest would push the legs too wide apart, again distorting movement. A reasonable width in direct proportion to the dog, and devoid of any narrowness, is what you are looking for.

A strong spine will give a level back from withers to tail. We have all sat at the ringside and

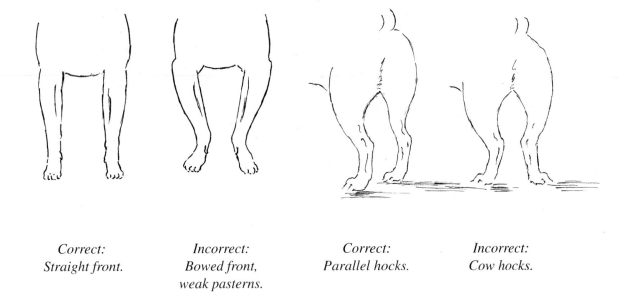

Correct:
Straight front.

Incorrect:
Bowed front,
weak pasterns.

Correct:
Parallel hocks.

Incorrect:
Cow hocks.

admired the dog with a sturdy level topline. It makes such a difference. So you will not wish to see a roached back, or one that is sagging. Having said that, although 'running downhill' from rear to forelegs is a fault in an adult, puppies often develop faster in the rear end than the front, but that is only while they are very young and still growing.

Hind angulation contributes to an effortless stride and a smooth flowing movement. Poor angulation tends to shorten the stride and make a dog's action stilted or choppy. This is particularly noticeable if a dog is straight in the stifle. When bathing your dog, part the wet hair at the back and note if the limbs are parallel when viewed from behind. Is there any bowing out, or a tendency to being 'cow hocked', or are the hocks twisted at all?

The coat is the over-mantle that covers the frame and, although it is often considered the crowning glory, you would be doing yourself and the Maltese breed a great disservice if you believe a beautiful coat outweighs an inadequate frame.

The Maltese coat should be single, without an undercoat, straight and silky in texture, and not crimped. It is written that the coat be of 'good length' and the exhibitor may grow it to whatever length he or she desires. Some prefer to grow the coat to the ground only, while others consider it more attractive to see it extended much further. Too great a length can impede action and can also present an unbalanced picture as it flows out behind when on the move, especially on grass. So this is a matter of personal judgement. Without doubt there are few more breath-taking sights than a free-moving Maltese proudly gaiting round the ring, with a supple coat flowing with the movement.

The colour: white, but slight lemon markings should not penalise. Puppies often have lemon ears and these lighten as they grow.

Now to the tail. Personal preference often applies here, because some like the tail to have a definite high arch, while some others prefer it simply to curve over the back and fall away to the side. Both are acceptable. However, the setting is the all-important factor. If the tail is set too low it will totally spoil the outline. A tail to avoid is one that has the bone twisted tightly in a circle, which is sometimes called a 'pig's tail'.

A well-made Maltese is a joy to watch on the move with the typical jaunty, smooth-flowing action. A Maltese is quite a fast-moving dog on comparatively short legs and at speed you will notice a natural slight swing in, which is called 'kinetic balance'. It is the normal movement of a well-constructed dog that is moving at speed – and I stress, at speed. The whole leg moves slightly inwards in a straight line – not to be mistaken for, or associated in any way with, a dog that weaves, which is when the legs are seen to swing in, almost or completely crossing; this is an ugly movement and one definitely to be avoided. Lastly, a male must be entire (two testicles descended into the scrotum). This all adds up to a unique dog – a Maltese.

As I said before, get to know your dog; be totally honest in your assessment; acknowledge any imperfections and do not expect exact conformity. A good judge does not condemn a dog who fails in some small aspect or another – every dog does, even the Champions. Your Maltese will be judged as a whole, against fellow competitors who are not absolutely perfect either.

Repeat this examination from time to time to refresh your memory, for it can play funny tricks and be a little forgetful. If you have other mature dogs (not just showdogs) examine them all in exactly the same way when bathing, and write down what you find for comparison. All this will help you when choosing future breeding partners.

Chapter Six

EXHIBITING YOUR MALTESE

Grooming a puppy has been covered in an earlier chapter (Chapter Three: Caring for your Puppy). Now it is time to go through the whole routine of caring for the more mature dog – particularly one you hope to show. To maintain a long coat in good order takes total dedication.

There are no short cuts when owning a coated breed. Neglect leads not only to discomfort for your dog, but to skin problems and ruination of the coat itself. However, you must not be too hard on yourself by expecting to become an expert immediately. I have always maintained that you learn with your first dog and reap the benefit of that knowledge with your second. Of course, there are those with a natural gift who present their dogs to perfection right from the start, but for the majority it can take time to become proficient. So be patient, and always endeavour to allocate to yourself a certain amount of time every day for making grooming a pleasure for both you and your dog.

With a Maltese, preparation for the show ring begins the day you acquire your dog. Nourishment, maintenance, and environment are all contributory factors. This is not a breed that can be spruced up the day before a show. It is everyday care that reaps results.

THE COAT
Like everything else in life, poor conditions produce poor results, so a coat that comes from a healthy basis has the best start. One that is gloriously rich and supple is dependent on many factors, including genetics (the breeder would hopefully have chosen parents with as many 'good coats' in their ancestry as possible). After that, dedicated care with the grooming is paramount, and finally, not to be underestimated, comes nutrition, for this is vital in keeping the skin in a healthy, flexible condition.

Although there are many excellent preparations for treating hair externally, if quality protein is deficient from the diet, and associated nutrients inadequate, the result is likely to be poor hair growth. Although external treatments will certainly help improve the appearance of a poor coat, these will only assist in the short term, while masking the true situation. A further consideration, not to be overlooked, is that a healthy, flowing, silky coat is far easier, and less expensive, to maintain. The hair does not cling together as much, therefore it is easier to groom, and you do not have to purchase all those expensive external aids to make it look good.

Keeping a coat in good order is, as I have said, all-important. Regular grooming is a must, as neglect leads to tangles which, of course, have to be removed, resulting in coat breakage – and a broken coat is not what you are after.

As with human hair, every coat has a different texture, and all young coats are soft initially, strengthening as they mature. The coat of an adult bitch may be found to be softer than that of a male. It is therefore up to you to familiarise yourself with your dog's hair texture. The correct Maltese coat should be silky and straight and without an undercoat. It should lie gracefully on either side of the body from a centre parting, and that is what you are striving for.

Some Maltese develop a stronger coat; not one that is coarse or wiry, for this would be totally incorrect, but one made up of stronger, straight silky hair. These are a joy to maintain as they are less likely to tangle quickly and seem to withstand normal wear and tear without any problems.

On the other hand, fine hair needs much more care as it can fracture so easily, giving rise to a 'broken coat' that not only looks untidy, but results in a coat on which it is difficult to attain any length. Here I should mention that you NEVER use a slicker brush on a show coat, whatever the texture.

The perfect Maltese coat is, as I have mentioned, lovely and straight, but not all dogs are so endowed. A few years ago it was not uncommon to see a quality mantle that displayed a very soft open wave in it and this was acceptable: however, a crinkly or a very wavy coat is not desirable and would be marked down by the experienced judge.

BASIC EQUIPMENT
This is similar to that required for the puppy:

Grooming tools (left to right): Pin brush, guillotine nail-clippers, scissors, round-ended scissors, wide tooth comb, pure bristle brush (bottom row): tail comb and a face comb.

A wide-toothed (long pin) stainless steel comb with rounded ends.
A fine-toothed comb.
A good-quality pure bristle brush preferably with long bristles.
A pin brush with flexible round-end pins, set in a rubber-cushion base.
Scissors, both tapered and round ended.
Nail-clippers (the guillotine type).
Cotton buds and cotton wool.
A small bowl for water.
Paper rolls.
Cornflour and/or borasic powder.
A plastic spray-bottle containing water.
A toothbrush and toothpaste.
Tooth-scalers, which may be purchased from show stands and *must* be sterilised after every

session, or between dogs, by boiling for ten minutes.
Latex hair bands.
Absorbent tissues.
Paper or plastic for wrapping.

For use between show groomings there are many different types of sprays and conditioners available on the market. Trial and error will establish exactly which type best suits your dog's coat texture.

GROOMING

There are several methods of grooming a Maltese in mature coat. Some owners prefer to work with the dog on their lap, but here I will discuss the two most popular systems, using a table.

Never groom a totally dry coat, because this can fracture or split the hair. So, before proceeding, mix a very small amount of conditioner with water and give a light fine spray into the air above the area to be worked, then lightly spray each section as you go along. Do not overdo the conditioner or you will make the coat sticky. Should you find this combination does not agree with your particular dog's coat, then use water only in the spray. Keep your brushes and combs scrupulously clean. Wash them regularly so that they glide smoothly through the hair and do not snag. The light spray of water and clean tools will ensure there is no drag on the coat, which is your main area for concern.

An alternative to water while grooming would be a light oil spray. Here the choice is many and varied and, again, it will be a case of which suits your dog's coat the best. The very light oil sprays can be used as an aid to grooming, whilst at the same time helping to protect the hair when wrapped. The heavy oils are used by those who may wish to 'oil a dog down' between shows.

Method One: Lie your Maltese tummy-upwards, on your lap, and groom down each leg, both outside and inside, taking care not to catch the dewclaw in the comb, then attend to the remaining hair underneath the chest, paying particular attention to where the leg hair rubs against the chest, as this is where knots can form. When combing between the hind legs, on the inside of the thighs, protect the sensitive parts of the body with one hand, whilst combing away from them. Lightly spray the coat with a fine mist of water while working, and carefully separate any tangles either with your fingers, or by picking them apart with the tip of the comb.

While you have your Maltese in this position, it is a good time for a foot examination, and for clipping off any excess hair that is growing between the pads. This helps the dog take a better grip on slippery floors and prevents anything attaching itself to the underside to mar movement. The remaining hair should sit level with the cushions (or pads). Remember that some dogs have ticklish feet, and may jerk a leg away unexpectedly. Never allow the nails to grow long, as, quite apart from the discomfort this causes, it will also affect movement. Again, do not forget there may be a dewclaw requiring your attention too.

When this stage is completed, stand your Maltese on a firm table, with the head to your righthand side. An insecure table will be unnerving. The table should be fitted with a non-slippery surface such as a rubber mat, with a thick, folded, terry towel for comfort. The table should be set at an ideal height for you to work, either sitting or standing, whichever you prefer.

Brush and comb the tail hair and, as with puppy grooming, take care that the comb does not trap the fine bones at the tip of the tail. Hold the bone of the tail in one hand and groom away from it, then move on to the body hair, after ensuring that the whole area beneath the tail is tangle free. Work from the rear (tail) along towards the shoulders, leaving the head and the front chest hair under the chin (this is called the fall) until last.

Starting at the back, work on a small section of the body hair at a time, brush it right through thoroughly. It is best to begin at the bottom, or tip of the hair and, while gradually lengthening your stroke, move up towards the centre parting, completing that section by being able to brush or comb right down to the skin beneath, and from top to bottom, using firm but sensitive strokes.

By 'sensitive' I mean you must be conscious of what your hands are feeling all the time. Have a light touch, like that of a good pastry-maker. The moment the brush or comb meets any resistance, back off and separate the obstruction carefully. Never drag straight down.

Finish each section by being able to brush or comb right through the coat, from the spine right down to the tip, using good straight strokes, taking care not to damage the delicate ends. Work forward carefully, blending in this top hair with the previously groomed coat beneath. Once the shoulder hair has been reached and completed, turn the dog round and repeat the process on the other side.

The worst mistake you can make is to groom only the surface of the coat. By ensuring you have gone right through to the skin, you are not only doing a thorough job, but are also stimulating the dog's circulation. Then, to give a final smooth finish to the coat, comb through with the wide-toothed comb and put in a nice straight parting right down the back. I like to use a knitting needle or tail-comb to do the parting, but your ordinary comb will be just as effective.

Method Two: Instead of standing on the table, the dog is laid on one side, and the operation differs only in the method of dealing with the coat. Do the underside and legs in exactly the same way as described for the first method. Now place the dog on one side on the table, paws facing you, head to the right. Having finished with the tail, lift the whole coat up and lie it away from you over the dog's back, leaving a thin layer of hair from head to tail upon which to work.

Brush and comb this first layer, intermingling it with the belly hair you have already previously groomed. Once completed, bring down another thin layer in a line from head to tail to work upon, and continue with a layer at a time, ensuring you go right down to the skin.

When finished, turn the dog over, repeating the procedure on the other side. All other aspects of care are the same as with the first method of grooming.

THE HEAD

This is the same for both Method One and Method Two. To tidy the head, turn your dog to face you. This is where training comes into its own, for it is much easier – and safer – if your dog is accustomed to sitting quietly, or, as is my own preference, is used to lying down facing me, with chin flat on the table, allowing me to attend to the head, and put up the topknot, without a tussle. Some exhibitors like to use a small padded cushion upon which to rest their dog's chin while setting the topknots, and some dogs find this more acceptable.

This procedure does not please all dogs, but do persevere. If you are lucky, your Maltese may lie there quietly right from the start, but usually it takes time and much patience to get a dog to stay absolutely still while you fiddle about; but do not give up – your dog will understand eventually.

You will reap the reward of your efforts when your dog remains quite still while all the hustle and bustle of the show goes on around you both, and you are trying to put the topknot up with fingers that seem to belong to somebody else when you are under pressure!

To return to grooming the head: with the dog's chin flat on the table in front of you, brush the hair up, away from the eyes then down the ears and cheeks. Do not use the wide-toothed comb near the eyes in case you catch the eye-lid itself, but remove any debris from the corners with the fine-toothed comb. If this debris is hard, moisten with a little water on cotton wool, leave a moment or two to soften, then try again. If you are too hasty and do not wait, hair will be removed at the same time, resulting in unsightly short clumps as the hair grows again.

EARS

Maltese, with their hairy, dropped ears, do not have the advantage of free air continually circulating inside, as do their prick-eared counterparts. For this reason, it is best to remove all hair from the cavity, so enabling air to enter more freely and keep the ear dry and a healthy pink colour. Do this in exactly the same way as described for grooming puppies. If in doubt, it would be prudent to ask someone to hold the dog's head steady during your early attempts, and the routine will then be soon learned.

If ear wax is evident, this should be a golden brown in colour, and may be removed with a baby bud, but be warned – do not dig down into the ear itself as you can do irrevocable damage. Remove only the wax that can be wiped out easily – never probe deeply.

Should the ear appear red or swollen inside, this could indicate a mite infestation or a bacterial infection. Either of these conditions may be accompanied by a dark or evil-smelling discharge but, even if a discharge is not evident, seek veterinary advice quickly. Ears must not be neglected.

TOPKNOTS

Years ago one particular judge made it known that she disapproved of any kind of attachment to the hair when a dog was being shown. She liked seeing them in their 'natural' state, firmly believing the standard required a parting 'from head to tail', and those exhibitors who were not aware of her preference had quite a shock when she whipped the bows off their dogs before judging them.

Today, there are many attractive ways of dressing out the head, especially if the hair is nice and long. In the US two topknots appear to be the fashion, in England the single topknot seems to be preferred for showing, and on the Continent both methods are to be seen in the ring.

The first essential is to lift hair away from the eyes themselves as soon as this is practical. The earlier you accustom a puppy to having hair tied up, the better. At home between shows you can put it in a little bunch, or braid or plait the hair. Alternatively tie it in bunches, one on either side of the head.

Here are two accepted methods of securing hair for showing. To make the single, centre topknot, brush the hair back away from the eyes. Next, take the tip of your comb and draw a line from the outer corner of the eye. This should be a straight line but angled slightly inwards, finishing just before the edge of the ear. Then draw the line across the skull to the same position of the opposite ear, followed by another sloping line down to the outer edge of the other eye (see diagram).

Gather the hair within this area upwards and slightly backwards, away from the eyes, and comb it into a smooth bunch. Between shows you will wish to protect the hair from being damaged by the band that secures it, so cut a small oblong strip of acid-free tissue paper, or plastic, and wrap it round the base of the gathered hair. Then take a small latex band (the quarter inch orthodontic type that may be purchased at shows) and secure it round the bunch.

If the hair between the skull and the band is too tight your dog will try and rake it out, so very gently ease anything that looks as if it is being pulled. Of course the protective paper would not be used when showing. At that time you would just secure the gathered hair with the band and add the bow, finally combing the plume backwards.

Setting topknots takes practice, but eventually you will find the position that suits your particular dog best, though it may take many attempts. Each time you wish to remove the band, cut it off, taking care not to snip any hair at the same time. Simply pulling the band off will be painful for your dog and you will lose quite a few hairs each time. There are special scissors made with slightly hooked ends designed to remove bands. Again, these are available on stalls at shows.

The alternative method of dressing the head is to make a centre parting from the muzzle up

TYING THE TOP-KNOT

Gather the hair for the topknot.

Put the elastic round twice.

Add the bow.

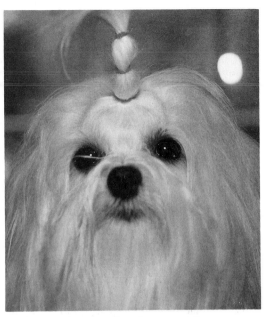

Am. Ch. Su-Le's Screech Owl, owned and bred by Barbara Bergquist. In the USA it is customary to tie the hair in two bows.

When you are not showing your dog, you can use this method of tying up the topknot.

Ch. Vicbrita Delight (Ch. Vicbrita Fidelity – Ch. Vicbrita Spectacular): Best of Breed Crufts 1966. Owned and bred by Margaret White. This is now considered an old-fashioned method of presenting a Maltese in the ring, but many owners use this style at home.

Photo: Sally Anne Thompson.

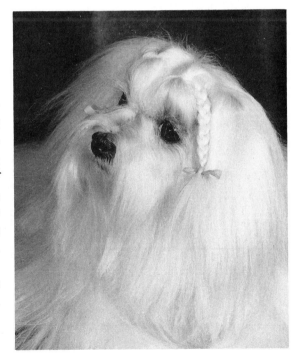

between the eyes, continuing across the skull between the ears. Again, draw a line with your comb from the outer edge of the eye up to just in front of the ear above, but this time go across the skull to the centre parting only. Comb this hair up and back from the eyes as before. Protect with a strip of paper or plastic. Fold the paper in half and secure by putting the latex band round once, or possibly twice, leaving a small knob, thus allowing the loose hair from this little bunch to lie between the eye and the ear. Make sure the hair between the skull and the band is not too tight by easing the hair away from the band slightly, drawing it towards the skull. Repeat the procedure on the opposite side and you will now have two little knobs, one over each eye (see diagram).

If a topknot is at all uncomfortable your Maltese will take the very first opportunity to try to remove it, thus ruining all your hard work, possibly slicing off the taut hair at the root, and disastrous if you are just going into the ring!

TEETH

Teeth should never be neglected and their inspection must be part of your daily grooming routine. There are types of toothpaste available made especially to be acceptable for dogs. In the past many breeders resorted to salted water, or a solution of peroxide and milk in equal parts as their cleaning agents, all to good effect, and still useful in an emergency.

Also available are special dog toothbrushes. These have long handles and are very effective in getting right to the back of a small mouth. Ordinary baby tooth brushes are also useful, and for a quick rub over, try using the finger brushes. These are made of a soft plastic with a raised area, and fit snugly over your finger – you can even just use gauze wrapped round a finger, as suggested when puppy grooming was discussed, to accustom a young dog to the teeth-cleaning process.

Always note the colour of your dog's gums. They should look nice and firm and a healthy pink. If the gums are receding, or are dark red and angry, this is a sign of danger, calling for experienced veterinary attention without delay.

Allowing tartar to build up will gradually push the gum away from the tooth. This could lead to an infection setting in which would endanger your dog's health, as problems in the mouth can adversely affect internal organs and, possibly, result in a loss of teeth. Toy dogs are not renowned for retaining their teeth into very old age, but the more care you bestow on them, the longer they will last.

Teeth cleaning equipment: Locking artery clamp, non-locking clamp, three different types of scalers, special enzymatic toothpaste, finger toothbrush, baby toothbrush, brushes for between the teeth, and a dog's toothbrush.

A badly neglected mouth with the teeth heavily coated with tartar. *Clean, healthy teeth, with the correct bite.*

TEAR STAINING

Tear staining on a Maltese can be the cause of much misery and worry to exhibitors. It has been the centre of discussion between owners of every white breed since the beginning of time but, sadly, a satisfactory solution has yet to be found.

Without doubt some dogs are more prone to staining than others and, in some cases, it may be possible to trace this problem genetically. The acidic makeup of the individual dog also has to be considered among other possible causes.

As I have said, puppies often stain heavily while they are cutting their teeth, and stress, wind, sun and dust may be contributory factors, as could the actual shape of the eye. It needs little imagination to realise how loose hair hanging across the eyes will irritate. Certain varieties of tinned and dried foods can also contribute to staining, so this should not be overlooked either.

I have often heard people complain at a show: "I can't imagine where this stain has come from. He was spotless last night when I bathed him." Since that bath, this little Maltese may have had quite a long journey to the show and is now thoroughly excited at the prospect of the day ahead – and excitement produces tears.

Occasionally, more sinister causes of staining may be determined. Low-grade infection is a common cause, and this is usually controlled with a low-level antibiotic. More seriously, ingrowing eyelashes or, rarely, blocked tear ducts are the culprits. Naturally these require experienced veterinary attention, but I must stress that most staining originates from the simpler causes detailed above.

Methods of dealing with this unsightly problem are varied. There are several products on the market that claim to 'remove staining'. By all means give every one a try. They obviously work for some, although, personally, I have not found them to be the whole answer.

Your daily grooming routine will help keep staining at bay. I prefer to remove any debris under the eye with a twist of cotton wool moistened with water. Clean the area and then – and I think this is the most important part – dry the hair completely, using either a tissue or any other absorbent material.

With the tissue between the finger and thumb take the damp hair and pinch and rub the hair strands until they are completely dry. Take a pinch of cornflour or cornstarch and work it into the stained hair, again with your finger and thumb or, using a small brush, saturate the area but ensure nothing enters the eye itself. Do this at least once a day, but more frequently if necessary. I do find that, by keeping the hair dry, staining is kept to a minimum.

Another method is first to mix together equal parts of boric acid powder and fuller's earth (white if possible). Store this in a jar to keep dry. Mix a small amount of this combination into a paste with water and, after cleaning the face as described above, plaster it under the eyes where the tears fall, taking great care not to get any in the eye itself. It will dry hard, and has proved to be very effective. The paste may be left on for two to three days before being refreshed. Great care must be taken when using boric acid. Ensure the mixture is not rubbed into the eyes by your dog, or that other dogs do not lick it off the face before the paste has dried hard, as this can have serious consequences. Cornflour or cornstarch mixed with Milk of Magnesia or other antacid cream is also useful if used in the same way. Again it hardens into a protective shield under the eye. This too can be left on until obviously needing replacement.

To remove either of the above pastes, soak well with water and sponge off. Never comb them off, otherwise you will damage hair. Whichever method you choose, keep a tissue to hand at all times, pinching the hair dry whenever you see it damp. This, together with the cornflour, will certainly help to keep staining down.

Male dogs often stain their coats when urinating and special whitening shampoos have been developed which can help with this problem between shows. It is a mistake to cut the hair at the end of a dog's penis, as it is this hair which helps to carry the water away from the coat itself.

Your brush and comb should glide smoothly through the coat. If you find drag building up then this is the time to bath your dog.

WRAPPING OR CRACKERING
Crackering, or as it is often called, wrapping the coat, is a matter of choice. Some exhibitors feel it is an asset, others prefer not to do it. It is a method used to help hair attain length. A coat that is left in its natural state is easily damaged by an active dog, once the coat grows long enough to reach the ground. By first oiling the coat, then taking small strips of hair and wrapping them in either paper or plastic, the coat is lifted out of the way, keeping it clean from staining at the same time.

To the inexperienced eye this procedure may appear easy, seeming an ideal way of growing the coat. It does, in fact, require knowledge and experience if you are to become proficient and not damage the hair. Remember no two coats are alike in texture, therefore the materials used may vary from one dog to another, and what is correct for the exhibitor whom you watch wrapping their charge at the end of a show, may not suit your dog.

Wrapping is an art that takes time to learn. It is in addition to grooming and not in place of it, therefore the packets should be opened and brushed through at the very least every other day, with some coats needing attention every day, otherwise the hair can become felted together, making loss inevitable as you separate it. A coat can be ruined if its texture is too fragile for the type of wrapping or bands used.

The choice of wrap is wide-ranging, from acid-free tissue paper, plastic, washed baby-wipes to

CRACKERING YOUR MALTESE

Photos: Steve Nash

Take a section of hair.

Lay the hair on the wrap.

Close hair within three folds, lengthways.

Fold the wrap in half, towards the dog's body.

Fold in half, once again lengthways.

Secure with an elastic band.

A fully wrapped dog.

Ready for the show ring.

ABOVE: he feet must be trimmed underneath to prevent excessive hair growing between the pads.

LEFT: The nails must be trimmed regularly, using the guillotine type of nail-cutters.

lightly waxed doughnut paper, perforated plastic bags, and so on. The idea is to select a wrap that is firm enough to retain the square shape of the packet when restrained with an elastic band, yet not so strong that it could rub and cut the hair when the dog is in motion, and this, naturally, depends on the texture of the coat. The restraining bands are also vitally important, for they must be of sufficient strength to prevent the packet coming out of the coat, but not so strong that they pinch the whole thing together, so damaging the coat within. Today, life has been made a little easier, as you can purchase bands of differing sizes and strengths that have been produced especially for wrapping coats.

By all means learn how to wrap the face whiskers and ears, as this is a good way to begin practising. If you have a boy dog, then wrapping the middle section of his coat will help to keep it clean when he urinates, but do not rush into smothering your Maltese in little packets, as, initially, a dog may object to having these strange attachments to the coat. Discomfort may encourage removal of the offending packet by rubbing along the sides of furniture or pens, therefore it is best to start with just one or two, in order to let the dog get used to the feeling, before attempting to wrap the whole body. It has been known for an active youngster to catch a loose packet on an obstruction, with disastrous results, and some take great delight in tugging the packet off themselves the moment your back is turned.

The method is to cut the paper, or plastic wrap, so that it is long enough to go beyond the length of hair to be worked on. The width may vary, for it depends on the amount of body hair you are taking into the wrap, but it should be roughly 4" wide. Holding the wrap lengthways, fold about a quarter of an inch over at the top, this helps to stop a raw edge cutting when in contact with the hair. Next fold the wrap lengthways into three equal portions. You should now have a long, narrow wrap folded in three. Open the wrap up and lay the hair flat within, ensuring the quarter-inch fold is at the top or root of the hair. Close by folding the wrap back lengthways over the hair. Turn the bottom end up to make a square and repeat until the packet sits comfortably against the body. See illustration. When taking each section of hair, lift the dog's limbs and ensure that nothing will restrict comfortable movement. The same applies to the ears; follow the shape of the ear round so that the head hair is not taken up in the same packet. There are two areas where extra care should be taken. When wrapping ears, make sure you can feel the end of the leather under the hair, and finish the packet so that the elastic is a good half-an-inch away from the end. If you cracker the tail hair, make sure the elastic is well away from the tip of the bone. It is possible to lose the end of both ears and tails if they are trapped within an elastic band.

BATHING

Never bath a Maltese with tangles remaining in the coat. If you take a short cut and leave the mats in place, they will just felt together and you will certainly lose more coat removing them later on.

You will need to have to hand everything you normally use to groom, together with these extras:-

A baby or puppy shampoo for the head and face.

A quality shampoo e.g. almond, coconut, or similar cream shampoo.

If the coat has been oiled you will require a shampoo to strip this out of the coat first. I have found a medicated product to be excellent for this purpose, but this should *never* be used on a dog's head or on a pregnant bitch.

Conditioner.

Jugs for mixing.

Plenty of towels.

A rubber mat.

A hair drier. A drier on a stand is a must when caring for a show coat, allowing both hands to be free to work.

Mineral oil (for the eyes).

Assemble your grooming equipment next to where you are going to do the drying, and if this is on a table, place a thick layer of towels ready for the dog to lie or to stand on. Next, place the shampoos, conditioners and wrapping towels within reach of the bathing area. Nothing is worse than completing the bathing only to find you have left the towels in another room. Ensure the rubber mat is in place to prevent slipping.

Inspect the coat and separate any tangles. Clean the teeth and if tartar has built up, gently remove it with your dental scaler. Put a small twist of cotton wool in the ears to protect them from an excess of water, and place a drop of mineral oil in each eye to protect them from soap.

If you are experienced in evacuating the anal glands, this is the time to undertake an inspection. This is not the most pleasant task, and entails identifying whether or not the glands need clearing. First stand the dog in the bath and soak the anus area in warm water. Move the coat to one side. The glands lie just inside the anal opening, and if they are full, they feel like two firm little marbles. Hold the tail up, place the thumb and first finger behind, and either side of the swellings within the anus and gently, but firmly, squeeze with an outward drawing movement away from the dog. The glands produce a foul-smelling liquid or paste that discharges from the anus. It may vary in consistency and in colour, from light cream to dark brown. It is imperative that you are ready to catch the discharge, which may expel very suddenly, into a tissue, or something similar. However, if you have never tackled this task before, seek experienced advice before attempting to clear the glands yourself.

Now on to the actual bathing. Place the dog on the rubber mat and soak the coat thoroughly with warm water. Make sure nothing is left dry. If you have been oiling the coat, this is the time to use the 'stripping out' shampoo. I thin this with a little water and squeeze it through the coat, never rubbing. Try to keep the parting in place throughout the bathing session.

Rinse well, then shampoo with the cream shampoo, again squeezing it through the hair.

If the coat has not been oiled but is simply dirty, you may wish to wash it twice with just the cream shampoo, followed, of course, by a thorough rinsing until the water runs clear.

Use the baby or puppy shampoos on the head, as these do not sting the eyes. Pay attention to the ears, as the hair there is usually more greasy than that on the face. Some Maltese object to having water poured over their heads, in which case you will have to sponge off around the eyes and nose.

There are many different conditioners on the market so only trial and error will establish which one suits your dog. Whichever is selected, make sure you have drenched every hair. Some conditioners are left on for only a short while before being rinsed off, but should you find you have damaged hair to deal with, you might wish to use the more penetrating type, which has to be left on longer. In this case, after saturating the coat, you should wrap your Maltese in warm towels to assist the conditioner's effectiveness and either have additional fresh warm towels ready to replenish, or direct warm air from your drier upon the towel, for whatever period of time the manufacturer suggests.

Finally, rinse and squeeze (never rub) as much excess water out of the coat as possible before wrapping the dog in a towel ready for drying.

DRYING

Regardless of whether I dry with my Maltese standing or lying on a table, or on my lap, I layer one section dry. This means drying a particular area thoroughly before going on to another part. Commence with the dog facing the left and dry the hair facing you, leaving the far side until last, as this is the side that will face the judge in the ring.

If you choose the lying down method, place the dryer so that it is blowing the hair downwards, away from the root towards the tip. Lift the body hair up and away from the legs and belly and cover with a damp towel. Taking your brush, concentrate on drying the tail, belly and legs; then, when they are perfectly dry, turn your attention to the body hair. Bring down a layer of coat from under the damp towel and begin brushing from root, or spine, to the tip. Keep the remainder of the wet coat covered by the damp towel. Gradually bring down further thin layers of the body coat from under the towel, until the whole side has been completed.

Remove the now-damp towel your dog was lying on, replace with a dry one, and turn the dog so the left side is now uppermost. Take care that the earlier dried hair remains flat and is not bunched up underneath the dog. Proceed as before.

Some people prefer to stand their dog during drying. This method does have the benefit of speed, but sometimes lacks finish if the angle of the dryer is too low, resulting in the hair being swirled and blown all over the place. To avoid this problem, make sure the nozzle of the dryer is above and slightly to one side of your dog, then work from the tail towards the head, moving the heat forward a little at a time, concentrating only on the area you are working. As with everything else, it is up to each individual to find which method suits best.

When you are satisfied that the whole of the body hair is dry, put your dog in a sitting position and attend to the head, protecting the eyes from direct heat with your free hand. You may find the ears take a little longer to dry. Do not forget to remove the cotton wool from the ears. Finally, secure the hair away from the eyes.

READY TO SHOW
It really is to your advantage to visit a few shows before embarking on this venture yourself, as you can watch procedures and question what is taking place, thus familiarising yourself with the intricacies of showing a dog. In any case, plan well in advance, to save panic at the last minute.

THE NIGHT BEFORE THE SHOW
Your Maltese is now bathed and prepared. The next step is to set out everything you will need for the show day itself. The following morning must be left free to give your attention to your dog and to ensure you have time for a good breakfast.

You should have considered, well in advance, what you will be wearing yourself, for today's exhibitor is much more conscious about appearance. So, a word of advice here on what to bear in mind when choosing your outfit. Spectators and judges alike appreciate an exhibitor who has given thought to wearing something that compliments their breed. Do not try and out-do your Maltese, as it is the dog that must catch the judge's eye, not you. Dress lengths have to be given considerable thought. I am sure that judges can cope with short skirts, but do remember there is quite a lot of bending down with a small breed, and the spectators are sometimes behind you. Then there are those calf-length, full skirts that waft all over the top of your Maltese, distracting the dog from the job in hand and spoiling the dog's outline. I have even been to a show and seen a Maltese totally eclipsed by the handler's ankle-length skirt, with only the dog's rapidly moving legs to indicate that there was an animal there at all. Blouses with tie fronts, and men's ties, can become an interference when you are crouching low over your dog, so hold them down with a pin or brooch. Do not wear noisy jewellery or chains that can dangle. Shoes, too, have to be thought about. If this is an indoor show with wooden floors, heavy clompy shoes are very off-putting as they stomp around and can certainly take attention away from your dog. Very high, pointed heels are also distracting – they may make you look terrific, but the audience and, possibly, the judge can find their eyes glued to your stiletto heels, terrified in case you accidentally step on an active dog.

When you have selected your outfit, set your alarm-clock to allow sufficient time for you to have something to eat, and for your dog to defecate and be made comfortable before travelling.

AT THE SHOW
Arrive at the venue in good time, buy your catalogue and check your dog is entered in the correct classes. If you discover a problem, no matter how small, go straight to the show secretary and sort it out there and then. A misprint, or mistake on the entry form, could cost you an award.

Identify where the benches are, which ring you are in, and establish yourself there. Some shows have 'grooming areas' in which you are asked to prepare your dogs; these are usually close to the actual ring. The reason you allow yourself plenty of time is so that you will not have to panic and so unsettle your dog. Remember you will transfer feelings, and your nerves can run straight down the lead.

Before going to the ring make sure your dog has attended to the call of nature and clear up after this if necessary. Have your dog ready in good time before you are summoned so that you do not hold up proceedings. You will either have found a duplicate set of numbers over your dog's bench,

A typical scene at a show. Some of the dogs are crated after competing, others are waiting for their turn to go into the ring.

The show dog must get used to being examined by a stranger. Here, the exhibitor is lifting he tail so that the judge can assess the dog's topline.

in which case one is for use in the ring, or you will be given the number by the steward when either entering the ring or when actually in the ring. Attach it to yourself in a position that can be seen clearly by the steward, the spectators and the judge.

If this is your first show, watch what everyone else is doing and follow on. If for any reason your dog is absent, tell the steward, as this needs to be marked in the judge's book. The steward will place the dogs present in a row, with the first dog facing the judge's table. This is the time when you stand your dog – it is called 'setting your dog up'. You will want your Maltese to be standing quite still, looking as good as possible, when the judge walks down the line for a first appraisal of all the exhibits. Any tidying of your dog's coat should be completed well before the judge reaches you both.

The exhibitors may then be asked to "take them round please" and the dogs will set off, one after another, in line round the ring. This allows the dogs time to settle to the task in hand, especially if they have been cramped in a travelling box beforehand. Give yourself plenty of room between your Maltese and the dog in front. The judge will stop the parade and indicate the first dog to be placed on to the table to be thoroughly examined.

Win or lose, you still have your beloved Maltese to take home with you.
NZ Ch. Villarose Sweet Sensation (Ch. Snowgoose Hot Toddy – Ch. Villarose Sweet September): Imported from the UK, bred by Chris Ripsher, owned by Sheila Allen.

When the dog before you has completed this table examination and is doing an individual walk for the judge, place your Maltese on the table, ensuring that you have set your dog up properly and that the lead is not going to interfere or get in the judge's way. Stand to one side so that you do not get in the way, but so that you still maintain control of your dog.

The judge will expect your Maltese to stand quietly while being examined. You should watch the proceedings and be ready to steady your dog if necessary. You may also be asked to show the judge your dog's teeth. This is quite common practice and you should lift the dog's lips sufficiently to display the whole bite. Do not talk to the judge unless you are spoken to first.

Hopefully you will have been watching the exhibitors who went before you and noted what was being required of them. Some judges just ask you to walk the dog away in a straight line in order to appraise the rear movement, then back, to assess the front movement. The art here is not to break your dog's stride as you turn, especially if the ring is on the small side. A bad turn may lose you several strides until your dog settles again, and the idea is to let the judge see as much of your dog's good movement as possible, so this is something you should have practised well at home.

You may be asked to make a triangle, in which event you would walk in a straight line at an angle away from the judge in the direction of the righthand corner, then move straight across the ring to the opposite side, making sure your turns are smooth and allowing your dog to keep stride, finally returning in a straight line to where the judge is standing. This movement also displays your dog in profile when in action. At no time should you put yourself between your dog and the judge, which means your dog should be moving on your left hand-side when negotiating the triangle.

Judges like to see the handler and dog moving in harmony and at a steady pace. Your Maltese's head must be carried proudly; the movement must not be slow or depressed with a head held so low that it is difficult to evaluate the front movement. The action should be animated and alive, yet totally under control in order for the judge to assess your dog to advantage. If a dog is all over the place, with the long coat bounding hither and thither, it can give the wrong impression. At the end of your walk, finish in front of the judge with your Maltese standing perfectly still, head up, tail over. Allowances are always made for puppies. A bit of mischief is understandable and forgivable – nobody likes to see an over-trained puppy.

Having completed this part of the proceedings, you now return to the line of dogs already seen, placing yourself in exactly the same position as before – that is, behind the dog that moved ahead of you. If you try to set yourself up at the front of the line of already seen dogs, this would be viewed very badly by your fellow exhibitors.

Now, a lot depends on the class size as to what you do next. If it is a huge class, then you can let your Maltese relax a little; but it is wise to remember exactly which dog will be the last to be seen on the table, because, when that dog's turn is getting close, you need to stand your dog again. However, usually the classes are reasonably small, so upon returning to your place, set your dog up ready for the last inspection.

Keep an eye on exactly where the judge is or you may find yourself nervously grooming hairs into place at the precise moment the judge reaches you, and passes on by, with the result that your Maltese will have lost that last, golden opportunity of being seen beautifully set up.

HANDY HINTS

Exhibiting looks easy but there is quite an art in keeping one eye on the judge at all times, while also making sure your dog is looking superb. Even though a judge may be studying another exhibit, an eye may still be cast along the line of seen dogs from time to time and, if you let your Maltese stand in a depressed, slumped manner, it certainly could go against you, especially if the one next to you is looking sharp and alert, so catching the judge's attention.

If you are baiting or using tidbits in the ring, do make sure you will not distract, or interfere in any way with the other dogs close to you. Make sure that food is not dropped on the ground when in the ring, as this can spoil another exhibit's chances. Keep your own dog under control at all times, but especially when your fellow competitors are concentrating on the job in hand. It is also unwise to take a squeaky toy into the ring as, if this is used, you will attract not just your own dog, but those around you, and the use of such a device could be the cause of much annoyance.

AFTER THE CLASS

If you are among the successful candidates, wait and see if the judge wishes to take notes, and only leave the ring when it is clear you should do so. Be gracious both with success and in defeat: this is a sport and every person involved is hoping for a good day. If you are fortunate enough to be successful, accept your fellow exhibitors' congratulations with grace and show your appreciation to your dog. If it has not been such a good day for you, show how much you appreciated your dog's efforts and remember others are happy, so it is up to you to compound that for them by applauding, while remembering it is that one judge's opinion and there is always another show another day. You still have your lovely dog and you have no doubt learned quite a lot by just being with other Maltese.

When packing up to go home, make sure you leave the area around you clear of rubbish.

Finally, before leaving the show ground, or immediately upon returning home, wipe, spray or dip your dog's feet in a mild disinfectant. If you have other dogs at home, change your shoes before entering the house and disinfect them too. You should take every precaution not to carry possible infection back to your other dogs.

Chapter Seven

BREEDING MALTESE

I am often asked how I embarked on breeding Maltese myself, and I suppose, as is the case with so many people, it was purely accidental. My ownership of dogs in the past had been quite varied, but mainly included gun dogs. About thirty years ago I felt I needed a small companion of my own, so, after seeing a local advertisement which offered a Maltese for sale, I made enquiries. In fact it was pity that overwhelmed me when I saw this sad little bitch, who was obviously so unhappy that my only thought was to bring her home.

She just blossomed like a flower but unfortunately, along with her improved health and condition, she developed an obsession about me. She just could not bear to have me out of her sight, which became distressing for both of us. I discussed the problem with my vet who suggested that, as she was now such a beautiful Maltese – with, in fact, a superb pedigree – and in a fine condition, I should mate her, and keep one of the puppies. She would then divide her attentions between her offspring and myself.

Not only did this work perfectly but, in seeking the right stud for her, I was introduced to the breed as a whole in the UK and became totally besotted. I retained a bitch from this mating and she, in turn, brought me into the world of dog showing. More often than not, though, the reverse is the usual route, for breeding is frequently a natural extension of successful exhibiting and, although it may not have been your intention to involve yourself in this side of the dog scene initially, if you now find yourself the proud owner of a lovely, typical Maltese, what is more pleasurable than to consider letting her have puppies?

MAKING THE DECISION

It is not a decision to be undertaken lightly, however, as many factors are involved. It goes without saying that your prospective mother must be of as high a quality and as true to her type as possible. She might be your show dog, on the other hand she may be a companion who is not quite perfect, or who does not display all the required virtues of a show dog. She may even have a small imperfection that would flaw her for exhibition, but as long as she is totally fit and sound, with the true Maltese temperament and typical of her breed in every other respect, then breeding is worth considering.

Breeding from inferior stock is not only self-defeating but indicates an indifference to the breed itself, to say nothing of the fact that it is an expensive up-hill task attempting to improve on poor-quality dogs, a true waste of time and effort. In any case, you should not overlook the fact that there is a certain amount of risk to your bitch in having puppies. Maltese do not always give birth like 'shelling peas', and complications can occur – usually timed for the middle of the night!

The whole venture can also be quite costly. First, there is the stud fee to consider, then extras to nourish your bitch before and after she has had her puppies. You will have to provide a whelping box and, if necessary, heating equipment. A degree of veterinary attention may be required, either during or after whelping. Finally, there is the cost of feeding and maintaining the puppies themselves.

Luck also plays an important part. In fact, dog breeding is a mixture of knowledge, intuition, enthusiasm and luck. Those who have been associated with the breed over a long period of years do have the advantage of personal knowledge of many of the dogs and their pedigrees, so any advice offered to you should always be taken seriously. Talk to as many people as possible, always bearing in mind that opinions can be biased one way or another, and it is up to you to separate fact from personal preferences, in making your decisions; but I also believe that if you have an instinctive feeling about doing something, you should follow it. This instinct may produce a litter of stunning winners; on the other hand it may be disappointing in your eyes, but take my word that the lessons you learn will be of lasting value.

Perhaps I had luck on my side many years ago, when a breeder of long standing was visiting my home. At that time I had three showable bitches: two were very much the type in the ring at that time, and one was a fraction larger. The visiting breeder pointed at this latter bitch and said: "Well, I would get rid of that one for a start, her legs are too long." I did not consider myself vastly experienced in those days and could so easily have complied with her comments. However, I liked the types of dogs behind this particular bitch and my instinctive feeling was to keep this dog for her overall quality, and I did just that.

I loved showing the other two bitches. They were great fun and they both retired with multiple CCs to their credit, one even being awarded the RCC at Crufts. Yet, not one of their subsequent offspring has played any part whatsoever in the success of my ongoing dogs. They each had lovely babies, but for one reason or another they were not what I was looking for.

The bitch I was advised to part with, however, although not then currently 'fashionable', was of such quality that when first mated to a half-English half-imported dog, she produced a Champion son who was Best of Breed at Crufts and went on to win the Group outright. The next time, she was mated to a completely outcrossed dog, and produced a Champion daughter, who went Best of Breed at Crufts the following year. Finally she was mated to a heavily line-bred dog and produced another Champion son in that litter. He, in turn, won the RCC at Crufts, then the CC the following year, and finally, CC, Best of Breed and Group finalist the next. All three then went on to produce Champion offspring of the highest order. Following her third litter this bitch was retired and spayed, to remain my companion into her seventeenth year.

The fact that I did not follow the advice from that older breeder all those years ago was certainly not based on experience, but on an instinctive feeling that I should keep that bitch. Had I been persuaded otherwise, and concentrated on the two bitches I was currently showing, then none of my subsequent successful Maltese would have been born.

Usually it is the stud that is credited with any virtues in the offspring and although the three, very different, dogs to whom I chose to mate this particular bitch were lovely, this little tale illustrates perfectly that a bitch can also be strong in her ability to reproduce certain qualities. I was very lucky, for prepotency (as this ability is called) is not an obvious virtue, but something only time can reveal, but intuition also played its part. To try and breed what you think is today's winning type is fraught with danger, for if you think about it, you will always be a show year behind and, by the time your puppy is ready to come out, the subtle differences that put one good dog above another that particular year, could have changed.

So yes, listen to every possible piece of advice, but do your homework, study the dogs and their pedigrees, aim for the qualities you most admire and keep your ideals high. Anybody can breed a

Mother and daughter: Dulc Tara's Triumph and Dulc La Heim Acer. Owned and bred by Marie Harper.

little white dog with a leg at each corner and some may even have a modicum of success in the ring, but think long term. Look upon this, your first litter, as a foundation, something you, or perhaps others can take pride in. In the end let the final decision as to which dog to use or which puppy to keep be yours.

BREEDING AGE

So, the time has come for you to consider breeding from your lovely sound Maltese, with the typically delightful temperament. The age at which a bitch may have her first season will vary, as every Maltese has a different pattern. She could come in at six months of age but the usual time is around nine to eleven months. You may at some time have been told that Toy dogs mature more quickly than the larger breeds. This is quite true. However, it is not wise to mate a bitch until she has had her second season. This allows her fully to finish maturing herself, both physically and mentally. Mating a bitch too early can interfere with her own growth rate.

At the other end of the time scale, if you are showing a bitch and therefore do not wish to breed her on her second season, then you should be thinking of mating her at around three years of age for her first litter, primarily because her bones are hardening and there is more chance of complications setting in if you delay too long. Thereafter, future litters may be considered on alternative seasons, thus ensuring complete recovery between deliveries. At whatever age a bitch is mated, she must certainly be in the peak of health and not overweight.

CHOOSING A STUD DOG

There is always a great temptation to use the most successful dog currently gracing the show ring. But is this really the ideal dog for your bitch? This prospective litter could be the foundation of your own bloodline so, in the months prior to mating, study and research the pedigrees of all the dogs that have taken your fancy and note the quality of their offspring to date. Naturally your chosen stud must, himself, be as fine a specimen as possible, but his greatest value is in the overall quality of his progeny. If you admire a particular dog but for some reason he is not available, consider using his sire. Try not to fall into the trap of 'following fashion'; be an individual. You might well have to travel far to reach the dog you want, but it will be worth it in the end. Lack of thought could lead to an expensive blunder. In making this very important decision, you are not only founding your own kennel, but bringing new life into the world, so give it the attention it deserves.

*Ch. Snowgoose Hot
Toddy: BIS at the
Maltese Club Ch. Show
1985, and a top sire
over many years.
Owned and bred by
Vicki Herrieff.*

Photo: Diane Pearce.

*Ch. Snowgoose First
Love, breed record
holder in the UK, with
his son, Benatone Love
on the Rocks, who later
became a Champion
and top winning male
in 1995.*

BREEDING PROGRAMMES

You will have heard that there are different methods of breeding. The terms I used earlier, such as in-breeding, line-breeding or outcrossing, may confuse you and appear to complicate matters, so perhaps the following will help a little.

In-breeding is a term used when immediate or very close relatives are mated together, like mother and son, father and daughter, or brother and sister. It is a speedy way of fixing certain characteristics within the resulting puppies. Experienced breeders only adopt this course of action when they have personal knowledge of many generations behind the dogs concerned, and are fully aware of both the faults and the qualities that lie behind the lines. In-breeding is a sure road to disaster if undertaken by those new to the breed, and is best left to safe, experienced hands.

Line-breeding is another frequently-heard term, used when a particularly influential dog appears on both the male's and the female's pedigree. Line-breeding is the most usual, or acceptable, method of improving your stock. The concept is that, by doubling up on the good points of this particular line, you are likely to consolidate them within the puppies. The majority of successful

Am. Ch. To The Victor of Eng:
Top sire in the USA with some
80 American Champions to his
credit.

kennels build their lines with this method but, once again, you must be aware of faults that may arise, for these will also double up. A dog's influence very much depends upon position within the pedigree. The closer the dog is to your potential dam and sire, the greater the influence. By the same token – the further away, the weaker the influence.

Out-crossing is the term used when two dogs come together from unrelated backgrounds. In the Maltese breed it has been used to give added vigour, or strength in one form or another, to a limited gene pool. Anyone wishing to establish their own line would be ill-advised to follow this path initially, as a random mating produces no set 'type' of off-spring. Its value is greatest when introduced into a strongly line-bred kennel, to strengthen some aspect that may benefit from a boost of complementary genes. Selected puppies from this mating can then be reintroduced to the founder line, thus still maintaining that kennel's 'type'.

GENETIC INFLUENCE

I stated earlier that a certain amount of luck is involved in dog breeding and that is what makes it so exciting. How boring it would be if we could totally predict the outcome of a mating. The genetic make-up is carried in a dog's genes, which are themselves packaged within the chromosomes. Man has twenty-three pairs of chromosomes while dogs, on the other hand, appear more complex, for they have thirty-nine pairs, thirty-eight of which are identical, with the thirty-ninth being the sex chromosome. The male has either an X or a Y sex chromosome, but not both, while the female carries just the X sex chromosome. Should the male's sperm carry the X chromosome when it encounters the female's X, the result will be XX, a bitch. If the sperm carries the Y chromosome the outcome will be XY, a male puppy. Curiously enough, that Y chromosome seems somehow to be more vigorous in its journey to meet up with the ova, as the percentage of males born to Maltese bitches appears relatively high.

The chromosomes in your bitch's ovaries and in the dog's testes divide in two during sexual reproduction, so that the fertilized egg comprises half the genetic information from the sperm of the dog and half from the ova of the bitch. This random mixing of genes accounts for the differences between one puppy and another. It also follows that there is certainly no guarantee that repeat matings necessarily will result in identical litters.

The genes themselves can be divided into two main groups: 'dominant' and 'recessive'. Within the millions of genes involved in any one union there will be the dominant genes, which can be carried by just one parent, and which are capable of being totally effective i.e. consistently determining, say, the eye colour or coat texture; and the recessive gene which is not effective unless it is carried by both parents. The recessive gene is usually responsible for the majority of undesirable characteristics and hereditary defects. Difficulty arises when the dominant gene masks the recessive gene.

Serious breeders of long-standing are in a better position to analyse a pedigree, as they will remember some of the obvious dominant, or recessive, characteristics that have appeared, over the years, in certain dogs or lines.

The fruits of a successful breeding programme – four generations of winners. Pictured left to right: Am. Ch. Stan-Bar's Spark of Glory, Am. Ch. Myi's Siin Seeker-Shinohara, Am. Ch. Myi's Ode to Glory, and Am. Ch. Myi's Ode to Glory Seeker.

Bear all this in mind when you, as a novice exhibitor who has had a degree of success in the ring, with a bitch whose overall quality pleases, come to make your decision. It would be to your advantage if the stud dog of your choice was line-bred, in one degree or another, to your bitch, through a well respected common ancestor.

So, after considering all the pros and cons of the available dogs, and having made up your mind about what you want to do, approach the owner to discuss details. We are assuming in this chapter that you have a maiden bitch, so do mention this fact, as she will require extra-sensitive handling. Give plenty of warning, do not leave it until your bitch is in season before discussing it, or you could find the dog of your choice is not available, leading to disappointment. Ascertain in advance the mating fee and any other details required.

THE IN-SEASON BITCH
One sign that a bitch is coming into season is a coloured discharge which can vary from quite heavy bleeding to only a faint sign if the bitch is intent on keeping herself clean. Young bitches sometimes appear quite shocked when they have their first season and become quiet and withdrawn. Another indication is the plumping up of the skin immediately behind the vulva and the gradual swelling of the vulva itself. It may also be noticed that a bitch will urinate more frequently throughout the course of her season.

The season is divided into two parts. At first the vulva will swell as the discharge continues, then after nine or ten days the flow may slacken off and the vulva becomes soft and receptive, often accompanied by the tail switching and curling when you touch the bitch near the rear.

Unfortunately some bitches have what is sometimes called a 'blind season', or colourless season. This is where there is no colour to the discharge accompanying the swelling. These are the most difficult seasons to read correctly in order to judge the optimum day for mating. Having the bitch swabbed at the vet will give a reasonable indication as to when she is ovulating, but your own careful observations are the most important. Note any change, no matter how small, in your bitch's vulva around the time she is due in season, otherwise it is quite possible for her to be well into it before you are aware at all.

Most bitches come into season every six months, but now and again you can come across some that are irregular. I had one who was a 'once a year' girl. Clearly, had she also been the type to have 'blind seasons' this would have complicated matters dreadfully!

The most receptive time for a bitch to be mated is, on average, following cessation of colour, from the tenth to the thirteenth day, although some bitches are mated successfully while still showing just a little colour, and a few go to the other extreme and only accept the dog at the end of the three week season. Unfortunately there is no set rule regarding ovulation, and every bitch varies slightly. I knew of one Maltese that was receptive around her eighth day and then only for forty-eight hours. Her owner had to be particularly observant or she "went over", and mating her past this time proved useless.

THE MATING

Unless there are exceptional circumstances, escort your bitch to the stud. If you have to travel, allow plenty of time so that she can relax in her new surroundings. Some bitches, especially maidens, are understandably nervous entering a strange environment, so meeting with an amorous dog can be overwhelming at this highly sensitive time.

If your Maltese is in full coat then, to facilitate entry by the stud dog, it is advisable to carry the hair away on each side of the vulva, and take it round over each hip, where it can be either plaited or secured with an elastic band.

The stud dog owner may prefer that you wait in another room initially, especially if your bitch shows signs of being temperamental and clinging to you. Some bitches are much better handled by a competent stranger, allowing everything to proceed smoothly without further fuss. In these circumstances no doubt you will then be called to witness the 'tie' a little later. On the other hand you may be asked to lend a hand right from the outset.

The bitch should be examined upon arrival to check her state of readiness. It helps if a little light jell is inserted just inside, and smeared outside, the vulva in order to make entry easier. Before any examination takes place, hands and nails should be scrubbed thoroughly, and if an internal examination is necessary, the nail on this finger must be as short as possible.

I prefer to give my bitch the opportunity to familiarize herself with the room first, and then introduce the dog and watch their reactions. If they play and flirt this stimulates them both and usually leads to an easy and happy mating. Once this initial introduction has taken place the two will, when left to their own devices, indulge in flirtatious behaviour, boxing each other with their paws and nudging with their noses. The bitch may readily stand with her tail curled round to one side, encouraging the male to mount, only to dash off as he does so. She might even repeat this several times, this will stimulate both animals and, if she is absolutely ready, you will notice that she lifts her vulva in anticipation.

If the dog is too interested in licking the bitch rather than courting her, then this could indicate that she really is a bit early. Signs of untypical aggression on her part could mean this also. Just a few hours can miraculously change a growling, actively resisting bitch, who just does not want to know the stud, into an unrecognisable melting, receptive, flirt. On the other hand, you have to decide if her aggressive reaction is due to nervousness, or even if you are too late.

When mating actually takes place this is the time to steady both dogs. If there are two people present one can gently restrain the bitch, while the stud dog owner attends to the male. The joining of two dogs usually results in 'the tie'. This is when the dog's penis swells and is grasped by the muscles within the bitch's vagina.

Ejaculation takes place in three stages: the first being a clear liquid, the second carries the spermatozoa and the third stage is again a clear liquid that washes the sperm forward. Although this is taking place during 'the tie' the length of the tie is not necessarily an indication of success. In fact, some dogs never tie.

Having entered the bitch successfully, the dog will continue pumping for a short while. During this stage the dog's penis continues swelling, and the bitch may appear uncomfortable, but it is essential quietly to restrain any effort to break apart, thus avoiding injury to either party. When he is fully erected and held fast by the bitch's muscles, they are then 'tied' and can remain this way for a few minutes or a very, very long bone-aching hour or so for the handlers. The stud will at this stage be lying along the bitch's back, with his front legs grasped round her loins. After a while the dog may become restless and indicate that he wishes to turn. Ease his hind leg gently over the back of the bitch so that they stand stern to stern. Once again, the stud owner will assist. Make a note of how long the tie lasts, as you may wish to have this recorded. I have had both the dog and bitch lie down and go fast asleep during a long tie, but you must be very aware of any sign of the tie coming to an end, because an excited animal can break away too quickly and hurt the partner.

Once the two have separated make sure the stud's penis has retracted smoothly, without taking any long hairs back into the sheath with it. If this is the case, very gently ease the hairs out. Sponge him off with a warm solution of water and mild antiseptic before putting the dog to rest.

The sperm can remain active over several days and many bitch owners like to return for a second mating forty-eight hours later, to cover as much of the ovulating period as possible.

THE STUD DOG

As with the brood bitch, health plays an all-important part in the life of a stud dog. Never consider using a dog that is remotely unwell, or unfit, or on any kind of medication.

If you are the owner, then every effort should be made well before any mating to ensure he is in the peak of health, with plenty of exercise, fresh air and good food. Ideally he should have been able to grow to maturity within a group of Maltese, as this will give him confidence as he learns to live with the other dogs and is able to establish his position.

As the owner of a dog at stud you have a certain responsibility to the breed. When first approached with an enquiry, ask to see the bitch's pedigree in order to try and ensure that both dogs will go well together and not promote something to the breed's detriment.

It can be embarrassing, but you also owe it to the breed to refuse untypical or unfit animals – which can be difficult, especially if the bitch has actually arrived. Then there are those bitches that are being bred for the wrong reason, something that should be discovered discreetly beforehand, but this is all part of being a responsible stud dog owner.

The time of enquiry regarding using a stud is when you discuss the fee; also any conditions appertaining to the mating, and these conditions should be made in writing so that there can be no misunderstanding at a later date. This is also the time to clarify whether or not a free return mating will be offered if the bitch fails to conceive. The stud fee is for the use of the male's services and is not based on results; therefore it is up to the discretion of the stud owner as to whether return matings of this nature are part of the agreement.

A stud dog should be as excellent a specimen of his breed as possible, displaying the delightful temperament of the true Maltese even at this exciting time. Never use a dog purely for convenience sake, i.e. because he lives just around the corner, or because you have one of your own. A poor male, used indiscriminately, can do an awful lot of damage to a breed, quite apart from the fact that if it is not a good match it will waste both your time and your effort. The responsible owner would prefer to see, and properly evaluate, the quality of the puppies his dog sires, before offering him out to be used at stud on a regular basis.

Once a dog has been used, he will change. You will have set in motion a process within his body that will always remind him of this side of his life. His confidence will have been given a boost and he now has a very good reason to check out every dog he sees. Some males experience an alteration in their urine and it becomes strong, staining the coat and giving off an unpleasant odour. Once they have mated a bitch they are also more inclined to scent-mark, which can spoil the relationship of a companion dog in the home, and that is why it is best for all concerned only to use a stud dog whose owner is aware of, and accepts, these possible inconveniences.

Because toy dogs mature more quickly, young males are able to reproduce before they are a year old and many breeders advocate using a dog just once before this age. You may see your young male just as a puppy, but the fact that he is perfectly able to sire a litter is something to be very aware of. I recall a lady stating adamantly: "My Billy could not be the father of those puppies, he was only a baby of ten months at the time." Yes, he could – in fact he probably was very potent at that age.

Young males are best introduced to stud work for the very first time by an experienced in-season brood bitch whose quiet confidence will reassure and encourage him. She will flirt and tease and tolerate his amateurish and sometimes very funny, clumsy attempts.

A male that has been too 'humanised', although this mainly affects the slightly older dog, may refuse to even associate with an in-season bitch even if she does flirt His reaction will probably be to remove himself as far away as possible from this hussy, and return to the company of his owner. This difficulty is less likely to occur with a male that has been reared in the company of other dogs.

A more experienced stud will know the routine and if, by chance, it is not the bitch's right day, will tell you so by being less than interested. However, although I said 'the more experienced dog', they too can differ. I have one male whose impetuosity would frighten a nervous bitch if I were not careful. He would charge into the room with not so much as a 'by your leave', and fill the place with boisterous activity. Wonderful if it is a confident bitch who would thoroughly enjoy a rumbustious courtship, but off-putting, to say the very least, for a maiden, and therefore this would be a mating I would have to organise particularly carefully, to ensure happiness all round. But another of my dogs is such a gentleman that he has to have the bitch's approval before mating. He courts her gently and peers closely at her face to check she is quite happy. If she so much as gives the smallest grumble, well that is it, he just does not want to know, and nothing will persuade him to mount.

When you have a 'family' of dogs it is possible to find that some bitches will only mate with certain dogs and vice versa, which can be somewhat frustrating if you have a special match in mind that does not coincide with this particular pairing.

TACTFUL HANDLING

Everyone has their own individual way of conducting a mating. Some let the dogs join together on the floor and, when they are tied, they lift them onto a table to save the handlers' aching bones; others introduce them on the tabletop in the first place; while there are those, like myself, who keep the whole thing at ground level.

Because dogs are creatures of habit they quickly recognize the routine and any trappings associated with mating. I have a large rug which, once produced, sends my boys into a frenzy of excitement and, because they accept this is part of the ritual, it is not unknown for them to refuse to mount the bitch until she is actually standing on this rug, which can at times be awkward. Even when the bitch is at the height of her season, I have known the dog to flirt with her then rush back to the rug and bark vigorously at me to organize things better.

There is no guarantee that every situation will run smoothly. If the visiting bitch has not been socialised with other dogs since purchase, this can prove a difficulty. Owners are notorious for not getting the day right and a bitch that fiercely rejects her suitor one day may be totally receptive twenty-four hours later – but patience and a good sense of humour are essential tools of the trade when handling animals.

It certainly helps if one person can reassure and be ready to restrain the bitch, once the dog begins to take the task seriously. The helper should be prepared to steady her while at the same time making sure she will not turn on the dog; this will allow the stud owner to supervise her charge. If there is a discrepancy in size and, say, the bitch is taller than the male, then large books are nice and firm, and provide a solid platform for the dog to stand on, so compensating for the difference in height. Wrap a towel or something similar around the books to give a firm base on which to grip. If the person steadying the bitch is also able to hold the hair on the end of the bitch's tail, this will keep it from getting in the way.

KEEPING RECORDS

Above all, keep records. Write down every detail of your bitch's seasons from the very first one: the dates; if she is swelling or showing colour; whether or not mated; which day if mated, etc. These records will become invaluable over the years, not only in monitoring individual dogs, but for comparison, and as an accurate history of what has taken place. Memory is not always reliable.

While the dogs are resting after mating, this is the time when the owner of the stud dog writes out the stud receipt, giving the name of the bitch and her owner, the name of the stud, and when mated. If there was a tie, indicate how long it lasted. Work out when the puppies are due. Make sure that any agreed conditions are clearly set out and signed by both parties. This is also when the fee is paid, and the decision made as to whether or not you should repeat the mating in forty-eight hours.

As the owner of the bitch, it is helpful to write on your copy of the stud receipt exactly which day in her season the bitch came, how she reacted, and eventually what the result of the union was. Should this same bitch return the following year you will have a better picture on which to base her next visit.

It is only courteous to let the stud dog owner know when you are sure the bitch is in whelp and, when the time comes, what the eventual outcome was. Every country has their own method of registering puppies, so check that you have everything you require in this respect.

Chapter Eight

WHELPING

COAT CARE

In the weeks between the mating of your Maltese and the whelping, you will have to decide whether to keep her in coat, or whether to cut it short. Obviously there is much to commend in removing it but, for one reason or another, you may wish to try and retain her coat length, but wonder how to go about it. I prefer to keep all my bitches in coat – though everyday length, not show. It does make for a little extra work, but this is no problem if you have the time.

The coat can be left naturally loose if it is not over-long and, with a little common sense, grooming will not pose a problem. There will, in all probability, be some loss of hair after the birth, which can vary greatly from a negligible amount to a heavy loss, so a daily brush and comb to remove anything loose will only take a few minutes. Your main concern, apart from keeping your bitch clean, will be to avoid the hair matting. Leaving the coat loose does have the benefit of keeping the puppies warm and snug.

When birth is imminent I plait the tail and, taking the hair from either side of the dam's rear, plait this over the hip, so that nothing obscures the birthing. The hair is released once whelping has been completed.

Another method is either to plait, or wrap, the coat and tail, but this will require just as much observant attention as the loose coat in order to ensure that a puppy does not become caught up in the hair between the top of the plait, or wrap, and the body of the dam. No foreign substance, such as oil, should be put in the coat at this time either.

Exactly how you keep your dog's coat when she has her puppies very much depends on your lifestyle. I am in the fortunate position of being able to keep a constant, unobtrusive, eye on my puppies, but this is not the case for everyone, so when in doubt, do not take chances. The comfort and safety of the bitch and the puppies is your priority.

GESTATION

The gestation period, the length of time before your Maltese has her puppies after mating, is about sixty-three days. Do not be alarmed if she is a little early or a little late. Maltese often give birth early. I have had several litters up to five days prior to the expected date, with no ill effects whatsoever. On the other hand, I have twice experienced a bitch going just past the sixty-third day yet producing a perfectly normal litter. If possible it is better to avoid any form of medication during pregnancy.

Throughout the early weeks of pregnancy you will hardly notice any change in your prospective mother. She may become quieter and have a soft expression in her eyes. As time goes on, her nipples may turn a rosy colour and her vulva remain swollen, although this could also apply to a bitch having a phantom pregnancy. More often than not you will have to wait until about her fifth, or even sixth week before there is any noticeable sign. Up to this time her usual routine should be maintained, including the diet, but from the fifth week onward she should have two small meals a day containing a higher proportion of protein in the form of fish, eggs, cheese or meat, increasing her diet slowly to about one and a half times her usual intake – but no more. If she finds carrying her puppies uncomfortable, then feed her three or four small nourishing offerings, as she will not want bulky meals during this time.

The demands being made upon her body increase during this period. Some bitches refuse their normal diet and have to be tempted, favouring all sorts of strange alternatives. I had one who would only eat raw beef and green tripe. Another showed every indication of being willing to starve herself to death until, in desperation, I scraped some raw liver into a paste, and spread it thinly over her normal food, only to see every scrap vanish in a blink of an eye. I know of one bitch who refused food from a dish and for the whole of her gestation period would only eat off the floor. Do not worry, because they all return to normal behaviour in time.

BATHING

Maintain the usual routine of bathing your Maltese, lifting her in the prescribed manner of placing one hand under her ribcage and the other under her hindquarters, raising the whole body together. As she comes close to her time you will probably wish to give her a bath in preparation. The only types of shampoo to avoid for a bitch in whelp are the medicated ones. Continue using your usual shampoo, for it is unwise to use anything new or untried, as this may produce an allergic reaction. Use this opportunity to check that her nails are sufficiently short to avoid an accident if she continues rucking her bedding for a while after the puppies are born. This is also the time to carefully clip off all the hair around her nipples, keeping it short throughout the weeks she is suckling.

EXERCISE

Normal exercise is still important. Continue to encourage regular, gentle activities which will keep her muscles in tone right up to the day she has her puppies. Boisterous games, like jumping on and off furniture, or bounding up and down stairs, should be avoided. Great care should be taken when picking up a bitch in whelp. Never, under any circumstances, lift her by her forelegs alone, and restrain any unthinking guest from this common practice.

To illustrate the point: many years ago I was at home with my Maltese bitch, who was due to whelp within the next two weeks, when unexpected visitors arrived. Having left the room for a short while to prepare refreshments, I returned to hear a guest saying "And how is the little pregnant girl?" My anxious, wriggling Maltese was being suspended by her fore legs in the air, level with the guest's head. Although I immediately took the weight of her body in my arms, two days later the bitch went into premature labour and her puppies were lost. It could be argued that this was coincidence but I will take some convincing, as her previous and subsequent litters were perfectly normal.

WORMING

Even though you have been treating your Maltese regularly for worms, some larvae of the roundworm Toxocara canis can lie inactive, hidden away in the adult dog. These can be re-activated by the hormonal changes taking place within the pregnant bitch. Around the fortieth day of pregnancy the dormant larvae migrate from the bitch into the unborn puppies, so it is wise to discuss with your vet, well before this time, how best, and when, to worm her.

WHELPING BOX

Introduce your expectant mother to the whelping box about fourteen days prior to the date she is due. Choose a quiet place to set everything up in an area away from bright light and noise. If she will now sleep in the box, so much the better, for this will make it a familiar, safe place which she will accept once she has her puppies.

The whelping quarters must be totally draught-proof and large enough to enable your Maltese to lie flat on her side, head and legs extended, when feeding her family. The front of the box should have a removable section to give access to a pen when the puppies are older but, during these early days, it will remain in place, providing a snug, safe interior. If the box is made of wood it is important to sterilise it thoroughly before use, adhering strictly to the manufacturer's instructions, as some disinfectants can be too potent for this purpose. Make sure the box is thoroughly dry before allowing a dog to sleep in it. If it is made of one of the modern materials, then a wipe-over with a reliable disinfectant will suffice.

Whichever type of whelping box you choose, the principal criteria must be warmth and privacy, especially during the first vital days. The box can be either square, with high sides and a lid, or of the open type, similar to a dog bed, and placed inside a pen of reasonable size. Putting a whelping box within a pen, or purchasing a box that has a pen attached, will not only be invaluable once the puppies are up on their feet and eager to investigate the outside world, but it will keep your litter safe from undesirable intruders.

I well remember a friend of mine having a tragic experience a few years ago when one of the family dogs became over-excited. A ringing doorbell triggered this little bitch into dashing madly about, then, in the blink of an eye, she flew upstairs into the room where a young mother lay with her puppy. Without warning she snapped at the tiny puppy, injuring it fatally, then, just as quickly, she dashed down the stairs again. This was an ordinary family pet, without an ounce of aggression in her, and as the two bitches were the greatest of friends, no one could have anticipated such a tragedy happening, but it did.

It is so easy to leave a door open unintentionally, exposing an unprotected bitch and her puppies to all sorts of dangers. A little thought and planning beforehand will give you that extra peace of mind later on.

HEATING

You will almost certainly need supplementary heating once the litter arrives, as new puppies must be kept very warm. The immediate temperature around them should be about 75 degrees (23.8 C) for the first few days. Puppies can lose heat rapidly during these early days and a weaker one that has been thoroughly washed by its mother, then accidentally left out alone, can be at great risk if the surrounding air is not maintained at 75 degrees. This temperature can be reduced gradually towards the end of the second week, when an average of 60 degrees (15.5 C) should be maintained.

If you choose an open whelping box, then the supplementary heating can be either an infra-red lamp suspended by chains above the box, or a heated plate or pad underneath the bedding within the box. The infra-red lamp will have a metal shade directing the heat downwards, and should be suspended at a height that is sufficient to give comfort, but not overheat the occupants. Also bear in mind that your bitch will, at times, be sitting upright beneath the lamp, so make allowance for this. If you follow the angle of the shade down to the floor, this will give a good idea of the area it will warm; it may be larger than you think. The lamp must be of the type fitted with a safety guard underneath. The heated pad will obviously warm the bedding immediately above it, but great care must be taken to ensure that all connections and cables are dog-proof. The one method to be avoided for providing long-term warmth is the hot-water bottle. It is a fact that vets quite often see puppies burned as a result of their use.

Before your puppies arrive, test the warmth of the whelping box. Turn on whatever method of heating you are using, place a thermometer – the type you hang on the wall or in the greenhouse – first where the puppies will lie. Leave it for quite a while and note how hot it gets, then place the thermometer in the cooler part of the bed and make a note of this also. The experienced mother will snuggle down with her charges, but if this is a first-time litter it may take time for her to settle. The puppies could find themselves rolled away from the heat owing to her restlessness.

If your whelping box is the type with a lid then, unless the lid has an open wire grid window on the top, your choice is restricted to the heated plate or pad.

BEDDING

My heated metal plate, with its soft home-made cover, is specially made for dog beds. The cable supplying the electricity is attached through a hole in the wall of the bed so that the plate is flush to the side and no cable is accessible for chewing. This type of heater reaches, and maintains, exactly the right warmth to satisfy a puppy lying directly upon it. When placed under a large piece of the synthetic fur-like bedding, which is warm to touch and allows moisture to go straight through, this particular heater spreads a constant gentle warmth through the bedding.

Such synthetic material washes beautifully and I keep several fresh pieces close by, as well as extra covers for the heated plate, in order to change quickly any that have been soiled. This bedding is also used extensively by vets, as it is so versatile.

The heater and bed take up one end of the whelping box, with the remaining floor space being covered first with paper and then with a cooler material on top.

To make my cool bed, I found that if you take several small tabloid-size newspapers and open them flat from the fold, this gives a nice thick, oblong wad of paper, that will fit beautifully inside a pillow case. If the mother becomes too hot and leaves her babies on the soft warm bed, she can move to the cooler area, yet still be beside her offspring. If the puppies follow her they can get a good grip on the material of the pillow case as they struggle along. I have also found this a useful form of bedding should the bitch, as I mentioned above, insist on raking everything into a heap, as the thick wad of paper stays flat within the pillowcase. However, just as a precaution, stitch the open end lightly together to avoid losing a puppy inside.

GETTING READY

I decamp, together with my expectant bitch, into a quiet, heated, guest bedroom a week before her litter is due. I have a large, closed whelping box beside my bed, with a covered metal plate to heat it. Attached to the box is a small, floored pen, where a bowl of fresh water is placed, and the whole area is covered in white paper. Close at hand is a table on which a bedside light with a low wattage bulb stands. I use a child's red night-light type that can be left constantly glowing, as this gives just sufficient visibility in the dark to monitor what is going on in the whelping box without disturbing either the mother, or her offspring once they are born.

Let your vet know when the puppies are due. Prepare everything well in advance. Have a large pile of paper to hand and several old soft towels. Sterilise and prepare, by boiling for ten minutes, a pair of round-end scissors and a pair of locking artery clamps, as these can be a very good standby. You will also need strong cotton thread in case you have to tie the umbilical cord; a bowl and some disinfectant for your own use, as your hands must be scrupulously clean; a bottle of liquid calcium and vitamin D; and a plastic syringe (without the needle) for administering fluid by mouth. I also have standing by a homoeopathic preparation to help the 'fading puppy', a few drops of which, when placed on the puppy's tongue, have proved very beneficial if one arrives exhausted. Finally, the vet's telephone number should be placed in a prominent position.

Accurate scales are a must. The digital type is very precise and therefore excellent for weighing the new puppies. Have ready a small cardboard box with a covered hot water bottle and some bedding within, as you may need to put a puppy in there while another is on the way. Glucose and milk should be ready to hand to sustain the bitch during whelping. Your last, but also important, piece of equipment, is the notebook into which you write a detailed account of the whole whelping as you go along, such as when contractions started, the time between puppies, their sex and weight, and so on. This will be an interesting reference for the bitch's future litters and invaluable information for your vet, should help be required at any time.

TAKING TEMPERATURES

Around two weeks prior to the date your puppies are expected you will have introduced the bitch to her whelping quarters and, about ten days from the date due, you should start taking her temperature night and morning. Her normal temperature would be around 101.5.F (37.7-38 degrees C) but during the few days prior to her whelping the temperature will begin to drop. In fact, it will fluctuate, up and down, reading normal one time then 99 or 100 degrees the next, then perhaps back to normal, until twenty-four hours prior to parturition when it will drop dramatically to around 98 degrees F (36.6 degrees C). This drop may be transient, which is why you must take the temperature regularly, and it indicates that birth may be expected within twenty-four hours, although I must say that my own experience with Maltese has been that this dramatic drop indicates parturition will take place within the next few hours. You will probably note that the bitch is quieter and her body may even take on a 'pear' shape, as if everything is moving to the back. Some, but by no means all, go off their food.

WHELPING

As her time is imminent the bitch will evacuate her bladder and bowels frequently. She may begin tearing up the paper, and rucking the bedding into a heap. These activities can last all day; do not fuss her, because it is important to maintain a quiet atmosphere. However, a close eye should be kept on her so as not to miss the first sign of straining. She may be a very private girl and keep these initial contractions low key, testing your powers of observation to the limit, or she may let out a strong, throaty cry commanding your attention immediately, then remain increasingly vocal throughout. Do not panic, this is perfectly normal for many bitches.

The second stage of labour is when the contractions begin in earnest and straining occurs. These will become regular, increasing gradually. At this stage the puppy is being pushed towards the vagina, through the pelvis, and is still attached to the placenta. Your mother may choose to lie down during these contractions, or she may stand, or adopt her own preferred position.

I like my bitches to have space in which to wander, as the moving about helps to stimulate contractions, but a word of caution here – do choose carefully where you are delivering the puppies, otherwise when the time comes you may find yourself peering under a low piece of heavy furniture, trying to see what is happening to your now out-of-reach mother.

Note down the time when you saw the first contraction and keep an unobtrusive but close watch on her from now on. Maintain a calm, quiet and unfussed atmosphere, thus giving her confidence in your presence.

A normal puppy presentation is head first, the head being the largest part of the body. Once the puppy reaches through the cervix into the vagina, a reflex mechanism is triggered, causing the bitch actively to push the puppy out.

Maltese do seem to have a high proportion of posterior presentations, i.e. when the puppy is delivered hind feet first. These are unlikely to present great difficulties, although the delivery is often more protracted, especially if it is the first puppy. In this instance, instead of having the normal presentation with the hard, pointed head nicely opening up the pelvis, making room for the narrower end of the rib to follow through, you would have two legs and the soft round rear end coming through the pelvis first, followed by the wide end of the rib, and finally the head.

A posterior presentation is not the same as a breech. The latter occurs when it is a rear presentation but the hind legs are folded underneath the puppy's body, forming a large bulk to push through the narrow pelvis.

The bitch will lick herself vigorously and a first sign that the puppy is well on its way could be when a water bag appears. This usually presents itself like a small dark balloon and is filled with amniotic fluid, which protects the puppy during gestation. In the normal course of events each strain will push the bag and puppy further into the world until safely delivered. A novice might easily mistake the bag for the whelp and break it in error, so creating a dry birth. Leave well alone, unless it is very obviously the head of a puppy with a problem requiring help.

The bitch will rest between contractions and this is the time when she will welcome a drink of milk fortified either with glucose or, better still, honey.

There may come a time when you feel that there has been too long a period of inactivity. In this event, a short, brisk walk on the lead round the garden may help the bitch to hurry things along. If no puppy has appeared after an hour of strong contractions let your vet know what is happening so that they can be prepared for any eventuality. If, on the other hand, your bitch seems to have totally given up straining, then contact your vet for help.

Most deliveries are fairly straightforward, but if a portion of the puppy appears – either the head or legs – and progress seems to have come to a halt, carefully examine what you can see and make sure the puppy is lying in the correct position with the spine uppermost, towards the dam's back. If this is not the case, wait until you have eased out enough of the body to turn the whelp, very carefully, until the right position is achieved. A small amount of warm liquid paraffin syringed just inside the vulva, or a smear of KY jell, may ease the turning, but remember it will also make the whelp more slippery to grip.

When the whelp is in the correct position, take a small piece of the cloth or towelling and grasp the visible portion of the puppy firmly. Wait until the next contraction, then pull the puppy out and downwards in a curve towards, and through, the dam's hind legs. Do not let go, but keep a firm hold between contractions in order to stop the puppy going back into the bitch. Take more and more of the puppy into your grasp whenever you can. The most important thing is to work with the contractions, and with a downward curving movement.

The exception to working with the contractions is if it is a rear presentation, and the puppy's legs appear, out of the bag. Then you must not waste a moment. Grasp the feet, using a thin cloth to grip – not too tightly for it has been known for toes to be pulled off – but tightly enough to prevent the puppy slipping back inside between contractions. Extracting the puppy will require a slow, steady, firm, continuous effort on your part, both with – and here is the difference – also in between contractions. Again I emphasise the need to follow a line that curves down between the bitch's legs, towards her nose. Although time is of the essence in this situation, do not panic and rush the actual task in hand.

Under normal conditions, once the puppy and placenta are safely delivered the bitch will break the sac and begin licking the whelp vigorously to stimulate circulation. If, for any reason, she is reluctant to open the sac, this must be undertaken by yourself. Do not delay, as the puppy may drown in the fluid. Grasp the membrane tightly and tear it open as close to the mouth of the puppy as possible and remove the sac. Open the mouth and clear any fluid, also from the nose. Cup the whelp in the palms of both hands and very, very gently give a little shake, head down, to release any further fluid. While still holding the whelp in the head-down position, take a soft cloth and rub the body, up and down the back and the chest, continuing until the puppy can be seen to be breathing regularly. Confirm that all is well with the puppy. Now you can turn your attention to the afterbirth.

THE PLACENTA

Immediately following the delivery the placenta, or afterbirth, to which the puppy should still be attached, will be expelled. Your bitch may now busy herself severing the cord that attaches it to the puppy and, once this is done, she may then devour the placenta. Had this been a wild dog, the eating of the placenta, being rich in nutrients, would have sustained the mother after all her hard work, as well as removing all trace of the birth from the detection of any passing predators. However, neither of these situations relate to modern life, consumption of a placenta does no harm, although it can result in a bitch having diarrhoea later. Ideally, remove each placenta as you go along, to avoid temptation.

There are occasions when puppies arrive already detached from their afterbirths and if this happens you must note if the missing placenta is expelled later. Once whelping has been completed you should account for one afterbirth for each puppy. If a placenta is retained it can lead to a serious septic condition. Inform your vet, who will probably give the bitch an injection to fragment and expel anything undesirable within her.

An occasion might arise when a new-born puppy may need urgent attention, but the placenta to which the puppy is still attached has not yet been expelled. This is when you will find the artery clamps useful. Lock the clamp on to the umbilical cord as close to the placenta as possible, leaving at least two inches or more between the clamp and the puppy. Although you will be working in haste, do try not to catch hair round the vulva in the clamp, as this could be painful for the bitch. You will now have both hands free to open the sac and, if necessary, detach the puppy from the placenta by severing the cord between it and the clamp. The clamp will have prevented the placenta vanishing back into the bitch after the puppy is released, and it may now be drawn out firmly in a downwards movement.

THE CORD

A bitch may sever the umbilical cord herself, but then again you may undertake the task yourself, either by choice or circumstance. Do not cut straight through a cord immediately after the puppy is born or it could haemorrhage. You do not have to hurry. There are two widely used methods. One way is gently to squeeze any blood in the cord towards the puppy. Hold the part of the cord that is close to the puppy's body tightly between the finger and thumb of your right hand, and with the finger and thumb of your left hand placed similarly, but a quarter of an inch away, shred, using the thumbnails. Hold the left hand perfectly still and work the right hand nail back towards the puppy, picking through the membranes until separated (some can be very tough) leaving about a quarter of an inch of cord attached to the puppy. This will shrivel and drop off during the next few days. Take care not to tug the cord from the body as this could cause an umbilical hernia but, when severing, make all your movements towards the puppy's body.

An alternative method is to squeeze the blood in the cord back, as above, then, holding the cord tightly near the puppy, take sterilised scissors and carefully *shred* the cord.

Whichever method you choose, once severed, take a clean cloth which has been sterilised by being boiled and cooled, and pinch the section of cord attached to the puppy tightly for a few moments, until there is no evidence of bleeding from it. If you are at all anxious, take the cotton thread and tie the cord off about half an inch from the puppy's navel. Trim the thread back to avoid attracting the bitch's attention, otherwise she may try to remove it.

THE TRAUMATISED PUPPY

The bitch will appear to be dealing very roughly with her new offspring, licking and rolling the puppy back and forth. In fact, she is stimulating the circulation and ensuring the lungs are functioning properly. Should the puppy not seem to be responding quickly, or appears still-born, you must assist. Take the puppy firmly, but gently, between both hands ensuring the head is well supported, and swing them in an arc downwards, coming to an abrupt stop and thus shaking out any retained mucus. This method should only be used if the puppy appears 'dead' or fading, as recent evidence indicates that, if overdone, it may result in brain oedema. Clear any fluid from the nose and mouth, then roll the puppy from hand to hand. Using a small terry towel, rub vigorously up and down the pup's back and between the front legs until you are rewarded with a gasp or cry. Keep working until you can feel the puppy has a hold on life. It is at this point that I would commence using the homoeopathic remedy for 'fading puppies' – as frequently as every ten minutes on a very weak whelp. Give each puppy a quick check. Open the mouth and look at the roof to make sure there is no evidence of a cleft palate or any other defect. Ensure the severed umbilical cord is not leaking blood; then weigh the little one and record your findings.

THE NURSERY BOX

I like to have a small cardboard box standing by in which is placed a *covered* hot-water bottle. This is useful if you have a fragile puppy or if you just need to keep a still-wet puppy warm while the mother concentrates on the next contraction.

The removal of puppies between deliveries depends greatly on the individual bitch. To remove a new puppy, distract the mother so that she does not see the little one going. You can give the puppy back to her later on during her quiet periods. Again, just let the puppy re-appear; try and not let her see you take it from the box containing the hot water bottle. If you find removal agitates her then, of course, it is better to leave well alone, provided the puppy does not become cold or is in danger of being trampled upon. In fact, a suckling puppy stimulates contractions, so a lusty puppy can be a great asset in preventing everything slowing down. If a puppy shows any sign of debility or weakness then heat is vitally important, and if you place a soft light cloth over the puppy on the bottle, leaving space for air, this will give comfort and help to keep the pup quiet.

DURATION OF WHELPING

The physical condition of your bitch has a great bearing on how she copes with the delivery of her puppies. However, unsuitable bone structure and age also play an important part. A well-exercised, well-nourished Maltese with a good pelvis could produce one puppy every fifteen minutes, while another in equal condition may take much longer. However, if one hour has elapsed and you are convinced there is another puppy to come, again it is wise to discuss the situation with your vet, as inertia – a state when the bitch ceases to make any effort to deliver the puppy and contractions appear to have stopped completely – may have set in because of exhaustion.

It is often difficult to know exactly when a bitch has completed delivery of her puppies. If you palpate the abdomen a large lump may be felt within her, convincing you that there may be another puppy to come. However, this could well be the now-swollen uterus which can remain in this condition for several hours.

POST WHELPING

Once all the puppies have been delivered your bitch will wish to curl up contentedly with her family. Encourage her to go outside to relieve herself while you remove all the soiled bedding and replace it with clean items. If necessary, clean the mother. Check that all is well with the puppies once more. Offer your bitch, who will now be very tired, another drink – this time, warmed milk and honey – and leave her to rest.

It is not unknown for some bitches to continue raking up their beds, puppies and all, for quite a while, so vigilance is all-important under these circumstances. Take heart, for she should quieten down given time.

PANTING

Many bitches also pant heavily for the first couple of days after producing their puppies and this can seem somewhat alarming if you are not prepared for it. Before your bitch whelps, ask your vet to recommend a calcium and vitamin D formula to have standing by, as I recommended on the list of things you would need. A daily intake of one teaspoonful of liquid calcium and vitamin D will help calm the panting, which is quite normal. Even so, you should regularly check the temperature in the whelping box and, I repeat, bear in mind the fact that, if you are using an overhead lamp, your bitch will be closer to it when she is sitting up.

SIGNS OF ECLAMPSIA

Should the panting, however, be accompanied by shaking or staggering, or should your bitch become depressed, with first a high temperature that then drops to sub-normal, contact your vet without delay as she could be suffering from eclampsia, a complication that can occur after whelping due to the level of blood calcium dropping to a dangerous level. If this is the case, you cannot do any harm by straightaway giving temporary first aid in the form of an additional dose of your liquid calcium. It may assist a little, but her urgent need is for a large immediate infusion of calcium given intravenously by your vet. So do not delay, seek help quickly, as this condition is serious.

THE FIRST FEEDS

A first-time mother may not settle quickly. It will be up to you to make sure she lies quietly so that her puppies can have their first feeds. Put the puppies on to the teats yourself, if they have not found their way there already.

Flatten the skin behind the nipple by gently pinching it together between your finger and thumb and encouraging the puppy to suckle. Do not take this hand away. Hold the puppy with your other hand, placing a finger firmly behind the head, and hold it on, making sure the nipple is right to the back of the puppy's throat. This is very necessary in order to create the suction required to draw the milk in. A normal puppy will clamp its tongue tightly round the nipple, including the area of skin behind, so creating a perfect suction. The puppy will then draw the milk in sufficiently strongly for you to see the skin behind the nipple being pulled with each intake. Occasionally the tongue may already be clamped to the roof of the puppy's mouth, especially when hungry, so make sure the nipple is on top of the tongue and not underneath it. A weak puppy will just hold on to the nipple with jaws moving up and down, giving the impression of feeding, but in fact receiving no nourishment at all and, if you are not diligent, the puppy could fade away quite quickly. Should you have such a puppy, make sure the nipple is in the correct position and follow the advice offered in 'Care of the Puppies' in Chapter 9 as it may help.

Not every bitch lets her milk down immediately, so the sucking should set everything in motion.

A Maltese bitch contentedly feeding her litter.

This little puppy is feeding strongly with his tongue firmly clamped around the nipple. The dam is Ch. Whitesilk Showpiece (Aust. Imp), and the puppy went on to become Ch. Milky Way's Fair Dinkum. Owned and bred by Carin Larson (Sweden)

At first the puppies receive a special type of milk called colostrum. This is secreted immediately after whelping and for three or four days subsequently. It is particularly rich in fat and protein, and contains concentrations of vitamins A and D together with the antibodies which provide the puppies with their first temporary protection against infection.

CARING FOR THE BROOD BITCH

You may find your Maltese has rather loose stools for a short while after whelping, and it is not uncommon for her to have a discharge from her vagina for a few days. Her temperature will also be higher than normal for a day or so and it is best to keep her on a light milky diet during this time. Water must always be available, as the milk she produces can relate directly to the amount of fluid she drinks. After the second day she will readily enjoy light meals, which you can increase according to the size of her litter.

The bitch should be taken to relieve herself about four times a day. Obviously she will be reluctant to leave her family, so do not keep her from them any longer than a few minutes at a time initially. To compensate for them losing the comfort of their mother while she is away, place a soft light cloth over the puppies (leaving room for air to enter) each time you remove her. Do ensure you remove it upon her return. Continue using the cloth over them until you feel they have reached the age when they will no longer fret at her departure.

NOTES

Your notebook should contain a complete picture, indicating when contractions started, the length of time before the first puppy arrived, descriptions of sex and weight, and your impressions at that point in time, and so on. Your documentation will be an interesting reference when that bitch is next mated, although it must be said that no two whelpings are identical, even if it is the same bitch involved.

Chapter Nine

REARING THE PUPPIES

Without doubt, there can be no greater joy than the sight of a proud bitch nurturing her plump, contented puppies. It does not matter how many litters one may have had over the years, the thrill and wonder never diminishes, and these beautiful new arrivals will completely take over your life for several weeks, becoming more and more interesting as they develop. On the whole, Maltese mothers are relatively problem-free but, just as a precautionary measure, it is wise to have a proprietary dried milk formula to hand – one that is made especially for dogs – just in case this is needed to help out in the early weeks.

THE NURSING BITCH

Maltese are excellent mothers, being devoted and attentive to their puppies, sometimes right into adulthood. The experienced bitch will quickly settle and be relaxed, comfortable with your attentions. The first-time mother may take a little longer to settle and may need just that extra reassurance, but your patient presence will do wonders. Occasionally the primitive instinct comes to the fore and although your attentions may be grudgingly allowed, this type of mother may be very disturbed by the introduction of outsiders. If this is the case, her wishes should be respected. The protective instinct is strong in most dogs and you may find that your bitch rests her head heavily on your hands as you try to put a puppy on the nipple. She is just reminding you whose litter this is – and, please, to take care.

At first the more highly strung bitch may not lie quietly for long enough to allow the puppies to suckle, but will rise to her feet and change her position every few minutes once they start. She is probably anxious, or tender, but in the beginning you must make sure she stays down long enough for the puppies to take a good feed. Firmly, but gently, restrain her in the lying position, reassuring her the whole time that all is well and that she is doing fine. Keep her there until you feel the puppies have had a satisfactory feed. Within a very short time she will settle down of her own accord.

When you test to see if your dam's milk has arrived, you may be alarmed when it appears she has nothing. Do not immediately panic, as some bitches release their milk more slowly than others. However, constantly putting lusty puppies on to suckle will encourage the milk to come down. If the condition persists, then contact your vet who may be able to help things along. In the meantime, sustain the puppies with the proprietary dried milk formula or, in an emergency, give boiled water that has been cooled and has a little (in order of preference) honey, glucose or sugar added, until you are able to obtain the milk formula. Dehydration is something you should be very aware of and, in order to test for this, gently take the skin on a puppy's neck or back between your finger and thumb and lift it, then release. Should the skin stay high, in, a peak, as your fingers left it, this indicates the puppy could be dehydrated. Normal skin is elastic and will quickly return to its original position.

DIETARY REQUIREMENTS
In the weeks following the birth of her puppies, your bitch will require several small meals a day. She has used up a lot of her own resources in producing and delivering her puppies and lactation will make further demands on her. The minimum, even if she only has a singleton puppy, is a milky gruel for breakfast, a light nourishing lunch, a similar meal in the evening and a milky gruel at bedtime. As her puppies grow, so the demands on the nursing mother increase, therefore it is vital that she is fed regularly and receives nourishment which is appropriate to the size of her litter and of the highest order. A daily supplement of one teaspoonful of liquid calcium and vitamin D supplied by your vet should also be included.

   Liquids are vitally important, especially if she has a number of puppies. Fresh water must be available at all times and, as long as she can tolerate milk, this should be provided in various forms night and morning. Cow's milk can give some bitches loose motions. If you have this difficulty then I suggest you use goat's milk. The majority of stores keep this in stock. I have always used unprocessed goat's milk, as I am fortunate in having an attested herd reasonably near. Goat's milk is highly digestible and closer in composition to bitch's milk than cow's milk. I have never experienced upset stomachs with either adult dogs or weaning puppies using goat's milk.

CHECKING THE MILK SUPPLY
As Maltese do not have large litters you must keep a close eye on the bitch's milk supply during the first few days. If the litter is very small, or just a singleton puppy, make a twice daily check, as the teats can become congested with a superfluity of milk and the area behind the nipple can become extremely hard and very painful, especially those at the very back between her hind legs. Keep a close watch to see that no one gland is becoming too hard with milk if her supply continues to be generous.

This litter is just two days old.

Photo: F.C. Sturgiss.

RIGHT: If there are problems with the bitch's milk supply, the puppies will have to be bottle-fed.

BELOW: This nine-day-old puppy has not opened its eyes yet. She is being hand-reared, using a pipette with a 'cat nipple'. This was a very sick puppy when this photograph was taken, and her poor health is clearly illustrated in her 'open', lifeless coat. She did, in fact, make a full recovery.   Photo: Pierre Bourque.

The problem with a singleton puppy is there is a choice of glands to feed from. If the area behind a particular nipple is too congested, the puppy will become frustrated by being prevented from taking it easily to the back of the throat and will seek out the softer ones that release their supply more readily. In order to help the situation you can either carefully flatten the area directly behind the nipple just a little, and firmly hold the puppy on to the over-full gland to start sucking and reduce the build up, or resort to manual expulsion, by massaging with cotton wool down from the congested area out through the teat. This will relieve the situation until nature takes over – which will happen – and adjusts the supply to match the size of the litter; but this may take two or three days. If, however, the milk build-up persists and the teats become red and hot, as well as hard, then consult your vet, as mastitis could set in.

During the days following delivery your bitch will probably continue to have a red discharge (sometimes tinged with green). This is quite normal. The only time to become worried is if the discharge darkens considerably and smells foul. Under these circumstances seek professional advice.

HYGIENE AND CLEANLINESS

Never allow visitors to disturb the new family. Your bitch will settle more quickly if left in peace, with just yourself in attendance, for the first day or so. When the time does come for you to show off your little family, if the puppies are still 'in the nest' discourage visitors from handling them unless they have washed their hands, as infection can so easily be unwittingly transmitted to vulnerable young babies from other sources.

Cleanliness is also important for your bitch, with regard both to hygiene and to her own well-being. When she has been out to relieve herself, always check that she is clean before returning her to her puppies, and although you would not wish to over-fuss her, make sure her coat is kept groomed and wholesome.

Removing a mother to be clean may sometimes cause her puppies to cry, so remember to cover the litter, as prescribed in the chapter on whelping. Again, remember to whip the cover off before returning her to the puppies.

ECLAMPSIA

Although the symptoms were highlighted in the chapter on whelping, it is important you are aware that this serious condition can manifest itself at any time. Eclampsia can strike when your bitch's puppies are only one week old, but it is more usual for it to occur when they are three or four weeks of age, which is why a dam with a litter should be regularly observed, and liquid Calcium with vitamin D kept readily to hand, to be given as an interim measure, at the first sign of staggering etc., while you seek urgent help. Delay in contacting a vet could possibly be fatal.

Once the puppies are fully weaned it is quite in order to cut back on your bitch's liquid intake, as you no longer need to stimulate the supply of milk, but do leave fresh water down. However, her body will still require building up as the puppies and lactation have been a great drain on her. The additional nourishing food should be maintained for a further month at least, the period of time required will very much depend on how quickly she returns to her former condition.

Having kept her growing family spotlessly clean these past weeks, your bitch should be wormed once she has regained her former strength and health.

CARE OF THE PUPPIES

Daily inspection is essential in order to pre-empt any problems that might be brewing. Puppies are tough, so do not be frightened about handling them. You will have already reassured yourself that there are no deformities, so all you have to do now is check that the umbilical cord is drying up nicely, eventually to shrivel and drop off.

As you watch the puppies feeding, note which are the strong ones and put these on the less full teats to begin with, as they will make sure they will have enough to satisfy them. Encourage the weaker puppy to feed from the nipples at the back, between the hind legs, as these usually offer more milk. The weaker puppy will tire more easily and may possibly fall asleep while still apparently feeding, but if you are watchful you can give a little nudge to keep the pup sucking until you feel the intake has been sufficient. To encourage a sleepy puppy to feed, squeeze a drop of milk from the nipple onto the tongue to get the puppy going again. This is the type of puppy that could quickly become dehydrated, so keep a check on the skin's elasticity. However, also remember that a puppy has only a very small stomach and therefore don't over-do the boiled water and honey. Milk must have priority. In these circumstances the water is supplementary and only given if deemed necessary, and must not over-fill the little stomach as this could result in a weak puppy feeling full and being disinclined to bother with struggling for the milk, so a few drops, at regular intervals between feeds, is the best course of action.

If you feel it is necessary, use either an eye dropper or syringe (without the needle) to supplement a dehydrated puppy, until the skin feels pliable once more. The main thing is to replace moisture quickly. Care should be taken to avoid inhalation into the lungs when administering any form of liquid to very tiny babies. Place a drop at a time on the tongue and allow the puppy a moment to swallow.

It is well worth giving extra time to watching, or even holding puppies on to feed in these early days. Never assume that because a whelp is holding a nipple in its mouth and moving its jaw that milk is actually being received. Make sure you can see the pink tongue is round the base of the nipple and the skin behind the nipple is being pulled with each suck.

Healthy puppies knead and press the dam with their paws as they feed, working hard to increase the supply of milk. Success is plain to see, for they stop kneading, and their little tails begin to rise into the air, as they lie gulping down the increased flow. To see a row of plump puppies all with their tails arched in unison is incredibly satisfying. The strong or greedy puppy will work hard to bring this extra milk in, which is a great asset to those suckling alongside, especially the less able, as the increased milk is supplied to each feeding puppy at exactly the same time and lasts a minute or two, following which the whelps will either resume kneading in order to encourage the flow to come again, or fall asleep. By carefully watching your puppies you will be able to put a weaker puppy to suckle every time the strong pup begins actively feeding.

WEIGHING THE PUPPIES

The best indication of progress is to weigh the puppy at the same time every day. The minimum increase I would wish to see on a puppy weighing four ounces at birth, is a quarter of an ounce daily. Occasionally a puppy will have a little burst of activity and put on half an ounce or even a whole ounce, but as long as there is a steady increase then this is what you are looking for. I weigh my puppies every evening for two weeks (or longer if I am remotely anxious). Then I weigh weekly, and later on monthly.

Puppies that are not 'doing well' are easily detected. A puppy should have a lovely, round, plump, yet soft, stomach; if it is flat and flaccid this tells you that the puppy is not receiving sufficient nourishment. Then the coat, instead of lying close, will stand away from the body and appear 'open'. All being well, birth weight should have doubled by the time a Maltese is about eight days old and quadrupled at around three weeks of age.

EVACUATING BOWELS AND BLADDER

Very occasionally a situation may arise when you have to evacuate your puppies' bowels or bladder yourself. Fortunately this is easily accomplished by taking a ball of cotton wool that has been slightly moistened in warm water and gently massaging around the anus area until a stool appears. To stimulate a dog puppy to urinate, wipe the cotton wool along the penis from the tail forward, and with a female puppy it is the opposite, stroke from the tummy towards the tail. The slightly moist, warm cotton wool stimulates as if it were the dam's tongue encouraging evacuation.

KEEPING THE PUPPIES WARM

As I have emphasised before, heat is vital and the temperature in the bed must be maintained at 75 degrees for the first two weeks, then 60 degrees thereafter. If isolated, a puppy will lose body heat very rapidly and more puppies die from hypothermia than anything else. The control of this situation is very much in your own hands.

When puppies lie in a tight heap, they could be seeking warmth; if they lie beside one another they are comfortable. You will no doubt have also noticed that very young puppies twitch quite violently when asleep; this is perfectly normal and will gradually disappear over the following few weeks.

CLIPPING NAILS

Attention should be given to puppies' nails. A close inspection will reveal they have tiny hooks on the end of each nail which, one can readily appreciate, can cause much discomfort to the dam if neglected. From ten days onwards, clip the tip of the nails off. Remember, even though these are tiny puppies, they still have a quick in the nail, so take care not to catch it and cause bleeding.

WORMING

Once your litter has arrived discuss with your vet when it would be best for you to start worming your puppies and what type of medication you would require. It will possibly be suggested that you commence treatment when the puppies are two weeks of age, and then treat at frequent intervals until they are weaned and beyond.

CLEANING THE PUPPIES

Be sure that your mother is cleaning her puppies properly. If this is neglected, a puppy can be caused much distress by the anus becoming sealed with deposits from when the bowels were last emptied. Constant straining against the blockage can damage the puppy and, in an extreme case, even result in death. New mothers are sometimes a little negligent in this respect, or it may be the puppy has an upset tummy and the dam cannot cope. Take cotton wool and a bowl of warm water and sponge until the blockage becomes soft, thus making it easier to remove. Always dry the puppy thoroughly with tissues or a soft cloth, and if the anus looks sore from the straining, smear a little Vaseline over the area.

RATE OF DEVELOPMENT

No two puppies – or litters come to that – are the same but, on average, a puppy's eyes begin to open around ten days, followed a few days later by the ears opening. At around three weeks of age they are beginning to try out their rubbery legs and become a little independent. By the time they are a month old they are investigating their world and the little tails are curling over. This is when the front of the whelping box is opened so that the puppies have access to the pen. Soon the first teeth begin to appear through the gums and the puppies take a serious interest in the food on their mother's dish.

Play is very important at this time, so plenty of lightweight, interesting toys should be readily available. No doubt you will find your litter a terrible time-waster as you will be unable to pass the puppy pen without pausing to have a word with them, for they will now be very responsive to your presence.

WEANING

It is difficult to say exactly at what age puppies should be weaned, but usually at around three to four weeks they will be ready to sample either their dam's food or whatever you have prepared especially for them. Do not be alarmed if your dam regurgitates her meal soon after eating: it is not that she is unwell, but some dams revert to the primitive and perfectly natural instinct of providing semi-digested food for their offspring. This is not common to every bitch but is possibly more prevalent if you delay weaning.

Introduce your puppies to food gradually. One meal a day at first, then two, and so on. You could try starting your puppies off on a dish of milky baby rice, sweetened slightly with honey. Always

It is not long before the puppies develop into individual characters. This pup is Foursome's Surround by Love (Ch. Su Le's Cordon Bleu – Ch. Foursome's Loving You) – a blending of Continental and American lines. Bred and owned by Ingela Gram.

ABOVE: A litter of Tamilay puppies, bred by Maureen Foley.

BELOW: Maltese generally make very good mothers. Vicbrita Delectabell is pictured with her puppies. Sadly, this was the last litter bred by the famous Vicbrita kennel.
Photo: Sally Anne Thompson.

use a rich milk (Jersey or goat's) as the puppies have been used to the high fat content of their dam's. Alternatively, you could offer finely-ground beef or a well-soaked complete food or puppy food for their first meal.

In order to ensure every puppy has an equal opportunity to be introduced to food, place each puppy in turn on your lap and offer, say, the dish of rice gruel. Once this is being accepted well, introduce the meat or moistened proprietary food at the next feed. This is very time-consuming, but once the puppies have accustomed themselves to these new tastes, you can supervise them feeding from a small dish together. When puppies first begin eating out of dishes, they often overbalance forward into their food, then spend a happy few minutes vigorously washing each other's faces. Food, especially milky gruel, if allowed to harden around the puppies' mouths, needs to be well soaked before you endeavour to remove it.

Feeding young puppies from a communal dish has the advantage of encouraging competition, thus stimulating active eating. Of course, you should remain observant in order to make sure the strong youngsters do not devour everything and put the less dominant puppies at a disadvantage. When your little family is older you can then feed them individually and if possible within sight of their siblings, so reminding them of the competitive meals and in this manner you can keep their enthusiasm for eating high.

Weaning has been made so very much easier these past years as there are so many excellent proprietary puppy foods on the market. Puppies require four or five small meals a day – two of which should contain milk and initially be fed for breakfast and last thing at night – while, at the same time, still having access to their dam. She will gradually become less and less appreciative of their attention as their teeth come through, so now is the time to begin arranging for the mother's visits outside to be clean to coincide with you feeding the puppies from dishes in their pen. It is always best to put food down while the bitch is away. Keep her apart from the youngsters for longer and longer as the days go by. Make sure you remove any food not eaten by the puppies before she comes back because, if you allow her to clean the plates upon her return, she will fuss and fret to hasten back to the pen rather than enjoying a relaxing time away from her family.

The more solid food can be one of the proprietary brands of puppy formula or finely ground beef, either raw and on its own or cooked and mixed with sieved vegetables and moistened with gravy; it very much depends on your lifestyle. Make sure whatever you offer the puppies the very first time is moist. There is no excuse for having poorly-fed puppies nowadays, as the proprietary brands are totally balanced and therefore require no dietary additives. Your puppies will quickly show you which diet they are thriving on and this will be illustrated when you weigh them. There may be a slight set-back in weight when you first start weaning, but weight gain will quickly settle back into a regular pattern.

With the milk teeth coming through fast now, puppies will need plenty of suitable things to chew in order to help things along. Chewing massages the gums and strengthens the jaw. Keep to a regular feeding regime, the same time every day. By the time they are five weeks old, try feeding a main meal early morning and 5 p.m., then give the milky feed at mid-day and last thing at night.

Should a puppy have an upset tummy it could possibly be that the protein level in the diet is too high. This usually occurs when the meals are home-made and a greedy puppy is indulged with some favourite meat. If this happens, rest the puppy for one meal and give a small dose of kaolin mixture, suitable for children; this will help to settle the insides down. If the problem persists, seek professional help. With either sickness or diarrhoea, the greatest danger to your puppy is dehydration and the glucose water treatment should be started quickly.

Always have fresh water available.

Once the puppies are eating food on a regular basis you will probably find the dam is less conscientious about keeping their rear ends clean, therefore it is important you inspect your puppies at the very least twice a day, to make sure the coat, which is now growing quite quickly, has not joined together across the anus, so preventing the puppy's bowels from being cleared.

Your normal daily routine of inspecting or weighing the puppies is all part of their socialisation. The relationship between puppy and human is critical between the ages of four and seven weeks. If this time of life is full of negative experiences or little contact with the world outside the pen, this could result in an insecure, nervous Maltese who will lack the depth of character of a puppy that has been introduced to many good times, involving plenty of loving interaction and play with humans. It therefore follows that a life full of adventure, care and love will result in a well-adjusted Maltese.

ASSESSING THE LITTER

Naturally you will have bred your litter for a purpose and, more likely than not, it was because you were looking for a puppy to show. I find myself assessing the babies in the nest, from day one. To the uninitiated they may all look exactly the same at this early stage for, of course, they are all captivating, yet there are differences. After allowing time for the trauma of birth to pass, when those little bodies have been squashed and squeezed into the world, you can now see they have settled into lovely puppy shapes, and I reach for my log book which will already contain their weights and sex.

To these facts I now add 'off the cuff' impressions such as the size of the skull – is it small, narrow or broad? I compare the length of muzzle. The whole body shape can be seen, so is it cobby and round or longer and narrower? Feel the bone size, match it against other puppies in the litter, and note any individual characteristics – perhaps the tail may be extra long on one, or short and chubby on another. Is one puppy extra noisy or very active? While weighing the puppies, note down their development, for instance when pigmentation first appears and its intensity. Is it black, or brown, or grey or even blotchy? Compare the coat development and its texture.

By five to six weeks the puppies are very definitely individuals with personalities coming to the

Canadian puppies Kuri Bola de Nieve and Kuri Copo de Nieve. Bred by Flora Mackenzie from the English Floriana line.

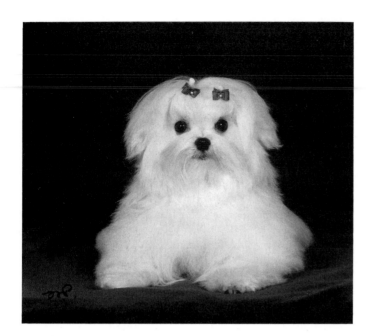

Ready to take the world by storm: Tennessa's Smashing in White (Am. Ch. Tennessa's Jon B of Hyler – Ch. Tennessa's Gadabout Glamour. Bred by Annette Feldblum.

fore. What one is looking for is the confident puppy, outgoing but not aggressive, whose tail is well over the back and who when standing naturally looks boxy, with the head carried well up.

By ten to twelve weeks the puppies can be assessed in greater detail. Spend as much time as possible just watching them play in a large open area, noting the general outlines and movements of each one, and often you will find you are drawn again and again to a particular puppy.

When examining your little family individually, you should look for a good breadth of muzzle – so that the teeth have plenty of room – and for a scissor bite. Jaws can change as the puppy grows and I have known those that appeared undershot at this age to finish with a perfect mouth, and the same applies to a puppy that appears overshot. I well remember one puppy that at first appeared as if it was going to be undershot. then a few weeks later it was overshot, finishing eventually with a perfect bite. There is no guarantee for absolute confirmation until the second set of teeth have actually come through.

Muzzle length differs too: you do not want it too short, nor too long. With the head in profile, examine the stop – it should be well defined. A shallow stop that obviously leans backwards is to be avoided, but too high and deep a stop will give a totally wrong head. Looking at the head from the front, the skull should be slightly curved, not high like a round apple. Hopefully the ears will be reasonably low set, rather than right on top of the head; however, bear in mind that the puppies may possibly be carrying their ears higher at this time because they would be cutting their teeth. You should be looking for a good-sized, dark eye; a small eye cannot give that ultimate soft expression, and a bulging round eye would be totally incorrect. Pigmentation should be well established, with black, unbroken eye rims and, possibly, 'halos' (the pigmented skin surrounding the eyes). Allow a leeway for seasons, as pigmentation may vary in intensity from summer to winter, but it would still be nice to see some sort of indication that halos are present.

Some puppies pigment up much more slowly than others; with these puppies it can come in blotches and take time to fill in, but they can often finish with the same black noses, mouths and pads as their quicker counter-parts. This is where previous notes on litters are invaluable, to recall the slow starter who went on to become a beauty.

It is possible to see just how the puppies are going to use their necks at this stage too, and how they are going to carry themselves. Examine the frames of the puppies when they are wet after a bath and match them against the breed standard. Everything contained in Chapter 5 now relates to your puppies' structure. Familiarise yourself totally with your little ones. Tails can sometimes be a source of worry if they lift towards the sky instead of curving over the back – but if this is all that is amiss, take heart – as long as the actual tail is set correctly – for the weight of the lengthening hair will hopefully improve this by bringing the tail gracefully over and down. If your eye is drawn towards a boy puppy, check that he is entire. Here again puppies vary and some are much slower than others, but ideally one would wish to know a male is entire at this age. However, do not be too quick in discarding the slow puppy, if this is the one that you had hoped to keep, as he may very well only be slower to mature.

Finally, appraise the coat. All young coats are soft, but there are still different textures. A coat can grow perfectly straight for about three inches then suddenly develop a dreaded wave, then just as unpredictably revert back to the straight hair as it grows on.

Your potential show puppy should be square in stature with the neck running smoothly, not abruptly into the shoulder. The whole picture should give the impression of substance yet with refinement. Temperament is seldom a problem. A Maltese should be outgoing, yet very affectionate.

Keep only the best, especially if you hope to breed on from your choice. This is sometimes easier said than done, as sentimentality can lead you astray and tempt you into holding on to a puppy for the wrong reason. In no time, you can build up the number of dogs, possibly resulting in some painful decision-making at a later date. How much kinder it would be to place a puppy that is unlikely to make the grade in a pet home to begin with. The primary object of breeding and showing dogs is to keep the various breeds true to their type, while, hopefully, improving on your own stock at the same time. It should be the aim of every worthwhile breeder – no matter how small, or inexperienced – to breed something which will complement and – who knows? – even benefit the breed.

SELLING PUPPIES

Now we come to parting with your surplus puppies. Once more we are assuming this is the first litter you have bred and it is your intention to sell those you do not wish to keep. Bear in mind you are inexperienced and there is no way you can confidently predict a puppy's potential – it is hard enough for the experienced breeder to do this – so err on the side of caution. Naturally every one of your puppies is beautiful to you, and the very least you can do for them is to try to ensure that each puppy surplus to your needs is placed in the best possible home.

I recall a novice breeder selling every puppy from a litter as 'showable', for in her eyes these babies were perfect – only to be deeply embarrassed a few months later when they were matched against the other puppies in the ring. The problem here is that the purchaser could be so disillusioned that the offending dog may immediately be disposed of, and care as to the future home may be the last thing in this disgruntled owner's mind. Had these same puppies been sold for what they were, delightful pets, they would have, in all probability, had secure, loving homes for the rest of their lives, and the breeder's reputation would still be intact. This could possibly have been a litter of 'show dogs', but how unwise to sell them as such before they proved their worth. I am a 'Rescue and Welfare' officer for Maltese, and have taken in young dogs that have been carelessly discarded into unsuitable homes, because of just such a scenario.

So choosing the right home is in your hands, which is as it should be, for you started this life into the world in the first place. Draw up a set of requirements you would want for your youngsters. Ask prospective buyers: What sort of residence do they have? How many are there in their family, and, if there are children, how old are they? Do they have a garden? Is it secure? Does the inquirer work? If so, what arrangements will be made for the dog? Any other established pets? Does the inquirer realise the work involved in caring for a Maltese? And so on. I never mind parting with dogs to the older person as I believe that age, within reason, should not be the criterion as long as suitable arrangements can be made should a difficulty arise. After all, young people can fall ill, divorce, and even die; so. as long as the prospective owner is capable of caring for, or making arrangements for the care of the dog right from the very beginning, and having a suitable agreement with someone to take over the dog in the event of a problem, why should age come into it? Mind you, again it is up to you, the breeder, to give all the advice possible in this respect.

You may have gathered from the Introduction that I am not really in favour of homes where there are very tiny children, especially if this is the family's first dog. Many parents may not be aware that a Maltese puppy is very quick in its movements and could, in a flash, leap from an unwary child's arms without warning. Small children rush about, and fast-moving legs seem to attract and excite puppies. Therefore there is always the danger of a running toddler being tripped up, causing injury to both infant and puppy. In any case, the Maltese is such a kind breed that it is very vulnerable to misuse, albeit the unintentional misuse of fascinated children. It is for all these reasons that I am that little bit more careful when young families want one of my puppies. Naturally, if my anxieties are satisfied, there is no better choice than a Maltese to be the companion of growing children.

Prepare your paperwork well in advance, and provide the new owner with details of the present feeding regime applicable to this puppy. Written instructions on basic grooming should also be included, together with details of vaccinations or wormings, and advice on future care. Any official papers, for example a clearly written or printed pedigree, should be ready, and finally, the receipt giving full details, including any specific agreed arrangements. Agreements should then be signed by both parties, and a copy is, of course, retained by yourself.

Make sure you give a small supply of the type of food the puppy has been eating, so that any change on to another diet will be gradual. Make it known that you are interested in the welfare of this puppy and are on call for advice if necessary. I also make a point of saying that I will have back any of my puppies should the new owner be in difficulties and have to part with the dog. Any re-homing would then be my responsibility .

Chapter Ten

HEALTH CARE

The Maltese is, in general, a tough little dog where health is concerned. If anything, they thrive better the less medication they receive, but it would be foolish in the extreme to say there are not some conditions that occasionally befall the breed, to a greater or lesser degree. Many of the conditions listed are not necessarily breed specific, but are common to the majority of small breeds and therefore warrant inclusion.

Maltese respond very well to both herbal and homoeopathic treatments. With this in mind a few suggested remedies have been included as useful additions to your home First Aid kit. (See sections headed Herbal Remedies and Homoeopathic Medicines.)

HEALTH CHECKS

TEMPERATURE: The body temperature of a dog should normally be between 38.3 and 38.7. degrees C (l00.9 and l0l.7 degrees F). The temperature is normally taken by placing a round-nosed thermometer in the rectum. In non-whelping situations a temperature of 102 would be indicative of ill-health.

PULSE: The normal pulse rate for Toys is 100 per minute, and can be determined by placing a finger on the inner side of the hind leg. The rate may increase in illness to around 150, but it sometimes decreases.

MUCOUS MEMBRANES: These are normally salmon pink and are easily observed by looking at the gums under the upper lip, or inside the eyelid.

THE EXTREMITIES: The ears and feet should feel warm.

CANINE CONDITIONS AND AILMENTS

ACCIDENTS: Always be aware that an injured or frightened animal may bite – even your most faithful companion. To move an injured animal, slide a blanket beneath so that the dog is lying on one side. Make sure that there is no airway obstruction. If unconscious, pull the dog's tongue forward. Keep the head and neck extended. If bleeding is evident, cover the affected area with a sterile wound dressing. Place a pad of cotton wool above it, then bandage firmly. If the bleeding persists do not remove the first dressing but apply another above and on top of the first and seek professional help quickly.

ALLERGY: As with humans, dogs may be allergic to a wide variety of substances, ranging from food to the sap from cut grass, house dust or flea bites. Tracking down exactly what is causing the problem is very complex and in the meanwhile remedial treatment usually takes the form of various cooling mixtures of calamine and sulphur or similar preparations to treat the immediate area, or one of the various forms of corticosteroid or antihistamine may be given by your vet. Should you find your dog is continually licking and biting at the affected area, try fitting a small 'Elizabethan' collar, which is obtainable from your vet. This trumpet-like hood will prevent the dog reaching the affected site and avoid aggravating the situation.

ANAL GLANDS: Two glands situated one on either side of the anus, under the skin. Providing a dog has sufficient roughage in the diet these should pose no problem; however occasionally they can become blocked, and should be expressed by either a vet or an experienced person, if you have not been shown how to evacuate them. Any inflammation should not be neglected. (See Herbal Remedies.)

ANAL ABSCESS: An impacted anal gland may become infected resulting in an abscess developing to one side of the anus. It may not always be immediately apparent. The first indication that an abscess is gathering may be that your dog seems unusually quiet. Soon a hard round lump will slowly appear next to the anus. Once you have identified the problem, if you wish to hurry things along, then sponging the abscess in its early stages with very warm (not hot) water will help. When an abscess is gathering, it will often come to a head following a bath. Once the abscess has burst there will be a heavy discharge. Keep the abscess open and free from crusting over by frequently bathing with warm water and a mild antiseptic solution or salt water. Should it become blocked, it will prevent the infected matter being totally discharged. It is an unpleasant messy condition, but not life-threatening. Your vet will be able to supply a short course of antibiotics. (See Homoeopathic Medicines.)

BAD BREATH: As with many Toy breeds this is reasonably common and can be the result of indigestion. Very occasionally it may be related to the kidneys, but more often than not tooth problems are the cause (this will be covered under Gingivitis and Stomatitis). If the offensive breath is the result of digestive problems then charcoal tablets or granules can sometimes help, also chlorophyll tablets help to mask odours. (See Herbal and Homoeopathic).

CANCER: Because Maltese are regularly groomed, anything out of the ordinary in the way of lumps or bumps is quickly detected. A growth, no matter how small should not be neglected. Bitches' mammary glands, in particular, should be regularly examined, as this is the most common form of cancer.

CANKER: A term used to describe ear disease. Scratching or rubbing the head is often the first indication that something is wrong, or the dog may carry its head on one side. Inspection may reveal a reddening, or even thickening, of the inside of the ear and the presence of a dark evil-smelling discharge. Clean the inside of the ear gently with cotton wool moistened with a mild antiseptic liquid or warm liquid paraffin, or better still an epiotic or other ear cleaner. Do not dig down into the ear but apply ear drops warmed by standing the bottle in a dish of hot water, then heat-tested on your wrist. Veterinary attention should be sought if the condition persists. In summer be very conscious that grass seeds can enter the ears and this will need immediate treatment. (See Homoeopathic).

CAR/TRAVEL SICKNESS: This may take the form of vomiting, or heavy salivation and panting. Accustom puppies to the interior of a car as early as possible. Should a puppy show signs of distress, make time to sit with the puppy in the vehicle while it is stationary and just play together, making it a friendly place. It is best to restrict food before travelling. If you know your puppy is going to be distressed, before setting out on a journey replace the drinking water with a small amount laced with glucose. A teaspoonful of Milk of Magnesia or any tummy-soothing preparation may help to settle the stomach. If all else fails, half a child's travel tablet will quieten the puppy and bring on drowsiness. Stronger sedative tablets must only be given following veterinary advice. Equip yourself with an ample supply of kitchen roll paper and towels. Sickness and salivation means a loss of fluid; this is when the glucose/dextrose and water is an excellent replacement. (See Herbal and Homoeopathic.)

CASTRATION: This is seldom necessary. It does have the advantage of making a male immediately infertile, if that is what is required, but should castration be advised for any other reason, then allow several months to elapse before expecting any hoped-for benefit.

CLEFT PALATE: This is a birth defect, when the two sides of the roof palate of the mouth are not united. It is sometimes accompanied by a hare lip. It is usually attributed to the coming together of two recessive genes and is considered to have a familial tendency. However, there is also another school of thought that it may be the result of a dietary deficiency. A puppy born with either defect must never be bred from and the dam should be partnered with a different sire when next mated.

COLITIS: Inflammation of the large bowel (colon) manifesting as diarrhoea or frequent mucus or blood- stained stools. Weight loss, abdominal pain, or fever can accompany the condition. The onset of acute colitis is sudden and brief in duration. Chronic, or long-term colitis is much more serious and can disrupt your pet for several years, even a lifetime. The exact cause may never be determined. In the case of acute colitis it may, among other things, be food-induced or bacterial. The chronic state may be caused by allergies, foreign bodies, tumours and so on – the list is very varied. Diet is all-important in dealing with this condition and it should be low in fat but high in fibre. Today there are excellent low-residue diets that are highly digestible and of value in this situation. Your vet will probably wish to monitor the dog's progress over a period of time to evaluate how it is responding to medication. (See Homoeopathic Medicines.)

CONJUNCTIVITIS: The signs are inflammation and discharge from the eye, possibly due to infection, dust or any fine particles irritating the eye. Bathe with a warm saline solution as an immediate treatment. If the condition does not respond, your vet will be able to supply a suitable remedy. (See Homoeopathic Medicines.)

COUGH: Maltese are not prone to coughs (the exception being kennel cough following a stay in a boarding kennel); therefore, if it is persistent, the matter should be referred to a vet. A cough could be the symptom of several illnesses including a heart condition, although this is more usual in the older dog. Nevertheless it is a symptom that should not be neglected. The displacement of the soft palate is sometimes mistaken for a cough. (See Palate) (See Herbal and Homoeopathic.)

CYSTITIS: Inflammation of the bladder, usually caused by an infection. A dog may be seen trying to urinate frequently without success, or to pass only very small amounts on each occasion, sometimes blood-stained. This condition more commonly affects bitches than dogs. A course of antibiotics may be advised, but your vet will certainly need to see her to eliminate a urinary blockage, which would need urgent treatment. (See Herbal and Homoeopathic.)

DIARRHOEA: This condition can have many causes: worms, an infection, a change in diet, too rich a diet, even stress. Treatment must be immediate. Give a kaolin mixture three times daily, and withhold all food. Fluid loss is something you must be aware of at this time and a mixture of salts and glucose will help in an emergency. Replace the drinking water with a solution of 5 grams of salt to 30 grams of Dextrose to 1 pint of boiled, cooled water. Young puppies may sometimes be helped if you add half a teaspoonful of cornflour or arrowroot to a feed. If the diarrhoea is persistent, or if blood is present, seek veterinary advice immediately. Once the dog has settled down and been free of the problem for twenty-four hours, start feeding small quantities of food, avoiding milk for the next day or so. It is wise to isolate a dog with this condition from any companions until the stools have returned to normal, in case it is infectious. (See Herbal and Homoeopathic.)

DISTEMPER: A highly contagious virus that affects a dog's respiratory and nervous systems. It generally spreads as an air-borne infection. Vaccination is the only effective control.

ECLAMPSIA: Sometimes called milk fever (See Chapter Eight).

ENCEPHALITIS: A term used to cover inflammation of the brain, possibly due to a virus, infection or accidental damage and resulting in convulsions. Keep the dog quiet and confined in a safe, quiet, dark place. Seek veterinary advice immediately.

EYE ULCERS: This condition is usually the result of a knock or a scratch received accidentally when playing and will require expert attention. Your vet will be able to assess exactly how severe the damage is by putting a drop of coloured liquid in the eye, and will then treat accordingly.

FLATULENCE: Excessive passing of gas, usually a sign of poor digestion. Charcoal in the form of biscuits, granules or tablets will help, but attention should be given to the fat content of the diet, as it may be too high. A teaspoonful of bicarbonate of soda in a little warm water may help. (See Homoeopathic.)

FLEAS: The dog flea (Ctenocephalides canis) is a rapid breeder, laying its eggs in the dog's bedding, on the dog itself, around the edges of fitted carpets – in fact everywhere. The eggs eventually produce small maggots which quickly pupate and two weeks later – though it could be a year or so – the flea itself emerges. It is a small, flat-sided parasite that can leap great distances and sucks the dog's blood. In addition to the great discomfort it causes, the flea larva carries the eggs of the tapeworm. These in turn can, of course, infect and lead to more problems when ingested by the dog. It is reasonably easy to determine if a Maltese is infested, as the dark grains of 'flea dirt' will be seen on the white hair. If these grains are placed on wet paper they will leave telltale small brown stains. Today there are many treatments, but prevention is better than cure. Thorough grooming is essential, and all bedding should be regularly laundered. Central heating and fitted carpets are heaven-sent for fleas, so occasionally treat the edges of all soft furnishings with a spray recommended by your vet. Alternate your normal shampoo with one of the specially made insecticidal shampoos, but keep it away from the eyes. *Do not use this type of shampoo on a pregnant bitch.* As long as you keep this as a regular routine it should not be necessary to resort to the use of flea collars, which have been known to produce skin irritations and allergic symptoms on Maltese. Today, new genetically-engineered products render the maturing flea infertile, widening even further your armoury against this pest.

GASTRITIS: This is very often caused by over-eating, or a diet not suitable for that particular dog, resulting in diarrhoea. Starve for twenty-four hours, allowing access to water (preferably the saline/dextrose solution described for diarrhoea) then return to a light diet, avoiding milk until the symptoms have passed. Seek advice if the condition persists. (See Herbal and Homoeopathic.)

GINGIVITIS: Unfortunately this disease and similar allied diseases are often associated with small dogs. They have variously been attributed to the feeding of soft food in the diet or to a build-up of tartar on the teeth. Gingivitis is the name given to inflammation of the gums: it displays itself as a dark red line along the gum, adjacent to the teeth. The gum bleeds easily when touched and the condition is sometimes accompanied by unpleasant breath. It is an infection that is treated with antibiotics. A diet containing a proportion of hard or chewable food is recommended, together with regular tooth cleaning in order to keep tartar at a minimum. There are now excellent toothpastes available that not only clean the teeth but incorporate enzyme treatments and they are very worthwhile using. Cleansing the gums with a solution of salt and water or equal proportions of hydrogen peroxide (10 vol) and water will also help. All dogs have two glands in the throat, situated just below the back of the jaw. If infection is present these glands swell and feel like two small hard round lumps, clearly indicating there is a problem that needs attention. (See Stomatitis.)

GRASS EATING: This is a very common practice amongst dogs, who instinctively know the benefits of eating grass, particularly the couch grass variety. The practice may produce a bout of vomiting, which is a perfectly normal bile-cleansing procedure and not an indication of ill health. A cautionary note: public grass verges could, quite possibly, have been sprayed with weed killer which will make your dog ill, and are therefore best avoided. Couch grass has been used by herbalists for centuries as a soothing preparation for minor urinary conditions.

GRASS SEEDS: Maltese are particularly vulnerable to picking up the barley-type grass seeds in their coat and long ears. The grass is found in both urban and country areas. It can be the same height as a passing dog, sometimes at the base of hedges, and thrives on any type of ground. This sort of seed is at its most dangerous during late summer and autumn, when the brown, dried, barbed flights may be taken up into the long hair of a dog at exercise. The pointed barbed darts travel through the coat with every movement of the body. They can penetrate between the pads, right into the skin, and even work their way into the body itself, where they will continue travelling, sometimes creating small abscesses as the body tries to discharge them. These cruel, sharp-pointed seeds have been know to be drawn up into the nostrils and gathered up in vulnerable dropped ears, where they are able to penetrate right down into the interior of the ear-canal itself causing intense pain and requiring veterinary attention. Should your Maltese appear distressed in any way after outdoor exercise, pay particular attention to these sensitive areas on the body and, again, always check carefully when grooming during this time of the year.

HAEMATOMA: A blood- (sometimes serum-) filled swelling. Usually found on the ear, especially with flap-eared dogs, and caused by excessive scratching or violent shaking often due to irritation within the ear itself. Haematomas can also be caused by a blow to any area on the body, and will require surgical intervention to drain.

HEAT STROKE: Even white-coloured dogs can suffer from excess heat if out in strong sun. In an emergency, to cool a dog down, seek shade and place wet towels, wrung out in water, on the neck, head and shoulders. If you have a fan, all the better, for this, combined with tepid water, will aid evaporation most effectively. Ice and very cold water can cause vessels to constrict and so slow down evaporation and can actually cause the temperature to rise. *Never, under any circumstances, leave a dog in a stationary car in hot weather.* Cars become ovens in a remarkably short space of time and even if windows are left open, a dog can succumb to that sort of intense heat very quickly, with fatal results.

HEPATITIS: Canine hepatitis is a disease of the liver and cells lining the blood vessels, causing high fever, oedema and haemorrhage, which affects especially puppies and aged dogs. It is highly contagious, spread by infected urine. A vaccine is available for protection.

HERNIA: This is a term generally used to describe the protrusion of an organ, or part of an organ, through its containing wall. An umbilical hernia is usually associated with puppies, when a bubble of fat protrudes through the abdomen. If small it will not have an ill effect. If large it must be corrected surgically. Either way, if a hernia is damaged or changes colour dramatically, seek veterinary advice. Inguinal hernia is a swelling to one side of the groin and is seen mainly in adult dogs. Perineal hernia is a condition seen mainly in elderly males and appears as a soft swelling close to the anus requiring surgery.

KENNEL COUGH: This is a respiratory infection that occurs especially where numbers of dogs are housed together, hence its name. It is an air-borne virus, characterised by a very persistent and irritating cough which may persist for a week or two. A healthy dog will recover with careful nursing, and possibly a soothing linctus from the vet, but older dogs are more at risk.

LEPTOSPIROSIS: There are two forms of this. One is a disease of the kidney, often called lamp-post disease because it is easily spread through the urine of affected dogs. The other form attacks the liver and is usually spread by infected rats. Symptoms include the characteristic yellow tinge to mucous membranes as well as vomiting and, possibly, diarrhoea. Protection is through vaccination.

LICKING: Although a degree of licking is not detrimental, it can commence with a minor irritation but develop into a habit, with unsightly and sometimes injurious results. If the paw is being worried at, first check that there is nothing physically wrong, e.g. a fungal infection or a damaged nail. Should you need to treat an area on any part of the body that is receiving undue attention, an 'Elizabethan' collar from your vet will help prevent a dog reaching the affected site. There are also various bitter-tasting preparations on the market, some of which can be sprayed directly onto an open wound to deter further molesting.

PALATE: The soft palate is situated behind the upper molar teeth and extends back into the throat. It is a muscle whose function is to close off the nose cavity when eating in order to direct food down the gullet. It is particularly long in the dog and occasionally may temporarily obstruct the airway into the nose if an animal becomes over-excited, resulting in noisy coughing or 'gagging'. This can occur both on or off the lead. Place your hand lightly over the front of the nose and encourage the dog to stand quietly for a moment; the muscle should then relax into its correct position, freeing the airway. 'Gagging' is not as serious as it may sound.

PARVOVIRUS: This is a relatively new virus-based disease which is easily passed from one dog to another. It is a disease of the bowel and characterised by acute bloody diarrhoea which quickly leads to dehydration and collapse. The virus is very resistant and can live in grass verges or pavements which an infected dog may have soiled up to twelve months before. Dehydration must be countered with Dextrose and salt water solution. Protection is by vaccination.

PATELLA: Dislocations (often referred to as slipping or luxating) of the patella (the knee-cap) may be congenital, or the result of a trauma. In a healthy knee-cap the little oval-shaped bone sits in a groove in the end of the femur and is held in place by the patellar ligament. Should the groove be too shallow it will allow the oval bone to constantly escape sideways, resulting in the ligament being over-stretched. The condition may not always be visually obvious, and many dogs adapt to live normal lives without discomfort. It can be easily detected when the joint is physically luxated, and is usually congenital. The more serious cases become obvious with the dog either limping occasionally or totally 'carrying' a hind leg. Surgical correction is possible. Dislocation can, however, be the result of an accident, when the knee-cap is knocked out of its groove, and often cannot be returned to its original position without surgical intervention.

PERTHE'S DISEASE: This is characterised by lameness in the hind leg, and caused by an interference with the blood supply to the head of the femur which becomes rough and painful. Perthe's is associated with children and young animals, therefore a dog around ten months of age showing increasing signs of lameness or limping, together with a marked deterioration in the muscle tone of the thigh, should be checked by a vet. The condition is thought to be inherited via a recessive gene or possibly the result of a trauma. Affected dogs are sometimes treated surgically, others have been known to 'grow through', with the affected femur reshaping itself; however osteoarthritis in the joints is a possibility in later years. Affected dogs should not be bred from.

PYOMETRA: This is an accumulation of pus in the uterus resulting in inflammation. Often associated with older bitches (including those that have not had puppies), but it can affect any bitch. It usually starts quietly during oestrus then becomes apparent with a high temperature, lethargy, off food and heavy discharge a few weeks after a season. This is a life-threatening illness that must receive immediate veterinary attention and usually results in the removal of the uterus and ovaries. (See Homoeopathic.)

SPAYING: Removal of the female ovaries and/or uterus for one reason or another. It is a major operation that is performed frequently, with success. The operation can be done at any stage in a dog's life but it is more commonly carried out when young. A bitch should be fully matured before being spayed, ideally halfway between either her first and second season, or her second and third.

SPINE DAMAGE: Although rare, it is possible for this active breed to damage its spine, resulting in the vertebrae calcifying together, mainly in the neck or lumber region, causing pain and sometimes complex side-effects. The spinal cord is enclosed within the spine, and any damage may result in a diverse set of symptoms ranging from simple stiffness to neurological problems. Anything to do with the spine is serious and best left to the experts. (See Homoeopathic.)

STINGS: Unfortunately stings are very common, usually sited around the head or lips.
Bee stings: a bee invariably leaves its sting implanted in the dog. If visible this should be removed with either your fingers or tweezers, and the area generously swabbed with a solution of

bicarbonate of soda (one dessert-spoonful to one pint).

Wasp stings: these should be bathed with vinegar. If the swelling is in the mouth or throat, or if the condition of the dog deteriorates over the following hour (some dogs go into shock), consult your vet, as antihistamine drugs may be required.

Dogs can also have a very painful reaction to stinging nettles; however, the discomfort will wear off. (See Homoeopathic.)

STOMATITIS: This is an extremely unpleasant disease, to which some Toy dogs are susceptible. It is associated with teeth but the inflammation is accompanied by foul breath, and in its most severe form the gums, cheeks and tongue become ulcerated and a putrid-smelling grey saliva leaks from the corner of the dogs mouth. The root cause has yet to be discovered. The onset of the condition often follows a stress situation; however, infection certainly plays its part and it is thought the disease is associated with the auto-immune syndrome. Any animal suffering from stomatitis is in great distress, especially when eating, and if the condition is neglected the body will be slowly poisoned. Treatment is usually a course of antibiotics; however, this is not a cure and some dogs may eventually become resistant to the various drugs. It has been documented that if every tooth (including the sound ones) is removed, the mouth immediately heals and the dog goes from strength to strength. Some veterinary surgeons leave the four canine teeth in position while continuing to monitor the situation. Should it be necessary to remove all the teeth the dog will be perfectly able to eat normally for the rest of its life. Research is still being carried out but until a definite answer has been found, animals affected with this disease should not be bred from. While your Maltese has healthy dentition, you can help keep this in good condition with simple regular oral hygiene such as rubbing the teeth and gums weekly with either a diluted mild antiseptic solution, salt and water or diluted hydrogen peroxide in conjunction with your normal cleaning or scaling sessions. The new slow-release cleaners and enzyme treatments are available from your vet. (See Gingivitis.)

STRESS: This condition is difficult to define specifically as it can vary from dog to dog. It is where a situation makes too great a demand for a particular animal to cope with. It is very individual. It cannot be seen, as it is emotional. In its simplest form stress for a Maltese could be something as straightforward as being put in isolation into kennels, or missing an owner who has gone into hospital. (See Herbal.)

TICKS: This parasite is common to the UK, USA and Western Europe. It sticks its mouth parts into the skin in order to suck the dog's blood. Ticks have large abdomens that enlarge as they feed. In removing a tick it is important not to leave the head behind, otherwise an abscess may form. You will want to get the tick to release its hold quite quickly, and there are several household remedies you can use. Try alcohol in the form of methylated spirits, or gin, camphor oil or flea spray. It is a case of trial and error. Soak the creature and leave for a minute, then pluck off with tweezers. Hopefully it will come away easily; if not, re-soak and try again; do not force, as the head will break off. Once removed, do make quite sure the tick is dead. Finally, cleanse the area of the bite.

WORMS: There are two common forms of internal worm infestation.

Roundworms appear as their name suggests, and as a preventative measure all puppies should be treated for this condition prior to weaning, after weaning and again at two and three months. Thereafter it should be a regular part of dog care, whether it be monthly or every four to six months, according to the preparation prescribed. The many products available for this purpose are constantly being improved.

Tapeworms are a more complex parasite that requires a drug to destroy them specifically, or you may use one of the better multi-wormers from your vet. The first indication of an infestation could be small segments, like grains of long rice, adhering to the coat around the anus. The intermediate host of this parasite is usually the flea. Eradication is not easy, as you must ensure that the head of the tapeworm has been evacuated and destroyed. Again there are excellent preparations available for this purpose.

SUMMARY: Having read through this list of illnesses and ailments, do not be alarmed. The Maltese is basically a tough, healthy dog requiring the minimum of veterinary attention, and the ailments listed here are some that can affect dogs in general, not Maltese in particular.

ESSENTIAL VITAMINS AND THEIR FUNCTIONS

A: Found in: oily fish, liver, kidney, dairy foods, margarine, green vegetables & carrots. Benefits: Eyes, bones, teeth & skin. Maintains mucous membrane. Deficiency: Conjunctivitis, loss of appetite, low resistance to infection, bronchial infections, ulceration. Excess may result in gingivitis or serious bone disease.

Bl: Found in: Yeast, wheatgerm, meat, beans, whole grain. Benefits: Safeguards against nervous disorders. Deficiency: Nervous disorders, inadequate gastric secretions.

B2: Found in: Eggs, milk, cheese, vegetables, yeast, meat, wheatgerm and animal by-products. Benefits: Cell growth, health, mouth, eyes, skin, essential for all growth. Deficiency: Dry hair and skin. Mouth sores, lack of stamina, nervousness, slow growth in puppies, loss of appetite.

B12: Found in: Liver, meat, eggs and animal by-products. Benefits: Healthy nerves, tissue, blood and skin, use of protein. Deficiency: Anaemia, skin disorders, lethargy, nerve disease.

C: Found in: Raw vegetables, fruit. Benefits: Gums, teeth, healing of wounds. Deficiency: Sore gums, low resistance to infection, slow healing, painful joints.

D: Found in: Fish-liver oil, sunshine on the skin, oily fish, butter, margarine, eggs. Benefits: Essential for puppies' bone growth, teeth, fracture repair. Dangerous in excess. Deficiency: Rickets, bone-related diseases, tooth decay, weak muscles.

E: Found in: Wheatgerm, wholemeal bread, egg yolks, green vegetables, vegetable oil. Benefits: Fertility, muscle health, process fat, body's defence system. Deficiency: Reproductive disorders, poor sperm production, muscular weakness, nervous disorders, weak puppies.

K: Found in: Yeast, liver, wholemeal bread, brown rice, eggs. Benefits: Necessary in the processing of fats and carbohydrates for healthy skin and hair growth. Helps blood to clot and helps to counter abnormalities. Deficiency: Alopecia, gastro-intestinal ulcers, liver problems, dry skin.

Niacin: Found in: Meat, fish, wholegrain.
Benefits: Healthy skin, digestion of carbohydrates, nervous system. Deficiency: Mouth inflammation & ulceration on tongue and mucous membranes lining the mouth, intestinal upset, skin disorders.

Zinc: Found in: meat, liver, kidney, green vegetables, cereals.
Benefits: Prevents skin problems, helps with growth tissues, helps many parts of the body.
Deficiency: Affects hair, skin and many other areas. Dangerous in excess.

Folic Acid: Found in: Meat, offal, green vegetables, yeast, wheatgerm, soya flour. Benefits: Essential for all growth, healthy red blood cells, fertility, production of red blood cells.
Deficiency: Anaemia, diarrhoea, weakness.

Biotin: Found in: Liver, kidney, wheatgerm, bran, oats, eggs.
Benefits: Healthy skin, nerves, muscles.
Deficiency: Dry flaky skin, falling hair, eczema.

Choline: Found in: Good-quality proteins. Benefits: Transports fat. Deficiency: Accumulates fat in the liver, impairing function, and metabolic process is slowed.

HERBAL REMEDIES
Seek professional advice before using home remedies

Anal Gland: (inflamed). Give a course of of Garlic or Garlic and Fenugreek tablets. Greenleaf tablets. Consult your vet if the problem persists. Bathe the area with Garlic Juice.
Appetite: (poor). Malted Kelp. Zinc. Elderberry.
Arthritis: While this is a complaint that cannot be cured, Garlic and Fenugreek tablets, seaweed, and Mixed Vegetable or Greenleaf tablets can relieve and make movement easier.
Bad Breath: Garlic and Fenugreek tablets. Charcoal granules.
Bladder complaints and Cystitis: Mixed Vegetable tablets. Barley water.
Catarrh and Coughs: Garlic and Fenugreek tablets. Lobelia.
Coat dull or with dandruff: Wheatgerm Oil or Evening Primrose Oil (in Summer) or Cod Liver Oil capsules (in Winter) and Kelp powder.
Constipation: Rhubarb tablets or Natural Herb tablets
Cuts, Bites and Scratches: Clean with Garlic Juice for minor abrasions.
Dandruff: Give Garlic, Seaweed and Elderberry.
Diarrhoea: Garlic/Fenugreek tablets and Tree Barks Powder as a first food.
Interdigital cysts: Bathe with Garlic Juice and Garlic and Fenugreek tablets.
Pigmentation: Kelp Seaweed tablets or Elderberry Tablets
Rheumatism: Give Garlic and Fenugreek tablets and Mixed Vegetable tablets. In younger dogs give Comfrey tablets instead of the Mixed Vegetable.
Ring Shyness: Skullcap and Valerian tablets or Yeast.
Skin complaints: Garlic and Fenugreek tablets, dried Parsley and Watercress or in severe cases replace this with the Mixed Vegetable or Greenleaf tablets. Kelp powder or tablets promote new coat growth.
Travel sickness: Scullcap and Valerian tablets
Whelping: Raspberry Tablets.

Worming: Garlic and Fenugreek tablets. If given regularly they will deter worms.

HOME-MADE REMEDIES
Honey Water: A wonderful reviver. Boil one pint of water and allow to cool. Stir in at least one dessert-spoonful of honey while it is still warm. Cool before using.

Dextrose (Glucose) & Salt solution: To compensate for dehydration following diarrhoea or vomiting. Boil and cool one pint of water. Mix in 5 grams of salt to 30 grams of Dextrose. Remove the drinking bowl and replace with this solution.

Barley Water: A health-giving drink, especially for animals suffering from kidney and bladder conditions. Good for all forms of skin conditions and helps to purify the blood. Bring one pint of water to the boil and add one tablespoonful of pearl barley. Simmer for twenty minutes. Cool, strain and add honey.

Seaweed and Garlic Poultice: This is a wonderful healing agent for injuries and wounds. Gently heat liquid garlic and mix the seaweed powder into a soft paste. Cool. Sandwich the mixture between pieces of gauze and bandage into place.

HOMOEOPATHIC MEDICINES
A growing number of vets practise Homoeopathy nowadays. Seek professional advice before giving home treatment. Homoeopathic tablets should be dissolved under the tongue or simply chewed, or crushed. Tablets should not be handled. The dose is so minute that it can easily be contaminated, so tip the pill onto a spoon and crush with a second spoon, but avoid touching with your fingers. You cannot overdose with homoeopathy.

Aconite: Good for the beginning of any illness. For emotional shock, fear and panic.

Acid-Benzoic: Urine odour, excess uric acid, cystitis.

Arnica: Number one remedy for any injury, physical shock, before operations or for wounds and injuries where the skin remains unbroken (as in bruising). Can also come as a liquid, ideal for helping bruising etc. Very versatile. Should be in every First Aid box.

Bryonia: For kennel cough, and bronchial problems, constipation and arthritis.

Cantharis: For burns and scalds before blisters form, sunburn, burning pain in bladder, dermatitis, exzema due to hormone imbalance, insect stings and mouth ulcers.

Caulophyllum: Whelping aid. Effective with difficult whelpings. Remedy given 7 days before delivery.

Cocculus: Can be used to overcome travel sickness.

Euphrasia: For conjunctivitis, inflamed burning eyes.

Graphites: For when the breath smells rotten and there are blisters on the tongue.

Hepar Sulph: A useful remedy for cysts between the toes, or abscesses in the anal glands, or any eruption.

Hypericum: Helps ease pain, cuts and wounds, also a very effective nerve remedy.

Merc cor: Valuable in the treatment of bowel conditions.

Merc sol: Treats bad breath, body odour, diarrhoea, abscesses. Inflammation of the mouth, simple or with ulceration. Inflammation of the kidneys, effective in skin and ear conditions and arthritis.

Nux. vom: Stomach disorders, flatulence, constipation, colic, bilious after rich food.

Physostigma: Useful for problems of the spine.

Pulsatilla: A very good female remedy when the seasons are out of balance, or false pregnancy. Helps skin conditions that are due to hormone imbalance. Helps to overcome salivation in the car, and offensive breath. A very useful and versatile remedy.

Rhus-Tox: For arthritis and rheumatic conditions, helps muscular and joint problems and eczema

Sulphur: This remedy is mainly used in skin conditions such as eczema etc. Also helps poor coat condition and loose bowels.

Thuja: For all types of warts and skin conditions due to ill effects of vaccination.

CARE OF THE OLDER DOG

This lovely breed gives us an extra bonus: it has a long life-span, remaining active and alert, with many Maltese maintaining a good quality of life until fifteen or sixteen years of age. In fact I know of one in England who died in 1995 aged twenty-one years, but that, I must say, is unusual.

A Maltese is very clever in disguising the fact of getting older. However, when you are close to a dog, you gradually become aware of the imperceptible changes taking place. It may not always be immediately apparent, but your companion is subtly winding down, little by little, as the multiple years roll on. These small changes may take the form of less tolerance towards younger animals or children, whose attentions may not be as welcome as they used to be. We do not always fully know what a dog is feeling, and a quiet animal may be one experiencing mild discomfort in some form or another. This is when an older dog becomes self-protective, and peace and comfort become the priority. The dog will know when to play and when to rest, and will be totally confident that your love and care can be taken for granted.

As enthusiasm for the more active side of life quietens down, rest and sleep will gradually take its place. This loss of activity may mean a smaller appetite. On the other hand, those little snacks between meals are habit-forming, so keep an eye on your dog's weight. Do not 'kill with kindness', as obesity is the greatest enemy of both man and dog, and will ultimately lead to a shortened natural life-span. Instead of feeding once a day, try dividing the meal into two halves and offering one in the morning and one early in the evening; this will help with digestion, and give an extra focal point to the day.

Sometimes, following illness or an operation, you may find your dog becomes choosy, so vary the diet using fragrant foods, even try frying tiny amounts of mince, or liver, and mixing it with meal while still hot from the pan. Should a dog be totally disinterested in eating but ready to drink, use the 'complete meal' liquid foods that are suitable for humans, or offer live yoghurt, sweetened with raw, unpasteurised honey. But whatever is acceptable, keep to small nutritious meals.

Some Maltese lose weight as they get older, becoming somewhat 'boney'. Having ascertained that this is not due to failing health, you can be assured they will remain just as energetic, eating well and having an excellent quality of life. Even so, changes in the weather will affect them more than their well-covered counterparts and, with less fat to keep them warm, this type of dog will benefit from being provided with a lightweight coat in cold weather when being exercised outdoors.

Maintain your grooming and bathing routines even if the coat does not appear dirty, as this stimulates circulation, which all helps towards keeping everything in good order. Should you find the skin becomes dry or flaky, try adding a little cider vinegar to the last rinse after the bath. Be aware of any lumps that may appear on your dog's skin. Keep an eye on unspayed bitches, as they are more prone to breast tumours. Do not neglect the nails either, as these are not being worn down quite as quickly now the dog is less active. Pay attention to the anal glands too, as any dietary alterations could affect them.

You may notice a change in the condition of your dog's eyes over the years. No longer are they dark, but appear to have a grey, opaque coating. This is not necessarily a cataract, but allow your vet to reassure you that it is just a change in the lens. Make sure the eyes are kept free from any sticky deposits by bathing them daily. This is just such an occasion when one of the herbal remedies will come into its own. Camomile or fennel tea can be used for this purpose as a soothing

Fortunately, Maltese are generally a long-lived breed. Quincey, Benjamin and Saucey are all over twelve years of age.

Snowgoose Quincey (Ch. Snowgoose Dark Horse – Burwardsley Stephiy Jayny of Snowgoose) pictured at thirteen years of age. She is the dam of three Champions, who all went Best of Breed at Crufts.

solution. Hearing very often deteriorates too as a dog gets older – sometimes very conveniently! This is something to be particularly conscious of when exercising in open public spaces, so keep your pet within reasonable reach. If you use the type of lead that extends, giving extra length to allow a dog more freedom, take care when walking along roads, as you have far less control over a dog with this type of attachment, and a deaf animal would not be aware of passing traffic approaching from behind.

Remember, an older dog may not be capable of walking as far as in the past. Nevertheless exercise is still essential, keeping limbs less stiff, and helping with the dog's circulation. It is just a question of keeping everything in moderation. Exercising in hot weather should be avoided as it will make too great a demand on the older dog, so lead walks are best undertaken first thing in the morning and last thing at night in these circumstances. Needless to say, taking an older dog out in a car on a hot day should be avoided if at all possible. If you simply have to travel, take plenty of water and some damp towels to cool the dog's body should it be necessary. Leaving a dog of any age in a car in hot weather is a sure recipe for disaster, as they can die very quickly from heat exhaustion, even if the windows are left open.

As your Maltese gets older, rising from bed may be somewhat slower, and it is quite possible the bladder will not be as strong as it was. This will all require tolerance on your part, especially if age means an unaccustomed puddle or two. This is a time when you have to adapt around your dog, by trying to anticipate problems, in order that life is tolerable and not stressful for either of you.

MAKING PROVISION IN YOUR WILL

When you buy a dog, the last thing in your mind is making provision in your will for the ongoing welfare of your new acquisition should anything unexpectedly happen to you. But tragedies can take place at any stage in our lives. Therefore this is something that should be given serious thought, and action taken to safeguard the future of any pets you may have in your care.

The first obvious consideration is specifically to include any companions in your will, and here it is important to discuss your ideas with family and friends. Find out who would honour your wishes and be willing to continue caring for your pets for the rest of their natural lives. Make a financial settlement, clearly setting out how you would like the money apportioned and what should happen to any surplus.

When travelling, make sure some method of identification is always carried on your dog, either in the temporary form of a tag on the dog's collar, or by one of the more permanent methods of identification, such as tattooing.

If you have an elderly relative with a companion, encourage them to make out several cards with information on as to whom to contact in an emergency, together with the telephone number of their vet, written in nice bold figures, and suggest they leave one by the telephone, and another in their handbag or wallet. This is not being morbid – in fact you will find it is something for which they will be grateful, as it gives the elderly person peace of mind knowing they have safeguarded their pet should they be taken ill at any time.

Write out a couple of cards for yourself for use on the occasions when you have to leave a dog alone at home, while you drive out somewhere. Carry one card in the car, and another on your person, stating 'Please *immediately* contact............' followed by two telephone numbers. These can be of friends or relatives who will have previously agreed to take care of your dog should you be unfortunate enough to have an accident. You will then have peace of mind knowing your pet will not be left unattended.

THE FINAL MOMENT

We all wish our animals could slip peacefully away in their sleep, in their own beds, at home, but it does not always happen that way. The ageing or sick dog may be experiencing such a poor quality of life that you have to make a decision yourself. Of course, the situation could be taken out of your hands, should it be necessary to act upon your vet's advice and have your dog painlessly put to sleep.

It will never be easy saying goodbye to a dear companion. This is where your compassion and love will give you the strength to do what is best. As your dog drifts off into a peaceful permanent sleep, cherish and value the memories of your life together, in the sure knowledge that this last unselfish act afforded your companion a dignified end.

I suppose death is one of the most difficult subjects to discuss as each and every one of us reacts in a very personal and different way to the passing of a much-loved pet. There will be those who can cope with the situation in a very stoical fashion, but for others it can be an overwhelming experience, difficult to come to terms with, whether the loss be through age, illness or accident.

The grief and the depth of loss created following a dog's death are sometimes difficult for others to comprehend, especially when they have not been privileged to enjoy the company of such a loyal companion themselves. However, recent studies have highlighted the fact that the trauma experienced can, in many instances, be paralleled to the loss of a close member of the family, and this realisation has led to a variety of counselling or bereavement support schemes being set up, accepting that it is very necessary to give yourself permission, and time, to grieve.

The final resting-place of a companion has also to be given considerable thought. Your lifestyle may not be conducive to staying in any one place too long, and in any case, not everyone is in the fortunate position of having somewhere suitable to bury a pet. However, there are excellent alternatives to consider.

Pet cemeteries specialise in collecting pets from home or surgery, and you have the comfort of dealing with people who understand your needs. These cemeteries offer personal plots of land, either for immediate use, or to be reserved by those who think ahead and wish to leave details in a will.

Alternatively, many pet cemeteries can arrange individual cremations with pleasant areas where the ashes may be either buried or scattered and memorials in the form of a headstone, or shrub can be placed. However, you may, if you wish, take the ashes home, in which case an inscribed casket or similar container will be provided. We have one such cemetery, quite close to London, which is set in beautiful woodlands; it is peaceful and serene, a very comforting, permanent place of rest in today's ever-changing scene.

Nothing will replace the dog you have lost. That unique personality enriched your life with a wonderful mixture of memories. However, do not deny yourself further love and companionship, no matter what your age, for to accept another dog into your life would not be replacing the one you have lost. This new companion will have a totally different personality and help to ease your pain, and you, in turn, will heal with the caring.

Chapter Eleven

THE COSMOPOLITAN MALTESE

For those of you who have lived through all the stages of owning and showing and/or breeding a Maltese there will, no doubt, by now be such a deep-rooted interest that you will avidly seek out anything connected to the breed, no matter from what part of the world.

The Maltese has always been a well-travelled dog and there cannot be very many countries where its presence has not been known. This chapter touches on just one or two anecdotes, together with pictures of dogs from various parts of the world, in order to give a very small insight into the benefits of looking at the Maltese further afield. Its popularity with connoisseurs is such that dogs are regularly exported from one country to another in order to either maintain or improve the indigenous stock. Although there are minor national differences in the dogs, dedicated breeders extract what is best from each for the betterment of their own kennel.

The majority of countries are able to purchase and exchange dogs with few difficulties. Today aircraft whisk them from destination to destination in a matter of hours, rather than the arduous sea voyages of yesteryear. There are, of course, still one or two countries – Britain, Australia and Hawaii for instance – who retain their quarantine restrictions, making the interchange of good stock difficult for their breeders; but regardless of such handicaps, the Maltese has tenaciously overcome most obstacles and this chapter celebrates just a very few, and I mean a very few, of the more recent progeny and dogs associated with these successful mixed marriages.

BREEDING INTERNATIONALLY

I can best illustrate how beneficial this interchange of dogs is by recalling the exploits of one particular Maltese very dear to my heart. He was not mine, I just had the immense pleasure of caring for him for six months. This little dog first became known to me as American Champion Su-Le's Great Egret, or rather by his pet name of 'Houdini'. He had been purchased by a friend of mine who lived in Australia. At that time one of the Australian authorities' requirements was that all dogs being imported from the US had to be resident in either Hawaii or England for one year prior to importation, as both these countries were rabies-free.

'Houdini' duly arrived in England, having first left champion progeny in the US, and was quarantined for six months, during which time I visited and watched over him. Upon his release he came to live with me for the statutory further six months, during which he sired a litter or two to my bitches. At the same time his coat was put into good order in anticipation of a show career in Australia. Of the puppies he sired here, one not only gained her British title but was Best of Breed at Crufts. Another became the foundation bitch for one of today's very successful British kennels, and yet another of these English/American puppies went to South Africa where her offspring was made into a SA Champion and became one of that country's top winning dogs.

ABOVE: Ch. Villarose Sweet 'n Saucey and Ch. Villarose Chocolate Charmer: A combination of English and American bloodlines. Owned and bred by Chris Ripsher.

TOP LEFT: Aust. Ch. Jamabeco Narayana, owned by Lee David. This dog is a grandson of Aust. Am. Ch. Su Le's Great Egret, combining Australian, New Zealand, American and British lines.

LEFT: S.A. Ch. Northwards Collington Diplomat (Vicbrita Maximillion – Vicbrita Judy Garland).

Australian Snowsheen kennels incorporating English and American lines (3 litters). Dam of all (3rd from left) Oelrich Fantasia (Imp. N.Z.). All Vicbrita (English) lines.
1st left: Aust. Ch. Snowsheen Skidadle. 4th.left: Snowsheen Splendifrus. 5th left: Snowsheen Scrumptious. 6th left: Aust. Ch. Snowsheen Twinkle Star. All sired by Aust. Ch. Vicbrita Avalanche (U.K.Imp). 2nd left: Snowsheen Sumwun Nice. Sire Aust. Ch. Boreas Bonitatis (U.S.Imp.).

ABOVE: Aust. Ch. Malthaven Su Leanne (Aust. Am. Ch. Su Le's Great Egret, imp US – Manalee Tamela).

BELOW: Aust. N.Z. Ch. Patrician Pistachio (imp. N.Z.). Owned by Robin Hurford, bred by Patricia Nicholson.

Swedish, Norwegian and Am. Ch. Barbarella Dixie, UK Imp (Ch. Barbarella Enchanteur – Barbarella Dallas). Bred by Barbara Miller. Owner/handler: Ingela Gram. Ashbey photography.

ABOVE: Swedish Ch. Milky Way's Fair Dinkum (Ch. Twin Tops Only the Lonely – Ch. Whitesilk Showpiece (Imp. Australia). Owned and bred by Carin Larson.

LEFT: Int. Nord and Am. Ch. Foursome's Extremely Lovable, aged nine years. (Nord Ch. Barbarella Xandoo (UK Imp).– Int Nord. Ch. Gosmore Snowdrop (UK Imp). Bred and owned by Ingela Gram.

Ch. Naysmith's Strut 'n Gabriel. Owned by Juan Cabrera, Del Zarzoso kennels, Spain. Bred by Beatrice Nysmith (USA.)

Lamsgrove Thistle Down, UK imp (Ch. Snowgoose Hot Toddy – Riells Annabel of Lamsgrove. Bred by Tom and Eva Lamb, owned by Renato Gogna of the Minuetto kennels, Italy.

His stay completed, 'Houdini' then continued his journey to Australia, where he gained his Australian crown. This little dog was now partnered with English/Australian and pure Australian lines, producing more Champions, and some of that stock then went on to New Zealand to claim even more success.

This was not some extraordinary or celebrated stud, but just a lovely, very good quality Maltese who, when partnered with nice, complementary bitches, enriched the breed in all these different countries. I, for one, will always be grateful to his breeder, Barbara Bergquist, for the legacy he left behind with me.

Reversing the direction of travel, Ingela Gram established a successful kennel of Champion Maltese in her native country of Norway, and later added to them by importing English dogs (Brantcliff and Barbarella), combining the bloodlines with equal success. When she emigrated to America she naturally took her dogs with her, and there her Foursomes prefix continued on its successful way, but now with the interesting addition of US blood. The progeny from these mixed marriages are now benefiting other lovers of the breed.

EUROPEAN CONNECTIONS

The Continent is particularly fortunate in that dogs may be exchanged with ease, to the benefit of everyone concerned. A good example of this is the successful Del Zarzoso kennel in Spain, owned by Juan Cabrera, which was established with Maltese from England and America, and it was not long before skilful breeding produced quality dogs from this combination.

Here is another good example of how a dog can be of benefit to several countries. This Maltese proudly carries the title of Finnish, Luxembourg, & International Ch. Del Zarzoso Papanatas. He is an elegant Spanish dog who left home to stay with Tarja and Maki Kulmala of the Maldonnas Kennel in Finland, where he was campaigned through to the Top Winning Maltese in that country, as well as being a successful sire. The following year he continued his career by staying in Holland with Wil and Harry van den Rijk of the Voorne's Home Maltese, themselves an influential kennel in Holland, whose dogs also carry a variety of skilfully blended imported bloodlines. There he also sired some lovely puppies. 'Papanatas' continued his career by winning in Holland, and several other European countries, before returning home for good. His bloodline has combined well with these kennels, an excellent example being his Finish daughter Ch. Maldonnas My Reflection, who also claimed the title of Top Winning Maltese during her career, and 'Papanatas's' name is now carried on a variety of pedigrees.

Because it is possible to move dogs easily from one Continental country to another, the breeders are able to be innovative with the excellent variety of bloodlines around, as with the two kennels that recently started in the Canary Islands. One based itself upon the Spanish Del Zarzoso Maltese and the other on dogs from the very respected Italian Minuetto Kennels, while a recently established breeder in Spain imported their first bitch from France, adding further dogs to their stock carrying bloodlines from Holland, Spain and England.

BREEDING IN NEW ZEALAND

Even if you live on an island, where importation is obviously much more difficult, dedicated breeders are still aware of the Maltese scene outside their shores, and if it is felt something elsewhere could benefit their lines, they work towards attaining it. A classic example of this is Patricia Nicholson of Patrician Maltese, New Zealand, who, finding her choices limited, studied the dogs abroad in order to maintain her type and quality.

Patricia had purchased her first Maltese in 1969. Within a few years she had developed a flourishing line to be proud of, but was in need of a different bloodline to complement it. She purchased a beautiful English dog, Ch. Vicbrita Park Royal, a grandson of the famous Ch. Vicbrita Tobias, who proved an influential sire.

Some time later a delightful little English bitch, Aust/NZ Ch. Ellwin Crown Jewel, who was sired by Vicbrita Maximillion, joined the Patrician kennels. Crown Jewel carried a magnificent coat of the correct silky texture, and was therefore of great value. Four more English dogs from

ABOVE: NZ Ch. Shaws Top Hat Amee (US import). Owned by Patricia Nicholson. Bred by Gerda Shaw, US.

RIGHT: NZ Ch. Shaws Stars and Stripes (US import). Owned by the Patrician kennels NZ Bred by Gerda Shaw, US.

various kennels followed, all with the same Vicbrita background. Patricia was also fortunate in being able to work with Ray and Joyce Powell of Caregwen kennels in Australia, who were themselves breeding to Vicbrita dogs, but along a different line.

The time came when a further outcross was needed, but care had to be taken not to lose 'type'. Patricia was very impressed with the elegance and neck carriages of the American dogs and contacted Gerda Shaw, who kindly sold her Ch. Shaws Top Hat Amee. This was the start of a fruitful friendship between these two kennels, with Patricia importing four more dogs from Gerda, which complemented the Patrician line and resulted in lovely puppies that achieved their aims. Patricia also sent Gerda homebred NZ/US offspring which also quickly attained their crowns in America.

What Patricia has done in blending her New Zealand lines with English, American and Australian stock is very exciting, especially when good kennels respect each other's dogs and work well together.

SUMMARY

Being able to travel to see Maltese in other countries is extremely beneficial when planning ahead but, if this is out of the question at the moment, it is possible to fuel your interest by joining complementary clubs and reading as much about other countries' Maltese as you can.

I would like to think that this chapter, depicting the exploits of just a few overseas dogs, most of which are blendings from different countries, will encourage you to watch what is going on in the rest of the Maltese world, for it is truly fascinating.

Once a kennel has established itself with a strong line of its own then what could be more exciting than adding a dog from overseas? The study of pedigrees, the seeking out of suitable contacts and the waiting is, in itself, wonderfully enjoyable, yet cannot match the exhilaration of finally receiving your thrilling new acquisition. Believe me, I know, for I speak from experience.

Chapter Twelve

THE MALTESE IN BRITAIN

It would be impossible to mention all those who have exhibited over the past twenty years, therefore the following will just touch on some of the kennels that have had a degree of influence on today's Maltese, or the show scene in Britain in recent years.

Although the large kennels of yesteryear are no longer around, in Britain we are fortunate to have more individual, dedicated breeders, each with just a few breeding Maltese. I say 'breeding', as many people also retain their retired dogs as companions. These breeders limit themselves to one or two carefully bred litters in any one year, maintaining all the very best elements of this lovely breed and, most certainly, proving their worth at the highest level of competition, yet retaining the essence of the true companion Maltese. The aspirations of the enthusiasts today are just as intense in achieving their individual aims and ideals, both in their breeding programmes and in exhibition. In the UK, once the decision is made to enter at Championship level, the first competitive goal is to try and qualify a dog, or dogs, for Crufts – the only Championship show for which a dog has to achieve a certain standard in order to enter. It is the one show that every exhibitor would like to handle their dog through to the top breed honours, and the going can be very tough indeed, as you cannot achieve that cherished CC unless you win over every Champion in your breed with which you are in competition that day. But oh! how sweet if attained – and that exciting goal sits quietly at the back of everyone's mind.

A STRONG FOUNDATION
The wonderful foundation provided by kennels such as **Harlingen, Sucops, Invicta, Fawkham, Gissing, Burwardsley**, etc. – all established during the 1930s and 40s – gave rise to the bloodlines still to be seen in pedigrees today.

LAMSGROVE
This kennel first came into being in the 1950s, in the hands of Eva and Tom Lamb. It was initially based upon Sucops dogs, later incorporating Burwardsley bloodlines. The most notable dog in the early pedigrees is Lamsgrove White Wonder, whose show career carried him through to win two Challenge Certificates and thirteen Reserve CCs. To be denied his crown by so narrow a margin on thirteen occasions must have been very disappointing. Nevertheless, it did not deter his admirers as this dog appeared on practically all northern breeding stock pedigrees at that time. This has been a small, but steady kennel and the Lamsgrove prefix can be found on a satisfying number of overseas Champions. Eva and Tom are still providing foundation stock for today's exhibitors by taking their bitches to complementary sires, producing Maltese that have attained their crowns in the hands of both the novice and the experienced at home and abroad.

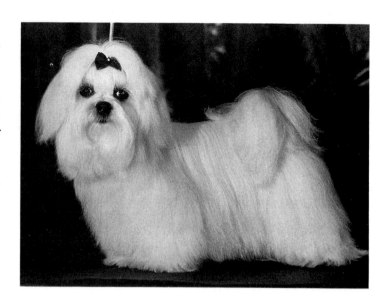

Ch. Lamsgrove Charmers Shadow, aged 8 months (Ch. Villarose Chocolate Charmer – Riels My Opinion of Lamsgrove). Bred by Eva and Tom Lamb. Owned by Jean and Fred Mann.

VICBRITA

Without doubt, this is one of the most well-known and respected of prefixes. The kennel was established in 1953, and the early dogs were purchased by Margaret White from the Invicta, Harlingen and Gissing lines. Although, sadly, this is not an active prefix today, its influence still prevails, with Vicbrita stock to be found in many generations of those in the ring today. Several of the Vicbrita dogs have made their mark in the history books, especially at Crufts, beginning with Ch. Vicbrita Spectacular who took the Breed and the Group in 1962. The following year the Champion twins, Fidelity and Frivolity, did the double at this prestigious event, with Frivolity going BOB. In 1964 it was to be Fidelity's turn to go BOB there and Reserve in the Group, and in 1965 Fidelity returned to Crufts and went one better winning the Group outright. This quality dog also proved to be an outstanding sire. His progeny won Best of Breed at Crufts three years in succession: 1966,1967 and 1968.

Ch. Vicbrita Tobias (Ch. Vicbrita High Society – Vicbrita Stitches): Winner of the Dog CC Crufts 1968. Bred by Gilly White.

Ch. Vicbrita Sebastian (Vicbrita Gambore – Ch. Vicbrita Samantha.): Top Toy 1970. Bred and owned by Margaret White.

Photo: Sally Anne Thompson.

Ch. Vicbrita Sebastian made 1970 his own with an impressive series of wins, including Reserve BIS at Hove (now Southern Counties), to be declared Top Toy of the Year. So many outstanding Champions were produced by this kennel, and their stock was exported worldwide affording prestige to their proud recipients. Every one of these beautiful British Maltese was prepared and handled impeccably by Gilean White throughout their careers.

IMMACULA

Founded by Ina Kirk in the 1950s, the successful beginnings of this kennel were based on Gissing and Sucops stock. Ina's first litters proved fruitful, containing Ch. Immacula Choirboy, a name to be found behind many good show dogs. In fact, his litter sister, Immacula Chanteuse, was purchased by Muriel Lewin as a foundation bitch for her Ellwin kennels along with Immacula Isola Bella. Isola Bella became the dam of Ch. Ellwin Melusine, who went Best in Show at the Maltese Club, under May Roberts, in 1967. Immacula Soloist also proved himself to be a successful sire with, among other attributes, an ability to improve pigmentation. Sired by Ch. Immacula Cantoris, he made his mark in the ring winning one CC and seven Reserve CCs, but, sadly, never gained his crown.

However, his son, Ch. Snowgoose Dark Horse, won the Dog CC at Crufts in 1975 and in turn, carried the genes on to further Champion offspring. The last Immacula to gain recognition at this particular show was Ch. Immacula Dawn Chorus of Snowgoose, who was the leading CC winning bitch in 1975 having first won the reserve bitch CC at Crufts that year.

ELLWIN

Muriel Lewin's kennel was established at the beginning of the 1960s, with Vicbrita Jasmine and the two previously mentioned, Immacula bitches. It was not long before the presence of this kennel was felt in the breed, especially at Crufts, where Ch. Ellwin Marietta won the bitch CC in 1965 and in 1967 Ch. Ellwin Pippelo won the dog CC, his breeding being a combination of the earlier Lamsgrove and Vicbrita lines. Ch. Vicbrita Fidelity was later chosen as the sire for Marietta, and the pairing produced Ch. Ellwin Victoriana, who carried the kennel's flag even higher in 1968 by winning the CC, BOB and Best Toy at Crufts, giving a great performance of ballerina twirls, swirling her coat at each corner of the show ring, to every ones amusement.

TOP LEFT: Ch. Ellwin Sweet Charity (Ellwin Little Jewel – Ellwin Albina Mia), winner of the Bitch CC at Crufts 1983. Bred and owned by Muriel Lewin.   Photo: Dave Freeman.

TOP RIGHT: Ch. Ellwin Touch of Magis (Ellwin Royal Envoy – Midnight Star of Ellwin). Owned and bred by Muriel Lewin.

Ch. Ellwin Leppu Zaza and Ch. Ellwin Gay Adventure took top breed honours at Crufts in 1971 and 1972 respectively, but it was Ch. Ellwin Sue Ella who outshone those around her by holding the (post-war) CC record, winning twenty-three – a title she held from 1973 right up until 1994. Sue Ellaalso won Reserve Best Toy in Group at Crufts in 1973. The more recent Champions include Ch. Ellwin Touch of Magic and Ch. Ellwin September Song, and the prefix is carried on by Champions overseas. Muriel Lewin has been the Chairman of the British Maltese Club for over three decades right up to the present day, and she still maintains an actively successful kennel.

FRANCOOMBE
The very first Maltese owned by Peggy Sturgiss was sired by Invicta Stormcock. According to Peggy, although he never graced the show ring, there will never be another Maltese to touch him for personality and intelligence. In 1961 Peggy acquired Space Charm of Gissing, a daughter of Ch. Spaceman of Gissing, and mated her to the leading Vicbrita stud dogs, so entering the show ring in 1963.

In 1967 Vicbrita Fancy Work joined the kennel and became a Champion two years later. Following the birth of her first litter, she once again entered the ring, this time for Crufts 1970, where she went Best of Breed. Returning to the Vicbrita line Peggy then produced Ch. Francoombe Pas Seul and later Ch. Fancy Me Too, followed by Ch. Francoombe Fancy Stitches and litter brother Ch. Francoombe Fancy Star Turn. When Fancy Star Turn was used at stud his more notable progeny included Ch. Snowsilk Othello and Ch. Snowsilk Iolanthe. Peggy Sturgiss was always an enthusiastic committee member of the club becoming Vice Chairman in 1985 and an Honorary Life President in 1987 until her death in 1994.

*Ch. Quantos Con
Tutto Chiaro JW
(Ch. Maytheas
Delmont – Quantos
Con Tutti Finezza):
Top winning
Maltese 1983.
Owned and bred by
Christine Turner.*

*Ch. Quantos Con
Vivacita JW (Ch.
Ellwin Gay
Adventure –
Quantos Vicbrita
Regina): Supreme
Best Toy in Show,
Crufts 1975.
Owned and bred by
Christine Turner*

QUANTOS

When Christine Turner set out to establish her Quantos kennel she had Vicbrita Regina as a foundation. From her very first litter she bred Ch. Quantos El Muneca. This little bitch gained her crown at Birmingham National, under Muriel Lewin, in 1967, a feat which Christine later repeated, as Ch. Quantos Con Vivacita also won her title at this show in 1973. Con Vivacita was also out of Regina, sired by Ch. Ellwin Gay Adventure. She commenced an exciting career in the ring by receiving her first CC at the tender age of eleven months under May Roberts. In 1973 Con Vivacita added Groups and Reserve Best in Show wins to her credit, closing the year as the Top Winning Maltese, and retiring with a flourish in 1975 after going Best of Breed at Crufts and claiming the Group.

Christine has consistently produced quality dogs, many of which have achieved the highest honours abroad. At home all the Quantos dogs are owner-handled, and their presentation is second to none. In 1983 Ch. Quantos Con Tutto Chiaro was Top Winning Maltese, going on to win the Dog CC at Crufts in 1994. This little dog was sired by Ch. Maythea's Delmont out of Quantos Con Tutto Finezza, and he held a very special place in Christine's heart. He sired, among others, Int. Ch. Quantos Elizabeth who was also a National Champion in Italy, Austria, Denmark, Spain, Finland, Luxembourg, Yugoslavia and the Republic of St. Marino. She won under thirty-four judges in thirteen countries and is mentioned in the *Guinness Book of Records 1994* for her achievements.

MAYTHEA'S

Around the same time as the Quantos kennels were setting forth, Dot Clarke fell in love with the breed and purchased from Marion Crook, Rhosneigr Ballet Shoes, a combination of Immacula and Rhosneigr bloodlines. With the registration of Ballet Shoes' first litter, so the Maythea's prefix came into existence. A bitch was retained to be mated at a later date to Ch. Immacula Cantoris, and this resulted in the very first Maythea's Champion, a dog named Zarrie, the sire of Dawn Chorus, mentioned earlier.

Later Vicbrita Zoffany and her son Vicbrita Vitesse were added to the kennel and Vitesse was mated to Maythea's Ablench Lilly of the Valley. This union produced one of the breed's most memorable bitches, Ch. Maythea's Delilah. She certainly left her mark on the history of the Maltese, going Reserve Best in Show at Leicester and Best in Show at Birmingham National (all breeds) in 1975, bringing the year to an end as the 2nd Top Dog All Breeds. Then came Crufts 1976 and Dot handled Delila through to Best of Breed, then won the Group and finally stood on the podium as Reserve Best in Show. As the photographers assembled a large piece of equipment fell to the ground making a terrible noise and setting the dogs barking, but Delilah, the true professional, didn't turn a hair.

Ch. Maythea's Delmont came next, winning the Best of Breed at Crufts in 1978, followed soon after by Ch. Maythea's Misty Chimes, who was made up at the Maltese Club Championship Show a year later. With the untimely death of Dot's husband Harry, both breeding and showing were curtailed for several years, although eventually friends did manage to tempt her back for a while. In 1984 she piloted Gosmore Janson through to Best in Show at the Maltese Club's Golden Jubilee Championship Show, just to demonstrate she hadn't lost her touch! Dot Clarke has had the honour of judging Crufts twice, once in 1982 and again in 1992.

SNOWGOOSE

My prefix came into being in the 1960s with the Gissing line, although the first litter was not produced until three years later. Then a daughter of the foundation bitch was mated to Ch. Joga Camino of Zurvic (whose breeding included several of the American Fairy Fay's dogs). This resulted in Snowgoose Bewitched, who was later paired with Immacula Soloist producing Ch. Snowgoose Dark Horse, winner of the Dog CC at Crufts in 1973 under Gilean White. Two more bitches from this kennel won the Reserve Challenge at Crufts in 1976 and 1979.

In 1982 Ch. Snowgoose Valient Lad, gained his title and was the Top Winning Maltese. The following year he was awarded BOB and went right through to claim the Group at Crufts. Valient Lad also goes back to American stock, in Am. Ch. Al-Dor Little Rascal. His champion daughters all reached high honours, with Ch. Snowgoose Buff Beauty being the Best Bitch in Show at the Club Championship Show in 1991. 1984 saw his half-sister Ch. Snowgoose Exquisite Magic, sired by Am. Ch. Su Le's Great Egret, awarded the Best of Breed at Crufts.

Ch. Snowgoose Valient Lad JW (The Migrant Snowgoose – Snowgoose Quincey): Best of Breed and Group Winner Crufts 1983. Owned and bred by Vicki Herrieff.

Ch. Snowgoose Apple Pie (Ch. Tennessa's Dancing Flurry of Snowgoose – Snowgoose Anna Marie): The most successful CC winning bitch in 1990 and 1991.

Ch. Snowgoose Firebird came on the scene next, (a son of Nivatus Mr Chips who carried Burwardsley blood), winning the Reserve Dog CC at Crufts in 1985, the Dog CC in 1986, and Best of Breed & Group finalist the following year. His half-brother, also sired by 'Chips', Ch. Snowgoose Hot Toddy, was Best in Show at the 1985 Maltese Club Championship show, and is to be found in the pedigrees of many of today's winning dogs, as he was the Top Sire over several years. His progeny have won either the BOB, CC or RCC at Crufts every year between and including 1988 and 1992. He was also the sire of multiple Group-winning Ch. Snowgoose Kings Ransome, the breed's leading Maltese in 1987, winning Best of Breed with every CC, a multiple All Breed BIS winner, BOB and Crufts Group finalist in 1988, and Reserve Top Winning Toy in the British Isles. Hot Toddy also sired Group winning Ch. Snowgoose Cori Magic who was BOB at Crufts in 1992.

Ch. Tennessa's Dancing Flurry of Snowgoose (US import, linebred to Great Egret) joined the

Ch. Abbyat Royal Rascle of Snowgoose:
Reserve CC winner Crufts 1991.

Ch. Snowgoose Cori Magic (Ch. Snowgoose
Hot Toddy – Fondant Frivolus Snowgoose):
Best of Breed, Crufts 1992.

Ch. Snowgoose First Love (Ch.
Villarose Chocolate Charmer –
Snowgoose Paper Moon):
Multiple all-breeds BIS winner,
Reserve top-winning Toy in the
UK, and the breed CC record
holder. Owned and bred by
Vicki Herrieff, co-
owner/handler Sarah Jackson.

kennel and quickly gained his British crown. His daughter, Ch. Snowgoose Apple Pie, was the most successful CC winning bitch in 1990 and 1991. That same year Ch. Abbyat Royal Rascle of Snowgoose, a son of Kings Ransome was the top winning Maltese overall and won the Reserve CC at Crufts 1991.

The last Snowgoose Champion could possibly be just that, as family health problems require a cutting back on all activities. However,, this last boy, multiple Group winning Ch. Snowgoose First Love, has had a spectacular career. Handled by young Sarah Jackson, who is now co-owner, First Love is a multiple All breeds BIS and Reserve BIS winner, the Reserve Top Winning Toy in the UK, and the Breed CC record holder, having been the Top Winning Maltese over two years. At Crufts 1994 'Pickle', as he is known at home, went Best of Breed and Reserve in the Group. He retired leaving one of his Champion offspring, Group winning Ch. Benatone Love on the Rocks, as Top Winning Male Maltese for 1995.

VILLAROSE
Chris Ripsher started breeding Maltese in 1970 and it was not long before her puppies graced the ring, affording her a degree of success, with two of her later dogs almost attaining their crowns. However, the Villarose prefix really came into its own with the introduction of a half American bitch, Snowgoose Calipso Magic of Villarose (Aust. Am. Ch. Su Le's Great Egret – Ch. Snowgoose Slightly Saucey). Calipso proved to be a super foundation. Her first litter was to Ch.

ABOVE: Ch. Villarose Sweet September (Ch. Snowgoose Firebird – Snowgoose Calipso Magic of Villarose): Bitch CC winner Crufts 1988. Bred and owned by Chris Ripsher.

RIGHT: Villarose Valentina (Ch. Snowgoose Dark Horse – Chryslines My Polonaise of Villarose. Bred and owned by Chris Ripsher.

Snowgoose Firebird, co-owned and shown by Chris, resulting in Ch. Villarose Sweet September, a Reserve Toy Group winner and joint top bitch 1987, and winner of the Bitch CC at Crufts in 1988, just four months after producing her first litter. That same year, a daughter from Calipso Magic's second litter, Ch. Villarose Mischief Maker (sired by Valient Lad) also gained her crown and completed the year as the Top Winning Bitch.

Sweet September, when partnered with Ch. Snowgoose Hot Toddy, produced NZ Ch. Villarose Sweet Sensation, a Group winning daughter with fifty-two CCs to her credit. A repeat mating resulted in Villarose Hot Chocolate, Reserve CC Crufts 1990, who is the dam of Group winning Ch. Villarose Chocolate Charmer, the best dog at Crufts 1992, and Top Stud for 1994/5. His Champion offspring include Ch. Snowgoose First Love. The year that Charmer, a son of Ch. Mannsown Remote Control, gained his crown, Ch. Villarose Sweet & Saucey made her presence felt winning two Reserve Toy Groups and being Top Maltese in 1992, and Top Bitch 1993. This little girl is a Sweet September daughter out of Royal Rascale.

GOSMORE
This prefix is well-known for its Champions in several other breeds; however, Audrey Dallison's first venture into Maltese commenced with a little Vicbrita bitch in 1969, to which she added, and made up Ch. Gosmore Vicbrita Tristan, the Top Winning dog for 1976. Ch. Ellwin Petite

Ch. Gosmore Maytheas Jannette (Vicbrita Vitesse – Malcolms Miracle of Barbarella): Reserve CC Crufts 1982. Bred by Dot Clarke, owned by Audrey Dallison.

Gosmore Busybody (Ch. Gosmore Tobias – Ch. Gosmore Maytheas Jannette. Owned and bred by Audrey Dallison.

Chanteuse, who was already a Champion, joined the kennel and was mated to Ch. Shenala Hamish, the Top Stud of 1975, which resulted in Ch. Gosmore Le Petit Chanteur. Later, partnering Chanteuse with Tristan resulted in yet another Champion, Gosmore His Majesty. In 1982 Gosmore Maythea's Jannette won the Bitch Challenge at Crufts, and the following year Gosmore Fairy Footsteps claimed the Reserve CC. Thus, 1983 proved a good year for the kennel with Ch. Gosmore Tobias also gaining his crown. His son, Gosmore Janson, then won the Maltese Club's Golden Jubilee Championship Show in 1984. The Gosmore prefix is to be found in winning dogs on the Continent, in Australia and New Zealand.

BARBARELLA

This is the home of Scotland's first homebred pair of Champions – a shapely young man by name of Ch. Barbarella Enchanteur (another 'Chips' son) and a little bitch called Ch. Barbarella Little Gem (sired by Gosmore Juniors Menace of Barbarella). Both were made up in 1984 handled by their breeder owner Barbara Miller. The Barbarella dogs are a combination of Maythea's, Vicbrita and Burwardsley dogs, and the prefix has been carried by Champions on the Continent and can now be found in the pedigrees of some American bred dogs.

BLAIRSKAITH

It is not easy for the enthusiasts in Scotland to campaign their dogs as they have to travel great distances and contend with difficult roads and weather conditions. However, yet another stalwart traveller from that part of the world is Stephanie Flemming who certainly made up her first homebred Champion, Fiddlestick, in style by winning his first CC at Crufts in 1990. Fiddlesticks was from Snowgoose Smokey Joe of Monalea, a Kings Ransome son. The following year his elegant daughter, Ch. Blairskaith Touch and Go (the sire and dam being both Blairskaith breeding) repeated the feat, after having gone BIS at the Maltese Club Championship Show the previous year.

MOVALIAN

This kennel was founded by Val and Ian Blore on Rhosneigr and Ablench stock. The delightful little Ablench Camino of Movalian, winner of two CCs and seven Reserve CCs proved a very valuable sire. In 1980 he was the top producer and the sire of Ch. Movalian Rhinestone Cowboy, who first gained his crown in l979, completing the year as the Top CC winning Dog and gaining the CC at Crufts the next year. In 1980 a Camino daughter, Ch. Movalian Sugar and Spice, won the Bitch Challenge at the Maltese Club's Championship Show. In 1983 her daughter, Ch. Movalian Sugar Puff (by Ch. Snowgoose Valient Lad), completed an exciting year as the Top CC winning bitch, claiming her title under Eva Lamb.

Ch. Movalian Sugar and Spice (Ablench Camino of Movalian – Rhosneigr True Star): Best Bitch Maltese Club Ch. Show 1980. Bred and owned by Val Blore.
Photo: Diane Pearce.

Ch. Movalian Sugar Puff (Ch. Snowgoose Valient Lad – Ch. Movalian Sugar and Spice): Best Bitch in Show Maltese Club Ch. Show 1983. Owned and bred by Val Blore.
Photo: Diane Pearce.

Ch Movalian Pierrot (Barbarella Polar Bear of Movalian – Movalian Super Trouper): Owned and bred by Val Blore.
Photo: Diane Pearce.

Ch. Movalian Troubadour made 1986 his year, taking the CC show after show, including the Reserve CC at the Maltese Club Championship Show, and finishing as the Top Winning Maltese that year. He then commenced 1987 by winning the Reserve CC at Crufts. Troubadour was sired by Ch. Movalian Pierrot, the most successful Maltese in 1984, also the sire of Ch. Movalian Eburacum Pantaloon. The Movalian prefix can be found in many pedigrees both at home and abroad, and their exports have proved particularly successful in Australia.

OTHER INFLUENTIAL KENNELS
Four kennels, **Snowsilk**, **Brantcliffe**, **Labellas**, and **Vairette**, although not active today, certainly produced some outstanding dogs in the 1970s and 1980s.

Jean Winkworth (later Kellard) was an artist at presenting her dogs. Her first Champion, Snowsilk Yum Yum, was sired by Ch. Brantcliff Snow Prince out of Snowgoose Distant Hope, litter sister to Dark Horse. In 1977 this bitch won almost everything in sight, commencing with Crufts. In 1980 Jean produced Ch. Snowsilk Othello, who was quickly made up and won the Maltese Club Championship show, and then the Reserve CC at Crufts in 1981. That same year Ch. Snowsilk Iolanthe entered the ring (a Yum Yum son sired, as was Othello, by Ch. Francoombe Fancy Star Turn). This delightful little dog was Best In Show, all breeds at Richmond, finishing as the Top Maltese. Ch. Snowsilk Pitti Sing closed 1985 as the Top Winning Maltese and won the Bitch Challenge at the following Crufts.

June Murphy's most outstanding dogs were Ch. Brantcliffe Snow Prince, who was the top stud dog and Reserve CC at Crufts in 1976, and Ch. Brantcliffe Cherub who stayed at the top of the breed for two years in succession, winning the CC and BOB at Crufts in 1979. Again, the Brantcliffe prefix figured prominently in pedigrees on the Continent at that time.

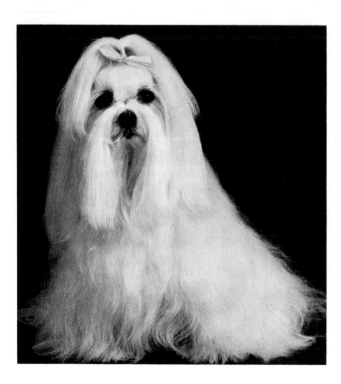

Ch. Snowsilk Yum Yum (Ch. Brantcliffe Snow Prince – Snowgoose Distant Hope): Top winning Maltese in 1977. Bred and owned by Jean Winkworth (Kellard).

Sharon Johnson bred some outstanding winning bitches under her Labellas prefix. Her Group winning Ch. Labellas Dream Baby went Best of Breed at Crufts in 1982, with Ch. Labellas Pearly Princess retiring with eighteen CCs. Ch. Labellas Petit Pearl then added the Reserve CC at both the Maltese Club Championship Show in 1981 and Crufts in 1982, followed by Ch. Labellas Love Pearl winning the Bitch CC at Crufts in 1987. Sharon was another exhibitor who presented her dogs to perfection. Eunice Bishop's Vairette dogs were founded on the Francoombe line. Her first homebred Champion was Vairette Truly Scrumptious who took the Bitch CC at the Club's Championship show in 1983, and repeated this feat at Crufts 1985. Ch. Vairette Mr Pastry came next, to be the sire of Ch. Vairette Angel Delight.

MANNSOWN

Jean and Fred Mann established their kennels in the early 1970s, bringing their prefix to the fore with Ch. Ablench Zaphni of Mannsown (Ablench Shamus – Rosanna of Yelwa). Zaphni was the winner of the Toy Group at Windsor in 1975, and dam of Ch. Mannsown Roman Warrior. Ch. Mannsown Don't Wanna Dance was the next to gain her crown. A daughter of Bleathwood Bobby Dazzler of Mannsown – Snowgoose Penny Farthing, she became the Top Maltese in 1984. Ch. Mannsown Special Delivery (sired by Ellwin Royal Encore of Mannsown) lived up to her name as a special girl, going Best of Breed at Crufts in 1989 and 1990.

Movalian Movie Queen joined the kennel and produced Ch. Mannsown Pause for Thought, winner of the Maltese Club Championship show in 1989. This was a good year for the kennel as their very successful stud, Ch. Mannsown Remote Control, was also made a Champion and later secured the title of Top Stud from 1991 to 1993. Remote Control is another son of Royal Encore and sire of Ch. Mannsown Nearly Missed It, who went abroad.

LEFT: Ch. Mannsown Don't Wanna Dance (Bleathwood Bobby Dazzler – Snowgoose Penny Farthing): Reserve CC Crufts 1984. Owned and bred by Jean and Fred Mann. Photo: Thomas Fall.

ABOVE: Ch. Mannsown Remote Control. (Ellwin Royal Encore of Mannsown – Mannsown Sudden Impact). Owned and bred by Jean and Fred Mann.

ABOVE: Ch. Paldorma Fancy Doll (Shenala Ambassador of Ablench – Playhouse Snow Queen): Owned and bred by Dorothy Palmer.

LEFT: Ch. Paldorma Fancy Showgirl (Paldorma Fancy Harvey – Emacee Babbette at Paldorma): Reserve CC Crufts 1986. Owned and bred by Dorothy Palmer.

PALDORMA

Dorothy Palmer established her kennel in the 1970s. She bred a lovely little dog called Paldorma Fancy Harvey, who entered the ring in 1979. Harvey was always in at the reckoning, but he just could not achieve the elusive CCs for his crown. He did win one CC and no less than twelve Reserves on his retirement. He made up for this by siring Ch. Paldorma Fancy Playgirl and Ch. Paldorma Fancy Showgirl. In 1989 his grandson, Ch. Paldorma Fancy Dylan, opened the year by claiming the Reserve CC at Crufts, then, later that year, his crown, and completing the pleasure of that day by also finishing Reserve in the Group. The Maltese Club's Championship Show saw him win the Dog Reserve CC. In 1988 he improved on this, winning the CC and Reserve Best in Show.

A later addition to the kennel was Ch. Variette Angel Delight, but the most recent Champion, Paldorma Fancy High Society (sired by Remote Control) made 1994 her year by going Best in Show at the Maltese Club Diamond Jubilee show and finishing as the most successful bitch in breed.

CARAMALTA

At the beginning of the 1980s Marlene Townes purchased Movalian Sugar Frosting and mated her to Ch. Snowgoose Firebird. The resulting litter founded the Caramalta kennel and produced the lovely bitch, Ch. Caramalta Sheer Delight. She was the Top Maltese bitch in 1986, winning the

Ch. Caramalta Sheer Delight (Ch. Snowgoose Firebird – Movalian Sugar Frosting): Owned and bred by Marlene Townes.

Ch. Caramalta Creshendo (Ch. Snowgoose Hot Toddy – Scenefelda Sweet Titania of Caramalta): Dog CC Crufts 1989. Owned and bred by Marlene Townes.

A lovely group of Scenefelda Maltese, owned by Jean Leggett.

bitch Challenge at the Maltese Club Championship show, where she had been awarded the Reserve CC the previous year. Scenefelda Sweet Titania at Caramalta was then purchased, and when mated to Ch. Snowgoose Hot Toddy she produced Ch. Caramalta Creshendo, who became the Top Maltese in 1988 and 89. Apart from being a multiple Toy Group winner, Creshendo won Reserve BIS at an all breeds Championship Show, BIS at the Maltese Club Championship Show in 1988, and the Best Dog at Crufts in 1989.

Creshendo's litter sister went to Holland where she quickly gained her title, and, together with other Caramaltas, founded the very successful Voornes Home kennel. 1991 saw Ch. Caramalta Calisto (a son of Sheer Delight – Hot Toddy), owned by Denise Vernon and Doreen Nixon, win

Ch. Caramalta Max in a Million (Ch. Mannsown Remote Control – Carmidannick Justa Jewel at Caramalta): Best of Breed Crufts 1993. Owned and bred by Marlene Townes.

the Dog CC at Crufts. That same year Group winning Ch. Caramalta Max in a Million also won his crown, and finished the most successful male in 1992, retiring with Best of Breed at Crufts 1993. Max is a son of Remote Control, out of a Carmidannick dam.

MARVESS

This is another successful kennel that came into being in the 1980s. This line has been mainly based on Francoombe and Mannsown dogs, giving Polly Reynolds her first homebred Champion in Marvess Jubilant Chiquitita, who won her title in 1987. A male came next, Ch. Marvess Silver Nugget, who was made a Champion in 1991, smartly followed in 1992 by Ch. Marvess Dream Dazzler (a Chiquitita – Ch. Francoombe Star Performer son). This fine dog is owned and was campaigned to his crown by Sarah Jackson of the Benatone kennels. Silver Nugget is double Francoombe and his daughter, Ch. Marvess Silver Sparkler, who won the Reserve CC at Crufts in 1994, is out of a Barbarella dam. Marvess Dazzlyn Tinsel was the leading brood bitch for 1994. She was the dam of Ch. Marvess Dazzlyn Starlet, a Mannsown Zebadee of Marvess daughter, and Top Winning bitch for 1995.

Ch. Marvess Silver Nugget (Francoombe James – Francoombe Fairy Snow): Owned and bred by Polly Reynolds.

Ch. Marvess Jubilant Chiquitita (Francoombe Tambourine Man of Regency Lodge – Mannsown Roman Lady of Marvess): Owned and bred by Polly Reynolds.

CRUFTS BEST OF BREED WINNERS
1975: Ch. Quantos Con Vivacita. (Group Winner)
1976: Ch. Maytheas Delila (R.Best in Show)
1977. Ch. Shenala Renoir
1978. Maytheas Delmont (later a Ch.)
1979: Ch. Brantcliffe Cherub
1980: Ch. Labellas Dream Baby (Group Finalist)
1981: Lilactime Love in a Mist (R.Group Winner, later a Ch.)
1982: Ch. Snowsilk Iolanthe
1983: Ch. Snowgoose Valient Lad (Group Winner)
1984: Snowgoose Exquisite Magic (later a Ch.)
1985: Ch. Vairette Truly Scrumptious
1986: Ch. Snowsilk Pitti Sing.
1987: Ch. Snowgoose Firebird (Group Finalist)
1988: Ch. Snowgoose Kings Ransome (Group Finalist)
1989: Ch. Mannsown Special Delivery
1990: Ch. Mannsown Special Delivery
1991: Ch. Blairskaith Touch and Go.
1992: Snowgoose Cori Magic (later a Ch.)
1993: Ch. Caramalta Max in a Million (Group Finalist)
1994: Ch. Firenzas Back with a Vengence
1995: Ch. Snowgoose First Love (Reserve Group Winner).

Chapter Thirteen

MALTESE MEMORIES

We who are involved with the Maltese today owe a great debt of gratitude to those who have unselfishly worked for the betterment of the breed in the past. Its greatest champion was, as we have seen, May Roberts whose foresight and determination rejuvenated the Maltese, not only in Great Britain, but by contributing to the dogs world-wide at a time when the breed was at a very low ebb.

A pen-picture of May Roberts displays a lady of determination, especially when she had a goal to achieve. However, her dogs always came first. She started to breed Maltese in 1910 with 'Frisky' and 'Barnet Jill'. Three years later she bought Snowflake of Esperance, who soon became a full champion. She gave advice, or physical help, to anyone, whether they had a Maltese or any other breed, and she loved and bred both Newfoundlands and Maltese from her childhood, since her parents had both. She worked tirelessly as a committee member of the Maltese Club and later as President until her death in 1977.

Her daughter Alice Kempster is still very active in the dog show scene today, being the editor of the Newfoundland Club Newsletter. I therefore feel it appropriate to include one or two anecdotes from Alice, recalling her life with some of those earlier dogs. She writes: "Reading an extract from *Hutchinson's Dog Encyclopaedia,* which states 'The vagaries of the weather do not seem to affect these dogs (Maltese), as they can stand extreme cold as well as heat', brings to mind a few instances illustrating the character of some of mother's Harlingen Maltese." Alice goes on to recall a lovely story showing clearly just how hardy some dogs are.

One of their then Maltese family, Leckhampton Blossom, was always an 'outside dog', just coming in the house on odd occasions, and even then it was not long before she was asking to go back outside once more. One night, in February, she whelped a litter, earlier than expected. She managed the whole event all by herself and, of course, when discovered the next morning she was quickly brought into the house, out of the cold. However, she would not settle, so eventually a nice cosy bed was made up for her in her

May Roberts (nee van Oppen) of Harlingen fame, with her Maltese in 1928.

One of Alice Kempster's Maltese taking the jumps.

outside kennel and she immediately settled down, cuddling up to her puppies happily and they all thrived well. In fact at five weeks of age they were running about in the snow having matured very early.

May Roberts loved relating the story that when Alice was a baby, a lady came up to the pram, leant over, and started tickling her, as people do, whereupon Tommy (Ch. Harlingen Snowman), who was also lying in the pram, lifted his head and snapped at her. The lady was most distraught, but May Roberts said she should not go about touching babies, to which the lady replied 'I didn't know it was a dog, I thought it was just a rug!'.

The family also had a spirited little dog called Teddy, or Ch. Harlingen Moonbeam. It seems that the neighbour bred rats at one time, some of which escaped into the wild. Now this was joy to Teddy who would burrow under the shed to get at them, and what a super little rat catcher he was, but you can imagine what his coat looked like at times! Unfortunately he never quite finished them off and Alice tells us that her father had to be called upon to issue the coup de grace. Of course steps were taken to eradicate the rats, much to Teddy's dismay.

The next little story is so typically Maltese: it concerns a little bitch called Flicka, Ch. Harlingen Mystic Moon, and what a character she was! On this occasion she had just produced a litter, of one puppy, and was comfortably bedded in the kitchen. However, apparently she objected to being left alone there and would suddenly appear in the lounge with the pup's head completely in her mouth, the rest of its body hanging limply down. She would then lie down at Alice's feet and cuddle her baby, utterly content. When her puppy grew larger Flicka would drag it along by anything she could get hold of and bring it to where the family was.

Impish Flicka was also reported to the police as a dangerous dog. It appears the postman was not an animal lover, and loathed dogs in particular, swinging his heavy bag directly at them. On this occasion Flicka had unfortunately slipped out before he arrived, resulting in him receiving a nip in the ankle. A representative of the police force duly arrived at the house demanding to see the

The Maltese of today retain their unique character and their stunning looks.
Ch. Paldorma Fancy Dylan (Paldorma Fancy Lahdeedah – Paldorma Fancy Stargirl): Winner of the Reserve CC Crufts 1989. Owned and bred by Dorothy Palmer.

culprit. In bounced Flicka, who immediately jumped up on the couch beside him and rolled on her back to have her tummy rubbed. All was forgiven, and he departed having considered her "a most docile dog".

Finally you will see from the photograph that the dogs were also very athletic. I doubt if there were such things as obedience classes in those days, and certainly agility had not been made popular; however, true to their temperament; the Harlingen Maltese loved performing. When a circle of obstacles was set up they would race round leaping everything in sight, ultimately to be rewarded with a choc-drop or similar treat when completed. Flicka, however, although she was more than capable of jumping the whole course would, if possible, hang back and then just nip over the last gate and join in for the reward! What an intelligent little girl!

These are just a few of the escapades of the Maltese of yesteryear. Thankfully nothing has changed. The dogs of today are just as mischievous, protective, tough and intelligent – and long may they stay so!

We who have been privileged to be involved with the breed, must never lose sight of the fact that we are just custodians in whose care the Maltese has been placed for temporary safe-keeping, to be treasured and maintained in good order for the generations to come.

Chapter Fourteen

MALTESE IN THE UNITED STATES

by Jacqueline L. Stacy

This chapter is devoted to Maltese in the United States, the top kennels, producers of importance, the top show dogs of the past who have had an impact on the dogs of today, and the top show dogs during this twenty-year span. One must begin by giving credit to the safe keepers of our dearly loved Maltese – the breeders. Without their devotion there would be no great producers or show dogs.

THE AENNCHEN LINE

An apparent beginning for some important United States breeders in the last twenty years starts with an ending. I refer to the death of Aennchen Antonelli on February 2, 1975. Aennchen and her husband, Tony, from Waldwick, NJ, are considered by many to be the most instrumental and influential Maltese breeders and exhibitors up until the mid-1970s. After Aennchen's death, Tony's active involvement with the breed ended. However, the influence of the **Aennchen's Dancers** breeding program on the American Maltese can be seen up to today. The name Aennchen in some form or another appears in many kennels The Antonellis were so highly regarded that, as a tribute to Aennchen, many individuals incorporated the Aennchen name into their own kennel name. As Aennchen's death became imminent, most of the younger dogs were given to friends. The late Mr. Nicholas Cutillo, a long-time friend, admirer and travelling companion to Aennchen, continued to use her prefix in his breeding program, fulfilling Aennchen's wish. Famous dogs of the Aennchen Kennel included Ch. Co-Ca-He's Aennchen Toy Dancer, who was a record holder for BIS in her time, the mid-60s, as well as the first Maltese to win the Toy Group at the Westminster Kennel Club. Toy was owned by Anna Marie and Gene Stimmler from Pennsylvania and handled by Anna Marie.

There are hardly any "old timers" who still don't think of the great Ch. Aennchen's Poona Dancer as one of the all-time greats. She was owned by Frank Oberstar and Larry Ward of Ohio, **Starward.** Poona was awarded 37 BIS and a Group 1 at the Westminster Kennel Club during her short two-year campaign in the later 1960s, owner-handled by Frank, who has now achieved great respect as a multiple group AKC judge. Frank has also judged the AMA National Specialty twice; in 1977 and in 1993. As safe-keepers of the Maltese breed standard during their time, the Antonellis were well known for keeping the breed small in size (under three pounds) with beautiful faces.

Am. Ch. Joanne-Chen's Maya Dancer: Winner of 43 BIS awards.

THE JOANNE-CHEN MALTESE

The Aennchen bloodlines were the foundation for Joanne Hesse's **Joanne-Chen Maltese.** Initially she used the Co-Ca-He's Aennchen prefix for her dogs, the most famous being the Stimmlers' Ch. Co-Ca-He's Aennchen Toy Dancer, described above. Later she used Jo-Aennchen and, finally, Joanne-chen. She bred many BIS and group-winning dogs, the most famous being Ch. Joanne-chen's Maya Dancer. Maya was shown by the then professional handler and now renowned judge, Peggy Hogg, for Mamie Gregory of Kentucky. Maya held the record for all breed BIS with 43 until 1992. He was well-known and loved by many. I can still see him in the ring. As soon as his feet hit the ground he was off and running. Besides being a beautiful little dog, he perhaps set the example of what show dog means for Maltese. He also won the Quaker Oats award in 1971 and 1972, the AMA National Specialty in 1972, the Toy Group at Westminster in 1972 and 1973. Peggy was honored by being asked to judge the sweepstakes at the AMA National Specialty in 1981.

THE PENDLETON MALTESE

While acknowledging some famous kennels of the past that have had an impact on the dogs of today, one must also speak of the **Pendleton Maltese** of Ann and Stewart Pendleton. They produced one of the first top winning Maltese in the history of the breed in the United States in the 1960s, Ch. Brittigan's Sweet William. His record was later broken by Ch. Aennchen's Toy Dancer. Their Ch. Brittigan's Dark Eyes also held the record for BIS for a while. Eventually it was broken by Ch. Aennchen's Poona Dancer. The most famous Maltese bred by Pendleton, Ch. Pendleton's Crown Jewel was owned and handled to her wins by Dorothy White, who chose **Crown Jewel** as her kennel name. Ch. Jewel won the AMA National Specialty three consecutive years (1969, 1970 and 1971), the Quaker Oats award in 1969 and 1970, and 29 all breed BIS. Dorothy is a past president of the AMA and was selected to judge the Sweepstakes at the 1985 National Specialty.

Darlene Wilkinson from Illinois formed a partnership with Shirely Hrabak using the prefix **Gayla.** After Shirley's death, Darlene continued to use this prefix, but later formed a relationship with Joanne Hess and, thereafter, named her dogs with the prefix of **Gayla-Joanne-Chen.** Freeman and Mary Purvis from Iowa purchased Ch. Gayla Joanne-Chen's Muskrat Luv from Darlene and began the very successful **Melodylane Maltese.** Melodylane has produced many BIS and Group winning Maltese, many sired by the very prepotent Muskrat, including Ch. Melodylane's Raggedy Any Luv, owned by Norman Patton and Chip Constantino and handled by Tim Lehman, and Ch. Melody Lane Lite N' Lively Luv (Lisa).

THE SAND ISLAND KENNELS

After a successful show campaign with Freeman, Lisa was purchased by the late Carol Frances Andersen of St. Paul, Minnesota, **Sand Island Kennels**. Lisa's show campaign continued under my direction. I started as a handler, and am now a judge. Lisa's show career was quite successful, winning multiple BIS and specialties. She will also go down in the record books as the dam of the top winning Maltese in the history of the breed, Ch. Sand Island's Small Kraft Lite, well-known as Henry. Carol Frances Andersen was passionate about dogs. Her first and everlasting love was with Skye Terriers, having been led down that successful path by Walter Goodman of Glamoor and Annie Boucher of Roblyn. I handled her Skyes to Multiple Best in Shows and National Specialties. With her success with these dogs, Carol's passion intensified and she decided to expand into another breed.

Since she was enthralled with the drop-coated breeds, it was not surprising that she chose the Maltese. I purchased a beautiful little dog with a gorgeous coat texture and an outstanding front assembly from Molly and Jeff Sunde for Carol. His name was Ch. Keoli's Small Kraft Warning. He was known as Ricky and he really set the standard for Carol's breeding program. He had the much sought-after refinement and small size of the Aennchen dogs, with the glorious coat of the Myi's dogs and the showmanship of Maya Dancer. Though he carried the Keoli prefix, the dogs in his background were Myis. He won multiple Best In Shows, as well as the breed and a group placement at Westminster. The highlight of his show career was being awarded Group 1 at the AKC Centennial Show under highly respected judge Melbourne T. Downing in 1984 over approximately 1000 other Toy Dogs.

As a stud dog Ricky, bred to Lisa, produced Henry, Ch. Sand Island's Small Kraft Lite. With my assistant, Jere Olson, I was Carol's kennel manager when Sand Island produced some 30-plus champions in addition to Henry. After my retirement as a handler, Carol employed Vicki Martin Caliendo Abbott to present Henry. Together they were most impressive. Under Vicki's beautiful presentation, not only did Henry win the National Specialty twice, and become the top winning

Am. Ch. Melody Lane Lite N' Lively Luv: Multiple BIS and BISS winner, dam of many Champion offspring, including Am. Ch. Sand Island Small Kraft Lite, Top winning Maltese in the US.

Am. Ch. Sand Island Small Kraft Lite: Top winning Maltese in the USA with 82 BIS, over 250 Group Ones and two National Specialties.

Am. Ch. Keoli's Small Kraft Warning, handled by Jacqueline Stacy, winning the Group at the AKC Centennial Show.

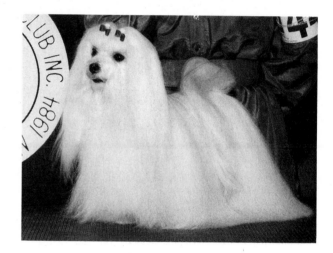

Maltese of all time, but he also earned the title for the top winning toy dog of all times with 82 Best In Shows and over 250 Group Firsts. He was the winner of the Quaker Oats award in 1991 and 1992 as well as the winner of the Toy Group at Westminster in 1992.

Carol's contributions to Maltese will go down in history books as remarkable. Unfortunately, the Sand Island Maltese ended abruptly with her death in 1992 from breast cancer. Her husband, Bill, was unable to continue Carol's breeding program, since he was left with the enormous responsibility of raising the three small children he and Carol had adopted from Rumania the year before she died. Thus, the Sand Island Maltese were sold to breeders throughout the United States, South America and the Far East. Hopefully they will continue to make their mark in the breed. Through the AMA the Carol F. Andersen Breeders Award is given to honor the breeder of the number one Maltese each year.

BIENAIMEE, MARTIN AND BAR NONE

Blance Tenerowicz from Massachusetts also has enjoyed much success as a breeder using the **Bienaimee** kennel name. She also purchased the lovely Ch. Joanne-Chen's Mino Maya Dancer from Joanne Hess. Mino was handled to top toy dog and 29 all breed BIS honors under the very capable hands of handler Daryl Martin. Together they won the National Specialty in 1980 and 1981. Daryl continues successfully to breed and show Maltese under the **Martin** prefix. Here again the influence of Aennchen Dancers can be seen.

Another offshoot from Aennchen Dancers are the **Bar None Maltese** of Michelle Perlmutter. Michelle actually acquired the Aennchen bloodlines through Joanne Hesse. The 1980s were good years for Bar None: there was Ch. Bar None Popeye, shown by handler Timothy Brazier, and Ch. Bar None Electric Horseman, shown by the late Gus Gomez, and Ch. Bar None Electric Dreams, shown by the late Dee Shepherd. The Bar None bloodlines were carried on by the late Brenda Finnegan from Oklahoma and others, particularly on the East Coast. The Bar None Maltese are well-known for their lovely heads and deep pigment.

MARCH'EN AND AL DOR

Continuing with the purity of the Aennchen Dancers' bloodline through the Joanne-Chen prefix is Marcia Hostetler of Iowa. Using the kennel name **March'en,** Marcia's dogs have been awarded several Dam or Sire of Merit certificates by the American Maltese Association.

Mrs Dorothy Tinker of Nevada has also had a large impact on the Maltese of today. At the time of her Maltese beginnings in the late 1950s she introduced Margaret White's English bloodline, Vicbrita, to the US. Her **Al Dor** Maltese have been the basis of several other well-known Maltese kennels, including Ann Glenn's **Rolling Glenn** and Agnes Cotterell **Cotterell's.** She actually combined the Villa Malta and Al Dor bloodlines and produced Ch. Cotterell's Love of Tenessa, who was owned and shown by Annette Feldblum. This lovely bitch produced seven champions and earned the MMA award from the American Maltese Association. The great stud dog and BIS winner, Am. and Can. Ch. Coeur-De-Lion was purchased from Agnes by Trudie Dillon of Washington. This wonderful little dog was very prepotent for beautiful coat textures. He was named the top producer, by siring 11 champions in 1974, by *Kennel Review* magazine.

MYI'S AND SCYLLA

Ch. Coeur-de-Lion was the sire of many top producers including Beverly and Dean Passe's Ch. Myi's Richard the Lion Hearted and Ch. Myi's Bit of Glory. Beverly should be credited with stamping silky straight coats and long arched necks on the **Myi's Maltese.** Beverly began breeding on a fairly large scale in the late 1970s, introducing some Aennchen bloodlines. An outstanding stud dog of importance for Myi's was Ch. Stan-Bar's Spark of Glory. He was a multiple BIS winner as well as a top producer. He won the Veterans Class at the AMA National Specialty in 1984 at the age of 10. He was the great great grandfather of the breed's top winning Maltese, Ch. Sand Island Small Kraft Lite. He was beautifully presented to his illustrious wins by Vicki Martin (Abbott), whom I have mentioned before as handling the Sand Island Maltese. She is also a Maltese breeder under the prefix **Scylla**. Her kennels are based on the Joanne-Chen (Aennchen) Bloodlines. The most famous is Ch. Scylla's Mino Maya Starfire, who was owner-handled by Vicki in the mid-1980s to several BIS. Vicki judged the AMA sweepstakes classes in 1988.

VILLA MALTA AND MALONE'S

While the Aennchen Antonellis should be credited with keeping the breed small, under three pounds, as the standard required up until the 1960s, Dr. Vincenzo Calvaresi, of the **Villa Malta**

Kennels, focused on breeding balance and soundness from the 1930s to the 1950s. After his retirement his breeding program was continued by Marge Rozik from Pennsylvania. The Villa Malta bloodlines have been used in conjunction with other excellent lines and are often seen in the pedigrees of a number of our very famous Maltese including, but not limited to, those of Barbara and Bob Bergquist from Michigan **Su-Le,** and the late Jenny Malone, **Malone's,** breeder of Ch. Malone's Snowie Roxann, handled by Peggy Hogg and owned by Mrs Nancy Shapland of Illinois, both of whom are respected judges today.

Roxann was bred just once, to Ch. Su-Le Flamingo but died during a caesarian section. Her three orphaned daughters were successfully raised by Peggy Hogg, who fell in love with Roseann, who became a multi group and BIS winner and remains her cherished house pet. The other two girls went to Beverly Passe of Myi's, who finished each of them and eventually sold them both to Carol Andersen of Sand Island.

The team of Shapland and Hogg also enjoyed great success with Ch. Maree's Tu-Grand Kandi Kane, who went BIS at his first show, won the Quaker Oats award in 1978 for Top Toy Dog and 11 all breed BIS.

THE SU-LE AND THE ENG KENNEL

Before we get into the Su-Le kennel, a bit of background is required. Their breeding program was based on the famous stud dog Ch. To The Victor of Eng and the BIS bitch Ch. Su-Le's Robin of Eng and Ch. Su-Le's Wren of Eng. The **Eng** kennels were owned by Ann Engstrom from Michigan and were primarily a combination of Villa Malta and Aennchen bloodlines. Ch. To The Victor of Eng sired some 80 American and many Canadian Champions. He holds the record as the top producing stud in the history of the breed. Su-Le also produced the top producing bitch in the history of the breed, Ch. Su-Le's Jacana MMA, the dam of 15 Champions. One of my greatest favorites was the lovely winner of the 1978 AMA Specialty and multiple BIS, Ch. Su-Le's Jonina. The Bergquists have bred well over 130 Champions and continue today as active breeders and exhibitors, and are very involved in the AMA. They are especially proud of the fact that their Maltese are all owner-handled – a feat most difficult to accomplish here in the US. Bob had the honor of judging the sweepstakes classes at the National Specialty in 1992. The impact they have had, and still have, on the breeding programs of today is enormous, as evidenced by the success of several kennels.

The **Crisandra Kennels** of Christine Pearson and Sandra Kenner from Florida foundation stock was primarily Su-Le. They have certainly enjoyed success with their Maltese in the 90s. Consistently they produce lovely typed Maltese with correct silky coats. With the assistance of the highly-regarded toy breed handler, Lani Kroemer, they were the co-winners of the co-breeder of the year awarded by the American Maltese Association in 1994. The Su-Le bloodlines were acquired through the Kathan Kennels of Kathy DiGiacomo of New Jersey. Kathy had the honor of judging the 1994 AMA National Specialty. Her partner, and aspiring judge, Elyse Fischer, judged the Sweepstakes classes at the AMA in 1995.

SUN CANYON

Miriam Thompson, **Sun Canyon Maltese** from California, has been involved in Maltese since the late 1950s. Her original bloodlines were Jon Vir; later she added Villa Malta and Aennchen. Famous dogs of this kennel include Ch. Sun Canyon the Heartbreak Kid, who was the top winning Maltese in 1976 and sire of 12 Champions. He was owned by Dr Jacklyn Hungerland, the first woman to sit as a director on the board of the American Kennel Club. Dr Hungerland is a multiple group judge, and in 1995 had the honor of selecting the Best in Show at the Westminster Kennel

Club. He was shown by Madeline Thornton. Mrs Sarah Lawrence, Mrs. Thompson's granddaughter, continues to breed and exhibit the Sun Canyon Maltese. Over the years they have produced over 100 Champions and they are not finished yet.

SAN SU KEE AND MANY OTHERS

The late Dorothy Palmersten from Minnesota bred Maltese under the name **San Su Kee**. Her original stock came from the Jon Vir part of Miriam Thompson's Sun Canyon lines. Peggy Hogg handled several top dogs for Dorothy, including Ch. Mike Mar's Ring Leader 11. His son, Ch. San Su Kee Star Edition MMA, owned by the late Richard Reid of Texas, was a multiple BIS winner as well as placing in the Toy Group at Westminster in 1975. In the late 1970s, Naomi Erickson, also from Minnesota, began her Maltese breeding program with the acquisition of a Champion San Su Kee male and a Champion bitch. From this mating the very successful **Gemmery** Maltese emerged, which later would be introduced into the **Merri** Maltese Kennels of Barbara Merrick. Barbara is the co-owner and breeder of Ch. Merri Paloma, the winner of the 1995 AMA National Specialty. Jason M. Hoke handled this elegant, correctly-coated bitch to this National Specialty win in addition to Best In Shows. The Merri Maltese kennel of Barbara Merrick began in the early 1970s. The predominant lines of its beginning were based on the Joanne-Chen lines. In the late 1980s David Fitzpatrick introduced his dogs to the Merri kennel. His Maltese were primarily based on the Gemmery Kennels. The combination of these two lines had led to over 25 Champions. Joyce Watkins, from Florida **Marcris**, purchased Ch. San Su Kee Show Off from Dorothy who, several generations later, produced the great producer Ch. Marcris Marshmallow.

At the 1982 AMA Speciality Marge Lewis, Maltese breeder **Al-Mar** and handler, awarded this doll-faced little guy Best In Sweepstakes. He was shown in many countries and, in addition to his American title, gained an FCI International Championship. He excelled as a stud dog, producing more than 30 Champions. Joyce should be credited with the AMA adopting the Maltese Merit Award, (MMA) created to honor and recognize bitches who have whelped three champions or more and dogs who sire five or more champions. Joyce judged the sweepstakes at the 1990 National Specialty. Marcris has also enjoyed a liaison with the **C&M** kennels of Carol Thomas, who is from Florida, and her friend Mary Day from California.

They added the Villa Malta bloodlines, and in contemporary circles are known to produce beautiful type Maltese with lovely silky hair, beautiful faces and excellent pigment. Mary owner-handled Ch. C&M's Totsey's-LollyPop to multiple BIS as well as a breed win at Westminster and two National Specialties, one from the Veterans Class. In 1994, Mary judged the sweepstakes classes at the National Specialty. Mary's bloodlines are behind the 1994 AMA National Specialty winner, Ch. Shan-lyn's Rais' N A Racous, bred by Lynda Podgurski, who was handled for his owners, Mr Joseph Joy II, Vicki Abbott, David and Sharon Newcomb, to multiple Best in Shows by Vicki Abbott. Macris has also enjoyed a very successful relationship with Glynette Class of **Wes-Glyn.** Glynette, like Marjorie Lewis, is a professional handler, so when showing, her client dogs must come first. As a result, she has not had the opportunity to campaign her own dogs to record-breakers, but has certainly made a significant contribution to the breed by consistently producing many Champions over these past twenty years. In 1991, Glynette judged the Sweepstakes for the AMA.

Faith Noble, **Noble Faith's** also from Florida, purchased her stock from C&M and bred to Ch. Coeur de Lion. The get was then bred to the famous Ch. Oak Ridge Country Charmer, and Ch. Noble Faith's White Tornado (Torrie) arrived. She won the National Specialty in 1983 and was campaigned through her career by the very talented handler, Barbara Alderman. Barbara was instrumental in the early show career of Country Charmer, handling him to his first few BIS.

Thereafter, he was handled exclusively by his breeder-owner, Carol Neth. Charmer won the National Specialty twice: in 1977 and 1979. Additionally he has sired at least 15 Champions, including the great Torrie for Faith Noble.

Helen Hood from Texas is the breeder of record of the 1985 National Specialty winner, Ch. Non-Vel's Weejun, owned by Candace Mathes (Gray) and the late Mary Senkowski, then from Michigan. Weejun was very capably handled to his wins by professional handler, and now judge, Bill Cunningham. In 1986, Bill judged the sweepstakes at the National Specialty. The **Le Aries** prefix was chosen by Candy and Mary as their kennel name. Candy was and continues to be a great friend of Madonna Garber, **Richelieu**, who is also closely aligned with the Marcris Maltese of Joyce Watkins. Though seldom seen aggressively campaigning her dogs, she is highly respected and considered by many as a true keeper of the breed.

Marjorie Lewis's involvement in Maltese goes back much further than the last 20 years. Her foundation stock was Villa Malta, but over the years she added additional lines to her breeding program, resulting in several BIS Maltese. One of the breeds all-time favorites is Ch. Al-Mar's Mary Poppins, a multiple BIS winner in limited showing, as Marjorie's first priority was her clients' dogs, since she was a professional handler, specializing in Maltese, Lhasa Apso and Shi Tzu. In 1975, the Texas **Pegden** kennels of Denny Mounce and Peggy Lloyd started their breeding program under the kennel name Valley High, with Aennchen bloodlines. In 1975 it changed to Pegden. They produced Ch. Pegden's Magic Touch, and sold him to Marge Lewis. He became the sire of the famous Mary Poppins – again, a nice example of combining Aennchen with Villa Malta. They also owned Am. Mex. Int. Ch. Mac's Apache Joray of Everon, a multi group winner and ROM sire of many champions. Peggy's Ch. Myi's Glory Boy Seeker, ROM, bred by Beverly Passe, was a multi group and BISS winner as well as AMA's Top Producer in 1987.

Patsy Stokes and Sheila Meyers from Texas began their **Pashes** Kennels in the early 1970s with the San Su Kee bloodlines. In the early 1980s they added Myi's bloodlines by breeding to Ch. Keoli's Small Kraft Warning (Ricky). A son, Ch. Pashes Smile Warning, became a BISS winner and later produced Ch. Pashes Beau Didley, who has already produced 15 champions at four years of age. They are breeders of over 50 champions, including 7 best in Specialty show winners, and tied with the Crisandra kennels of Florida for top co-breeders in 1994.

Carole Baldwin's **Fantasyland** Maltese from California started in the late 1960s with Villa Malta, Jon Vir and Invicta bloodlines. Over the years she added Aennchen and, today, the Fantasyland Maltese are well-known for cute faces and nice type. Ch. Fantasyland Pete R. Wabbitt is well-known as an important stud dog as well as best of winners at the 1981 AMA Specialty. Her Ch. Fantasyland Billy Idol was the winner of the Top Sire award given by the AMA in 1994. Carol was also the top breeder in 1994.

Rebecca's Desert Maltese began in the late 1960s with Ted, Freda and their daughter, Rebecca Tinsley. Their bloodlines, being primarily Aennchen and Villa Malta, have produced two AMA National Specialty winners. In 1976 Ch. So Big's Desert Delight, Missie was handled to this win by Rebecca Tinsley. In 1982 Missie's son, Ch. Rebecca's Desert Valentino, took these same honors, handled by professional handler, Don Rodgers.

Special credit must be given to the dogs listed below, each of whom won the American Maltese Association National Specialty in the year listed. No award is as respected as Best of Breed at the National Specialty.

National Specialty Winners
1975   Ch. Celia's Mooney Forget Me Not
1976   Ch. So Big Desert Delight

1977	Ch. Oak Ridge Country Charmer
1978	Ch. Su-Le's Jonina
1979	Ch. Oak Ridge Country Charmer
1980	Ch. Joanne-Chen's Mino Maya Dancer
1981	Ch. Joanne-Chen's Mino Maya Dancer
1982	Ch. Rebecca's Desert Valentino
1983	Ch. Noble Faith's White Tornado
1984	Ch. Myi's Ode to Glory Seeker
1985	Ch. Non Vel's Weejun
1986	Ch. Villa Malta's Chickalett
1987	Ch. Bar None Electric Horseman
1988	Ch. C&M's Toosey's-LollyPop
1989	Ch. Two Be's Hooked on Sugar
1990	Ch. Sand Island's Small Kraft Lite
1991	Ch. Sand Island's Small Kraft Lite
1992	Ch. C&M's Toosey's-LollyPop
1993	Ch. Melodylane Sings O'AlMar Luv
1994	Ch. Shanlyn's Rais 'N A Raucous
1995	Ch. Merri Paloma

THE FUTURE

Over the last twenty years the Maltese in the United States have evolved as one of the most competitive and popular dogs in the Toy Group. In earlier times there was an occasional "great" Maltese. However, now this breed is consistently quite good, from the puppy classes through the Best of Breed competition. In most Toy Groups the Maltese is a stand-out. The grooming of the Maltese in the United States is excellent and the quality of the dogs themselves is often outstanding. Certainly the grooming products have improved greatly, as have the grooming skills of our Maltese exhibitors, both owner-handlers and professional handlers. It is a true joy to observe a class of Maltese and an even greater pleasure to judge one. Thanks to the foundation laid by the Antonellis of Aennchen and Dr Calvaresi of Villa Malta, the safekeeping and breeding programs of Joanne Hess of Joanne-Chen, the Berquists of Su-Le, Beverly Passe of Myi's, Carol Andersen of Sand Island, Joyce Watkins of Marcris, and Mary Day and Carol Thomas of C&M, and Peggy Hogg, whose grooming created the glamorous look of the present day Maltese, this wonderful breed is better now than ever before in the US. The classes at the 1995 National were a perfect example of this. The depth of quality, particularly in the puppy and bitch classes, was outstanding. Based on this, the future for our beloved Maltese should be even better because the breeders are doing what they committed themselves to do long ago – keep this ancient breed safe.

Bibliography

Over the years I have read many books and articles on canine matters, and these, in their different ways, have added to my knowledge of the Maltese breed. I am grateful to all these authors who have, albeit unknowingly, helped me to write this book.

The following books have been an excellent source of reference:

Dog Breeding – The Theory & Practice, Frank Jackson, Crowood Press.
The Dog's Health From A to Z, John Bleby and Gerald Bishop, David & Charles.
Veterinary Notes For Dog Owners, Trevor Turner, Popular Dogs.

MALTESE
BREEDERS DIRECTORY

WALES
SAMOSSA
Mrs Gayle Yanez,
No 1 The Laurels, Cardiff Road, St. Fagans,
Cardiff CF5 6EB.
Tel: 01222-566668
Dogs at Stud/Puppies Occasionally for Sale.

EAST MIDLANDS
SWANDOWN
Peter Moorby,
18 Robinson Drive, Worksop,
Notts. S80 1AT
Tel: 01909-475578
Dogs at Stud/Puppies Occasionally for Sale.

WEST MIDLANDS
MANNSOWN
Fred & Jean Mann
Gaydonwood House, Gaydon Road,
Bishops Itchington, Royal Leamington Spa,
Warwickshire CV33 0QW
Tel: 01926-612043
Dogs at Stud/Puppies Occasionally for Sale.

SWANDOWN MALTESE

Photo by John Hartley

CH. LAMSGROVE LOVEBIRD TO SWANDOWN
with owner/handler Peter Moorby, Swandown

Photo by Peter Moorby

LAMSGROVE ON THE BUTTON AT SWANDOWN
a wonderful showgirl and multiple First prize winner, now doing extremely well with
breeding. Owner: Peter Moorby, Swandown

PETER MOORBY
18 Robinson Drive, Worksop, Notts, S80 1AT   Tel: 01909-475578

SWANDOWN MALTESE

Photo by Peter Moorby

BREEDING FOR THE FUTURE

A most beautiful litter sired by QUANTOS CON TUTTO AMORE ex LAMSGROVE ON THE BUTTON AT
SWANSDOWN, whose famous grandsires are CH. MANNSOWN REMOTE CONTROL
and CH. QUANTOS CON TUTTO CHIARA
Owner/breeder: Peter Moorby, Swandown

*Photo by
Peter
Moorby*

CH. LAMSGROVE LOVEBIRD TO SWANDOWN
seen here winning Best in Show at the Maltese Club Diamond Jubilee Autumn Show.
Sired by breed record holder CH. SNOWGOOSE FIRST LOVE.
Owner/handler: Peter Moorby, Swandown

PETER MOORBY
18 Robinson Drive, Worksop, Notts, S80 1AT   Tel: 01909-475578

Restinim Maltese

Representing the past . . . reflecting the present
. . . and ready for the future!

Photos by
Nigel Southall

RESTINIM BE MY LOVE (age 10 months)

'Winston' has had many First Prizes at Championship shows, and won four Best Puppy in Breed awards. He is one of the very few males in the ring today with a pedigree filled with the 'Royal Crowns of Maltese Hall of Fame'. His sire is CH. VILLAROSE CHOCOLATE CHARMER (sire of CH. SNOWGOOSE FIRST LOVE). The Grandsire is Eng. CH. TENNESSA'S DANCING FLURRY OF SNOWGOOSE, a USA import, and Winston's pedigree includes Eng. CH. SNOWGOOSE HOT TODDY, Eng. CH. SNOWGOOSE VALIENT LAD, Eng. CH. SNOWGOOSE DARK HORSE, Eng CH. CARAMALTA CRESHENDO and finally from the USA, CH. TO THE VICTOR OF ENG and the well-known dog USA and Aus. CH. SU LE'S GREAT EGRET.
A very special combination of many years of the finest breeding.
Winston lives at home with us and runs freely to his heart's content.
Groomed by CHRIS and handled by REV. ANDREW FAIRCHILD

The Manse, 28 Inholmes Park Road, Burgess Hill, Sussex RH15 0JE
Tel: 01-444-232285

MARVESS MALTESE

Photo by
Alan V. Walker

CH. MARVESS DAZZLYN STARLET
Bitch C.C. Crufts 1995 (age 15 months)

Photo by
Yvonne Kent

BREEDER OF FIVE U.K. CHAMPIONS
POLLY & IVAN REYNOLDS
'Yas-Ma-Pa', 50 Waldegrave Way, Lawford, Nr. Manningtree, Essex CO11 2DT
TeL: 01206-392581

TAMILAY

"Loves's wing moults when caged and captured,
Only free, he soars enraptured"

THOMAS CAMBELL 'Freedom and Love' 1777-1844

TAMILAY MALTESE and ITALIAN GREYHOUNDS
MAUREEN & MARINA FOLEY
Tamilay, Harris Barton, Frampton Cotterell, Bristol BS17 2ET
Tel: 01454-773011

Lilactime – Reg. 1946

"Freddie"

LAMSGROVE INSTANT REPLAY OF LILACTIME
J.W., 6 Reserve C.C.s
Photographed at 17 months of age.
Best Puppy in Show at United Kingdom Toydog Championship Show 1994
He is adored and shown by
Mrs. ELIZABETH HOWGILL
Lilactime, 22 Roland Avenue, Wilford Village, Nottingham NG11 7AN
Tel: 0115–9819029

SAMOSSA MALTESE
proudly present
Ch. SAMOSSA'S IT'S A KIND OF MAGIC JW

Sire: **TAMILAY RAINBOW WARRIOR AT SAMOSSA**
Dam: **BALLERINA GIRL AT SAMOSSA**

Bred and owned by:
Gayle & Eddy Yanez
1 The Laurels
Cardiff Road
St Fagans
Cardiff
South Wales CF5 6EB
Tel: 01222 566668

MANNSOWN MALTESE

Photo by Chris Ripsher

CH. MANNSOWN SPECIAL DELIVERY J.W.
B.O.B. CRUFTS 1989 & 1990

Photo by Chris Ripsher

CH. MANNSOWN NEARLY MISSED IT

FRED & JEAN MANN
Gaydonwood House, Gaydon Road, Bishops Itchington,
Royal Leamington Spa, Warwickshire CV33 0QW
Tel: 01926-612043

LAMSGROVE MALTESE

Photo by B. Rees

LAMSGROVE DEBUTANTE

Photographed at 10 months of age, having won the following awards under 10 months: 10 Firsts in A/V Toy classes at Open shows, 4 Best Puppy, 1 Best Minor Puppy 1 B.O.B., 1 B.O.S., 3rd Toy Puppy Group and 4 seconds at Championship shows.

LAMSGROVE MALTESE have been bred and exhibited since 1958, including overseas Champions.

MRS EVA LAMB
International Championship Judge of Maltese and Yorkshire Terriers LAMSGROVE, 7 GEORGE STREET, MANSFIELD, NOTTS. NG19 6SF TEL: 01623-22162

SHOBHANA MALTESE

Judge's critique from South Wales K.A. Ch. show 1995: "Junior Dog. 1. Pendle's Shobhana Bala, smart little dog of nice quality, excellent balance, good front, shoulder and hindquarters, elegant reach of neck, short compact body, level topline, good head, lovely dark eyes, good pigmentation, correct bite, nice silky coat, good tailset, presented beautifully and moved nicely. Should have a very promising future. Dr. S. Nishi (Japan)."

At SHOBHANA, my aim is to breed only the top quality, sound and beautiful puppies. All my breeding stock is checked to be free of hereditary problems. Through dedication, my hope for generations to come is that I can make a significant contribution towards the overall soundness and well being of this delightful breed. SHOBHANA is an ancient Sanskrit word for "Beautiful White Light". This, I believe, the Maltese are, and my goal, as a lover of the breed, id for Shobhana Maltese to live up to this!

SHOBHANA BALA
PATRICIA PENDLE
Moelfre Newydd, Cerrig-y-Drudion, Nr. Corwen, Clwyd LL21 0RS. Tel: 01490-420586

STUDS & CROOKS

The hidden history of Kilnsey Show

To Andy,

Best wishes

Victoria B_____

STUDS & CROOKS

The hidden history of Kilnsey Show

BY VICTORIA BENN

IN COLLABORATION WITH JAMIE ROBERTS

TICKLED TROUT PRESS

PUBLISHED BY TICKLED TROUT PRESS 2016

Kilnsey Park Estate, Kilnsey, Skipton BD23 5PS

Designed and typeset by Nic Butcher
Photographs by Stephen Garnett
Printed and bound in Slovenia by DZS Grafik/Latitude Press
A CIP catalogue record for this book is available from the British Library
ISBN: 978–0–9955076–0–9

To Angus, Beatrice, Louis and Seth

CONTENTS

FOREWORD

We are very blessed in Yorkshire to have so many agricultural and country shows, from the famous Great Yorkshire Show in Harrogate to the countless one-day shows. One of the highlights of the show calendar has to be Kilnsey Show, which I have enjoyed visiting for decades.

My first abiding memory was watching in awe as dozens of runners tore across the magnificent Kilnsey Crag that towers over the showground. The incredible strength and spirit of those fell runners tackling this fearsome cliff just overwhelmed me. I always love the way the show builds up to this unique and thrilling spectacle, creating a magical highlight to what is now one of the biggest one-day agricultural shows in Yorkshire.

Kilnsey Show is an event where people come together, not just to celebrate farming, but to see old friends. There's a story around every corner and you'll find an essence of the Yorkshire Dales wherever you look – from the farmers showing their prize-winning animals, to the patient drystone wallers, the talented crafts folk and the daredevil fell runners. All of this – and the passion of the people who take part – is beautifully captured here in *Studs & Crooks* for the very first time.

To me the secret of Kilnsey Show's success doesn't just lie in the variety of what it offers, but also in the beauty of its tremendous backdrop. Moving with the times, it has gone from strength to strength. Just like the steely spirit of the fell runners who take part, Kilnsey Show epitomizes true Yorkshire grit.

The show has survived many changes in rural life and in farming since it started in 1897, the year of Queen Victoria's Diamond Jubilee, and has continued to flourish into being a vital fixture in the national agricultural show calendar. Kilnsey Show has a special place not just in the heart of the Dales community but also in the heart of Yorkshire – and it always will.

Sir Gary Verity, Chief Executive of Welcome to Yorkshire, has been attending Kilnsey Show for many years and is renowned as the man who brought the Tour de France to Yorkshire.

Kilnsey sheep sale in the 1950s © NYCC Unnetie digital collection BU08426

PROLOGUE

A day at the show

To those of us born amidst the stony fells and lush river meadows of the upper Dales, the coming of Kilnsey Show attracts almost the same anticipation and excitement as Christmas.

Like the passing of the seasons, it always arrives more quickly than you expect. Just two weeks before the event it's impossible to imagine that these flat meadows beside the river Wharfe, home to oyster catchers, sheep and the odd fisherman, could ever play host to 15,000 visitors.

The week before the show linen-white marquees rise like mushrooms as the carnival descends on the sleepy valley: a steady stream of trucks arrive and offload, a rough symphony of clanking poles and pegs being hammered into the turf.

Further afield final preparations are made as cakes and pies are baked, jams bubbled and bottled, walking sticks whittled and varnished. On remote farms sheep are shampooed, cattle quiffs brylcreemed, Shire horse hooves lacquered so you could almost shave in them. Elsewhere vintage tractors are waxed and buffed, while fell runners spend evenings stretching their calves and dreaming about the ever-shifting screes.

The weather, always a Dales obsession, becomes even more acutely observed: "Forecast's fine for show day", "Showers I hear", "Sunshine and showers, with more of the latter no doubt", "Do you remember that year it were washed out?", "We were towed off by a tractor!" The speakers wear their stories with pride, like medals of honour.

Show day, and local children awake to slow-moving traffic and tannoy announcements echoing off the limestone crag. Kilnsey's hamlet-sized population swells to that of a bustling market town. Cars arrive, unloading families and friends; the red tunic'd brass band begins to play; and over ten thousand different versions of a single Kilnsey Show day begin.

Different corners of the showfield reveal their own distinctive character, each with its own time-worn etiquette and chatter. Drystone wallers compete before a keen gathering who know their topstones from their foundations. On a carpet of straw immaculate beasts are awarded rosettes and polished silver cups. People hover outside a buttoned-up marquee that warns 'Judging in Progress', trying and not trying to hear hushed comments about the texture of their sponge cake, the tang of their lemon curd.

To this day you will meet seasoned show-goers – perhaps sheepmen or vegetable growers – who have never ventured beyond the limits of their habitual area of the showfield. And that's just the way they like it, for they know and love their patch and it's where they catch up with old friends, year in year out.

If you close your eyes and listen, beyond the rumbling tannoy, sizzle of sausages and bellowing bookies, you can still hear curlews piping on the hills, the gentle flowing of the river and the cries of sheep – the regular sounds of the Dale, waiting to take back possession of their valley.

The day builds towards the fell race, when all showfield eyes crane towards the skyline as the intrepid runners tackle the screes and come tumbling back down the side of the jutting crag. By the river generations share a straw bale watching horse-drawn chariots speed around the ring. Later, as the sun sinks behind the fell, stalls close, weary animals are loaded up, car parks empty and the show meadows fall silent. Soon the marquees will be toppled, litter picked, and the fields left to grazing sheep once more.

You'd hardly know it had happened. Just one wonderful day, and then it's over. It's been like this ever since I was a child, and it's no less exciting all these years later.

Jamie Roberts is the fourth generation of his family to live and work on the Kilnsey Estate, which was purchased by Sir James Roberts in 1911. His family have always been closely involved with the show – his great great grandfather, grandfather and father were all Presidents and today Jamie is on the organising committee.

1

THE SHOW MUST GO ON

The history and origins of Kilnsey Show

Nestled under its magnificent limestone crag amidst remote moorland fells, the hamlet of Kilnsey in the Yorkshire Dales has been a picturesque destination for locals, walkers and travellers for many hundreds of years. To the uninitiated, Kilnsey may have the appearance of enduring tranquillity, but that is only a temporary truth. Since the 1800s, on a Tuesday when summer is giving way to autumn, this small hamlet of just twenty-one houses utterly transforms as 'Kilnsey Show and Sports' slowly buds and then gloriously blossoms into life.

Show jumping, parades of cattle, sheep on show, heavy horses and vintage tractors. Foot races, fell races, horse races. Produce, horticulture, handicrafts and walking sticks. Fly fishing, sheep shearing, drystone walling and sheep dog trials. Fun fair, candy floss, beer tent and food glorious food. Kilnsey Show is like a travelling circus, agricultural fair and mini-Olympics all rolled into one; and it's been this way for well over a hundred years.

Disappearing as quickly as it comes, it leaves behind unanswered questions… like, how has such a small village come to host an event of such proportions, which has attracted crowds of up to 18,000 in its busiest years? And, what was the spark that launched the first show well over one hundred years ago in 1897? Truly, Kilnsey Show is resilient – it has survived two World Wars, the Foot and Mouth crisis of 2001, a hurricane and, critically, the complete transformation of farming and rural life. In the face of such challenge and adversity why has this Upper Wharfedale show not only continued to endure, but flourish as one of the largest one day agricultural shows in the country?

Far from the crowd: Kilnsey Show in 1982 © Steve Haithwaite

In the early years of the show the driving purpose was all about the animals, whether they be farm ponies or local sheep. However looking back over the last 120 years it's apparent that Kilnsey Show is primarily a reflection of the people of the Dales – their interests, their passions and their spirit. The guardians of its flame are the generations of farmers and Dales people who've not only participated in the show but have been instrumental in safeguarding its heritage, ensuring that whatever the challenges 'the show must go on'.

This book is a celebration of the people who conspired to create and support the show, building it up year by year, into an established high profile event. The authentic voice of Kilnsey Show and the wider Dales can be heard here in first-hand accounts from some of the competitors and driving forces behind the show today – people whose passion, belief and dedication to their craft marks them out as truly unique.

He who laughs last, laughs longest...

When one considers the current size and stature of Kilnsey Show, it might be surprising to discover that it was one of the last agricultural shows to be established within the Yorkshire Dales, entering the fray in the latter part of the nineteenth century. Yet the show has become not only one of the longest surviving, but indisputably the biggest in the area.

In the year that Kilnsey Show was established, 1897, the Settle Agricultural Show had already been going thirty seven years, and the very grand Craven Agricultural Show for forty three years. The local paper of the time featured adverts for as many as twenty five agricultural shows across the district, plus numerous other sports and feasts.

During the late 1800s shows were big business as agriculture was thriving, with over one in five people working on the land, a statistic which was reflected by the popularity and prevalence of shows like Kilnsey. In 1876 when The Great Yorkshire Show held its thirty eighth annual show in Skipton, just twelve miles away from Kilnsey, it attracted crowds of nearly thirty thousand. Agricultural shows were as popular as music festivals are today.

The 'new' Kilnsey Show boasted a spectacular location in the shadow of Kilnsey's iconic crag, on the meadows beside the river Wharfe. Yet looks alone cannot explain its longevity, for its biggest competitor, the Craven Agricultural Show also boasted a picture perfect location in the grounds of Skipton Castle. There was nothing particularly remarkable about Kilnsey's programme of activities, which comprised the sheep, cattle and horse classes that were common to most agricultural shows of the time. With the exception of its famous gravity-defying fell race, the Crag Race, its sports – including a steeplechase for horses, trotting and wrestling – were likewise similar to those of neighbouring shows.

Yet there was always something distinctive about Kilnsey. More than just a show of animals, it was a day out, a chance to relax and have fun in the countryside – as the local paper reported, "It was a day's holiday pure and simple." Perhaps this is one reason why, when the boom years of agricultural shows passed, relative newcomer Kilnsey, in its remote Upper Wharfedale location, survived and came to flourish.

Best in show: Edwardian ladies strut their stuff in 1907

One characteristic that can be attributed to the early years of Kilnsey Show was its down to earth approach and lack of pretension. Contemporary newspaper reports described it as a show where the 'ordinary' farmer could showcase his stock – a show for "farmer farmers" as George Emmott, a long-time show attendee, now terms it. This grass roots 'no nonsense' ethos meant that hard-working farmers could literally walk their sheep or cattle down from the fields to the show, as indeed many did. Whereas at other agricultural shows there was a certain degree of 'showiness', at Kilnsey the animals were paraded before judges in their natural condition – a common sense approach that might well have helped to sustain the show through hard times. It was a philosophy that put the working farmer at the heart of the event. This is the way things have continued to be, as the stories of this book reflect, with passionate, hardworking, 'down to earth' people at the core of the show's longevity and enduring success.

The first Kilnsey Show took place in September 1897, and for many years it has been presumed that the event spontaneously appeared in the rural calendar with no antecedents. In fact the show's roots are deeper than anyone might have guessed, being associated with a local feast.

The first recorded mention of a 'feast' held at Kilnsey came in 1869, when a Lancashire newspaper noted that the event was 'well patronised and its sports excellent' – suggesting that it was already an established fixture. In 1884 an advert on the front page of the local newspaper alerted readers to the main attractions of the forthcoming 'Conistone with Kilnsey Gala and Sports', also known as the 'Conistone with Kilnsey Feast'. There was to be a quoiting match, trotting match for horses, fell race, foot races, sack races, jumping and a tug-of-war.

The 1884 advert also stated that "A large marquee will be erected, in which tea will be provided at 4 o'clock [with] Dancing immediately after" – a surprisingly grand affair for two small villages. More intriguing still was the report published in the paper the following week, which noted prize winners coming from as far afield as Halifax, thirty four miles away. In modern terms this is a modest car journey, but in the 1880s when transport was mainly by horse or by foot, and the closest railway station was twelve miles away in Skipton, travel to Upper Wharfedale from beyond the valley would have been a time consuming challenge.

Young Crag Race pioneers in the late 1940s (Roger Ingham)

Very little has been written about 'feasts' in the Yorkshire Dales, although they must at one time have been a significant part of rural life. Fortunately for Kilnsey well-known Yorkshire author Edmund Bogg documented his experiences of Kilnsey Feast in two books written about his travels in Upper Wharfedale, both published in 1904. Bogg recorded "the country people attending from near and far, racing, jumping, and dancing on the green, the echoes of music and revelry giving back from the walls of the old rock. One race is to the top of the western side of the crag... which puts to the test the breathing powers of the very strongest."

Bogg also witnessed something unexpected: "great feats of wrestling were performed, the dales people being mighty wrestlers." His observation suggests that the sport was flourishing at feasts like Kilnsey during the 1800s, and possibly even earlier. Wrestling still thrives in the Lake District to this day, although research suggests that unlike their Cumberland and Westmorland neighbours the Dales wrestlers of the time would have merely rolled up their trousers and removed their shirts, rather than don the Lakeland style long johns and embroidered vests.

Bogg suggests that Kilnsey Feast was already long-established in his time: "Kilnsey Feast has a great renown… Many are the records of the deeds of strength and agility performed by the stalwart dales men forty to fifty years ago…" The implication of this being that Kilnsey Feast, like many other village feasts in the Dales, had been part of the rural calendar since the early 1800s and possibly earlier. Nevertheless the question which still begs to be answered is, when and why did such a festivity start?

There is a strong likelihood that Kilnsey Feast was part of the tradition of religious feasts which were commonplace from the Middle Ages, when Britain was a Catholic kingdom. Originally feasts were attached to 'Saints Days' in the church calendar, and would have marked a week long local holiday celebrated with eating, drinking and sporting pursuits such as archery, wrestling and running. The parish saint at Conistone-with-Kilnsey was the Virgin Mary, whose day was celebrated at the Feast of the Assumption in the middle of August. A major change to the calendar in 1750 saw that date move to the end of August – around the time when Kilnsey Show is customarily held. It's possible then that the tradition of holding a festivity at Kilnsey stretches back centuries to the 1200s, when the monks of Fountains Abbey were farming their vast flocks of sheep on the surrounding fells and pastures.

Following the Reformation, from 1550 onwards, the Protestants didn't give as much importance to the worship of the Saints as the Catholic Church had done. Feasts continued to thrive, but as time passed their religious significance declined, so that by the 1800s most feasts were purely celebrated as local holidays with sporting events, which fits with what is written and known about Kilnsey Feast.

It's impossible to be completely sure if an ancient religious festival is the actual origin of Kilnsey Feast, and the show that followed it. However, what is unambiguous is that events in 1895 were pivotal in the evolution of a traditional and long-standing village gathering into one of the largest one-day agricultural shows in Britain.

Ready for service: The Luncheon Tent awaiting diners in 1907 (Ben McKenzie)

By 1895 Kilnsey Feast was a large well-established event attracting many hundreds of people from across the district, who travelled to the area to partake in the holiday spirit, the sporting competitions, and to catch up with family and friends. As that year's festivities gradually subsided, local residents and visitors retreated to the bar of the local coaching inn, the Tennant's Arms, for good company, good cheer and a drink or two. Under these convivial circumstances a Michael Fernley from Bradford, who owned a travelling stallion named 'Morning Star', decided to establish a little competition. To those listening he pledged fifty shillings [£2.50] as a prize at the following year's Feast for the best foal sired by his horse. The landlord Henry Inman also sportingly offered fifty shillings of his own money for a competition of lambs. Those in the pub might not have known it at the time, but this was a historic moment, as it was the origin of the modern show.

A newspaper advert for the 1896 Feast confirmed that there would be "Special prizes given by Mr Michael Fernley [of Bradford], for foals by his horse 'Morning Star'." It also recorded that prizes would be given for the best lambs from the local area [stated to be the villages of Burnsall and Cracoe to the south, and to the north Littondale and Kettlewelldale – the last a historic term for Upper Wharfedale that is no longer used].

It is not recorded how many entries there were in the foal classes – a number presumably dependent upon how popular Fernley's stallion was with the fillies – but the new event was clearly a success, as the report in the following week's paper confirmed that "Mr Fernley generously proposes to repeat the prizes next year." It was also reported that there was an intention to form a committee to run the show annually.

By the following year the Upper Wharfedale Agricultural Society had been established, with Mr James Hammond as President and Mr G.E. Clayton as Secretary and Treasurer, along with a committee who were to become the driving force for the new show. The early committee numbered a dozen and included many established local farming families, including members of two families still actively involved in the show – Mr Edward Carlisle and Mr Dick Foster. The show committee continues to this day, numbering anywhere up to thirty from the local area. Farmers showed their support and enthusiasm for the new venture by subscribing a total of £100 in advance of the first show.

The first 'official' Kilnsey Show took place on Tuesday September 7th 1897. It was billed as the precursor to a "gala in the evening", which was clearly still regarded as the main event – with a thousand attending this the previous year. There were 184 entries in total, spread across cattle, horses and sheep. Butter and cheese exhibits were staged in a tent on the field, and not surprisingly for an area of dairy farmers, the butter competition was particularly competitive, with sixteen entries. Other attractions included Skipton Prize Brass Band and tea in the marquee. There was also what the local paper called "the usual itinerant catch-penny arrangements associated with country fairs" and several sporting events including the fell race. The new event was well received, with the only criticism being that the show ring was too small for the horses to be shown properly. However as the paper said, "The main thing was to show," and with relatively high entries across the board for this new event, it illustrated resoundingly that the people of Upper Wharfedale had embraced the opportunity to do just that.

One of the earliest pictures of the show c1900 (Ben McKenzie)

The following year's show in 1898 was reported to be bigger, better attended and with higher entries, but beyond Kilnsey the boom years for agricultural shows were waning. By 1902 the show President Captain Roundell was noted as saying that "They had heard a great deal lately about shows going downhill, and decreasing gate receipts." He had little doubt about the cause: "The decreasing popularity of district shows was due to the fact that promoters did not cater sufficiently for the tenant farmer. At many of the larger shows the tenant farmers were supposed to be encouraged, whereas the people who were really encouraged were those who did no good to an agricultural district, but made prize getting the absolute business of their lives." The clear inference being that professional competitors were driving 'real farmers' out of the shows – yet almost uniquely this was not the case at Kilnsey Show, which continued to celebrate the achievements of the ordinary hard-working farmer.

Nothing is permanent except change…

The outside world came much closer to Kilnsey in 1902, with the opening of a new railway line to Grassington, only three miles away. This brought new opportunities for attracting show visitors, with adverts on the front page of the local paper promoting "Cheap Bookings from Leeds, Bradford, Otley, Ilkley, Bentham, Horton in Ribblesdale, Colne and intermediate stations to Skipton inclusive." With access so much easier, a crowd of 4000 was reported at the show the same year the railway reached the upper Dales. Only five years after its creation, the show was becoming an established fixture within the district.

When the First World War broke out Kilnsey Show had only been going seventeen years. War was declared on July 28th and despite the fact that certain local events were held throughout the month of August, a decision was quickly taken to cancel the show, which had been due to take place at the beginning of September. In the shadow of that calamitous conflict normal life was suspended, and all shows, feasts and fairs stopped for the full duration of the war. The only show-related activity during these years was a General Meeting of the Society held in Kettlewell in September 1916, at which it was confirmed that £500 had been raised for Red Cross funds.

Humorous cartoon from 1912, showing how the opening of the Yorkshire Dales Railway ten years earlier helped to reel in the mill workers to Kilnsey Show (Ben McKenzie)

Kilnsey Show re-commenced in 1919, billing itself as the "Eighteenth Annual Show and Sports". The newly expanded name – which continues to this day – better reflected the significant contribution that sports added to the proceedings. The first post-war event was judged a success, with crowds of 5000 attending, perhaps reflecting the determination of the local population that life should return to normal as quickly as possible. As the local paper reported, "it must be a long time since the sequestered little village [of Kilnsey] witnessed such scenes of bustle and activity." The earliest film footage of the Show – a Pathé news clip from the following year, 1920 – features crowds gathered around the ring watching showjumping followed by an excerpt of the Sheep Dog Trial Competition.

On the face of it everything was back to normal. However the grim reality was very different; things had changed immeasurably over the intervening five years. Families the length and breadth of the country had lost fathers and sons – and a generation of young farmers had been taken away in the mud and blood of the trenches. Portraits of fallen servicemen on the pages of the local paper soon gave way to pages upon pages of adverts for farms to let and job advertisements. The country as a whole had lost a huge proportion of its wealth and manpower, and the farming communities of the Yorkshire Dales had not been spared.

Somewhat ironically, it seems that the outbreak of the First World War might have indirectly prevented the destruction of the idyllic site of Kilnsey Show. In 1911 great concern had been expressed about the proposed extension of the railway line from Grassington north to Wensleydale. The new line would traverse alongside the River Wharfe, slicing through the entire stretch of fields used by the show. Following the war all plans to extend the line were shelved; and the branch line between Skipton and Grassington closed to passengers in 1930.

As farming slowly returned to normal, there was a new threat – over-production. Wise words were forthcoming in the 1927 luncheon speech, with former President Mr G.B. Holdsworth advising the assembled diners "not to glut the market all at once [but] to send their cattle at different times and not altogether." Such advice was no doubt borne out of fears that over-production and over saturation of the market would ultimately drive prices down.

In the 1930s the feared depression took hold – farms were put up for sale and many farming families left the land to find new work elsewhere. Kilnsey Show and Sports was deeply affected, with entries significantly down.

It was against this backdrop of an agricultural slump that, across the Channel, the clouds of conflict began gathering again. Kilnsey Show was advertised to take place on September 5th 1939, but was cancelled at the last minute following the declaration of war on September 1st. Sporting matches and events, shows, feasts and festivals were all swiftly abandoned as the country once again found itself at war.

Unlike during the Great War, when Kilnsey Show simply didn't take place, token events were held during the Second World War years, perhaps with the aim of retaining some sense of continuity. Activities included Sheep Dog Trials and a new event, the Dry Stone Walling Competition. The money raised was donated to the Red Cross and St. Dunstans Home for Blind Soldiers. The local community was clearly determined to keep normal life going as much as possible, despite it too being directly impacted by the conflict, experiencing rationing, conscription, a plane crash and a night-time bomb falling nearby.

Following the announcement of VJ [Victory in Japan] Day in mid-August 1945, the show was hastily re-scheduled and attracted a sizeable crowd of 5000. However the following year the lingering impact of the war was still apparent, the local paper reporting of the livestock classes that "naturally there was evidence of farmers' present-day difficulties in the feeding of their stock." The animals were in poor condition – but at least there was a show to enjoy.

Even with peace across Europe there was to be no reprieve from the challenges facing farmers. The 1940s and 1950s saw the widespread introduction of mechanisation to Dales farming practice. Jobs which had taken days and much manpower to accomplish could now be done in hours. Tractors were of course a godsend to farmers, but ultimately their arrival meant that farming started its inevitable evolution from numerous labour intensive smallholdings, into large mechanised businesses. The impact on a rural parish like Conistone-with-Kilnsey was clear – where there had been eleven farms, soon there would be just three. The story was the same the length and breadth of the Dales, and throughout the country at large.

Just two weeks before the event it's impossible to imagine that these flat meadows beside the river Wharfe, home to oyster catchers, sheep and the odd fisherman, could ever play host to 15,000 visitors…

Kilnsey village with the showfield in the background © Stephen Garnett

UPPER WHARFEDALE AGRICULTURAL SOCIETY

President: WILLIAM HOLDSWORTH, Esq.

Over £400 in Prizes and Three Silver Challenge Cups

TUESDAY
6th SEPT. 1949

THE 42ND ANNUAL
SHOW

SPORTS & SHEEP DOG TRIALS

WILL BE HELD AT

KILNSEY, near SKIPTON

Classes for Sheep (Open & Local), Cattle, Horses, Driving Turnout
Pigs, Eggs, Bread and Hams, Dressed Poultry, Horticultural Produce
Fruit Preserving, Vegetable and Floral Section,
Collection of Wild Flowers open to Children :: Sheep Dog Trials

ENTRIES CLOSE 30th AUGUST

SPORTS - All Open Events

CRAG RACE -to Top of Kilnsey Crag and back to Show Ground- **£23**

1 Mile Flat Race - 440 yds. Flat Race - 100 yds. Flat Race.

1½ MILE OPEN TROTTING HANDICAP **£23**   1½ MILE OPEN GALLOP **£30**

SPORTS ENTRIES CLOSE 30th AUGUST

DRY WALLING COMPETITION   JUNIOR GALLOP £8   PONY SCAMPER RACE £9

Official Parking Ground for Motors :

Char-a-Banc 2/6,   Car 2/-,   Cars on Show Ground (excluding Passenger) 5/- (Limited Accommodation)

LUNCHEON in Marquee on the Field, from 12-45 p.m. and TEA in Marquee at 4 o'clock.

"Games of Chance" Not Admitted to Show Ground

Apply to Secretary for Space on Show Ground for TRADE STALLS and EXHIBITS.

ADMISSION: ALL DAY 2/6   (After 5 o'clock 1/-)   Children under 14, Half-Price.

DANCE in Village Hall at 8 p.m. Admission: 2/-

Schedules and Entry Forms on application to : G. J. HARKER, Secretary, GRASSINGTON
Near SKIPTON,   Tel. Grassington 79

Ref. No.: 8B or 8G   THE SUN ENGRAVING CO. LTD., LONDON and WATFORD

Another important change to affect the Dales was its evolution from a working landscape to a leisure based one. The loss of people farming on the land coincided with people from towns and cities wanting to spend more time visiting the Dales, to take part in leisure activities such as hill walking. Throughout the 1970s and 1980s farmhouses and workers cottages increasingly became re-appropriated as second homes and holiday cottages. The outcome of this social and cultural change is not only that a vastly reduced number of people now work in agriculture, but also that many ordinary working people can no longer afford to live in the Dales. Whilst this has significant long-term implications for rural life, for Kilnsey Show it has meant a vastly diminished natural catchment of show competitors and visitors.

For those farmers who have survived, agriculture looks very different than it did to their ancestors. Farming is now a global business, with food being imported and exported on an industrial scale. The Dales, with its small hill farms and handful of surviving dairy herds, is no longer secluded from the outside world and relies on European subsidies to survive. The biggest peacetime crisis to hit British farming came in 2001 and meant that for the first time in its history – excepting war – the show was cancelled in its entirety. The reason was the catastrophic outbreak of Foot and Mouth disease which saw over ten million sheep and cattle culled across the UK, with 416 farms across the region of Craven and the Dales directly affected.

The aftermath of the 2001 crisis saw huge changes to farming practice, including new restrictions regarding the movement of livestock intended as precautionary measures to prevent future outbreaks. These restrictions mean that it is now a lot harder for farmers to show their animals; indeed in 2007 there were no livestock shown at Kilnsey following a Foot and Mouth scare hundreds of miles away in Surrey.

Casting an eye back across the social and cultural changes of the twentieth century it can seem like a roll call of blows to rural life and farming. Yet Kilnsey Show has endured, and now enters its twelfth decade in robust health.

Kilnsey Show poster from 1949 (courtesy of David Hill land agents)

Variety is the spice of life…

Kilnsey Show is steeped in tradition: the show ring, livestock classes, the Crag Race and even the huge white marquees have all been the ever-present sights and sounds of the show since it started in 1897. The appearance given by these unchanging elements is an evocation of timelessness and of things having always been the same. This impression contradicts the truth however, which is that over the years the show has altered enormously. It has had to; to reflect the prevailing interests and culture of the times it has found itself in, and also to attract new audiences.

The growing status of Kilnsey Show can be followed in the newspaper reports of the day. The 1920 show was headlined an "Event of Social Importance" by the local paper, which also reported that "the event is something a great deal more than a show… the day's programme is usually a lengthy one, and is only half over when the show exhibits have been removed." By 1927 the show was headlined "the leading agricultural and social event in Upper Wharfedale". A decade later the local paper again noted the growing reach of the show, not just within the Dales, but across the north of England and beyond, revealing that "two visitors from London had made the 200 mile journey especially to see the sheep dog trials." By the 1970s the show had started to be noticed by regional and national media, with the first of what was to become several television programmes and documentaries being made about it.

> *"Kilnsey Show is steeped in tradition: the show ring, livestock classes, the Crag Race and even the huge white marquees have all been the ever-present sights and sounds of the show since it started in 1897"*

As the prestige and breadth of the show's schedule has grown, so have the rewards. In the late 1890s there was three silver trophies and prize money of just a few pounds; by 1977 there were twenty one silver cups and £2000 prize money. Today there is £17,000 prize money and more than eighty silver cups and trophies awarded.

The silver cup for 'Best Cow either in Calf or Milk' won by Mr Leonard Carlisle in 1925

A true show character was John Willy Hebden of Cracoe (right) – 1920s wrestling star and local butcher, captured here with fellow judges in the 1960s (Ken Blakey)

The programme of Kilnsey Show day, which is now centred around the main attractions of the livestock, the Crag Race and the trotting, has actually fluctuated significantly through the decades – changes which cast light on society's values of the time, as well prevailing hobbies and pastimes. Sheep Dog Trials first appeared in 1899, Showjumping [referred to as 'leaping'] in 1903, and a 'weight judging competition' in 1913. Eggs then bread followed by cured pork and dressed poultry were also new additions to the Produce section in 1899, 1904 and 1913 respectively. Wrestling reappeared on the schedule in 1920, for the first time since the 1800s – an event which was won by John Willy Hebden, renowned as the village butcher at Cracoe in later years. There was also the re-introduction of several track events this year, including a 'scamper' and a ladies race – many of which had been popular events in the days of the old Kilnsey Feast.

By the 1920s the fell race up the western side of the crag, colloquially known as the Crag Race, had become the iconic event it is regarded today, and was reported as attracting "some of the cleverest fell runners in the country," including the winners of Grasmere Sports, considered the premier fell running event in the country. 1920 also saw the addition of the tug-of-war and high jump. New show classes that year included Pigs and Horticulture, with the variety of vegetable classes most likely reflecting the trend of 'growing your own' brought about by the First World War food shortages. The pig classes never really took off at Kilnsey – the Dales has never been a notable area for rearing pork – and were removed from the schedule altogether in the early 1950s.

Despite the severe economic problems facing the country during the inter-war period, the show reflected the growing social freedoms that people were now embracing, with events like the trotting and the gallops [horse racing] making a popular return, as well as some new events for motorcycles. In 1927 a motorcycle 'Gymkhana' arranged by Skipton and District Motor Cycle Club attracted thirty competitors, and included a 'potato race', 'musical chairs with lady passengers', a 'scamper race', a 'T. T. race' and a 'balloon bursting competition' – according to the local newspaper "much amusement was caused". The motorcycle events lasted just four years, making a brief return in the early 1950s, and once again as an attraction in 2007. Their downfall was that the bikes damaged the turf of the show ring too much, as well as perhaps not being in keeping with the relaxed atmosphere of a rural show.

Exhibits within the marquees were extended in 1927 to include the first ever class for children – 'A collection of wild flowers'. It would be nearly thirty years before the children's section was further extended, with new classes in 1958 including 'Best picture of a country scene', an 'Exhibit in wood or metal' and a baking class. During the 1960s the children's classes were expanded again, to include garment making and pottery. This era also saw the coordination of entries from all the local village schoolchildren, a practice that continued right up to the early 1970s, and which firmly established this educational and very popular aspect of the show, as well as being a means of keeping the community strongly engaged in 'their' local show.

Nineteen forty five brought the first equestrian events for children with a pony riding class and junior pony gallops, and 1949 heralded the first running race for juniors since the days of the old Kilnsey Feast, in the form of the Under 17s Crag Race. This event was won by Gordon Jackson of Cracoe, who contributed much to fell racing in Upper Wharfedale, and aptly the winner the following year was Kilnsey's own Bill Foster, who was later to become an established member of the show committee. Crag Races for children Under 12 and Under 14 were added in the 1970s.

There were also fads that came and went. The 1930s brought the new but short-lived events of 'catching the greasy pig' and 'pillow fighting'. More enduring was the introduction in 1932 of two classes "for members of the Upper Wharfedale Calf Club", the precursor to the Upper Wharfedale Young Farmers' Club. A version of this competition continues to take place, in the form of the Young Farmers' Sheep Judging Competition, which is held a week prior to Kilnsey Show, owing to the fact that the local Young Farmers play an important role in both the set-up and running of the show.

The social and cultural changes which took place in the post war Britain of the 1940s were reflected in other changes to the show's schedule. In 1948 a new class of fruit preserving was introduced, reflecting the war-time drive to preserve the country's fruit as jams and pickles, a massive enterprise coordinated by the Women's Institute. Recognition of the increased prominence of W.I.s following the war came in 1950, with the inclusion of a Women's Institute section "displaying the interests and hobbies of country women", which by 1959 was described in the local paper as a "notable feature of Kilnsey Show".

Pat Daggett (left) cantering into the prizes in 1945 (Ian Daggett)

A blooming good show: Exhibits from the Horticulture marquee © Stephen Garnett

All the fun of the fair: Winning a prize is the highlight of a young Dalesman's day

The 'fun fair' is mentioned for the very first time within the 1948 show report, as an "attraction for the younger generation". Although this is the first official mention of this aspect of the show, photographic evidence and personal memories confirm that some kind of fun fair had been an established feature of the early shows. The photograph from 1907 shown earlier on page 15 vividly shows a bustling and busy show with a child having a donkey ride.

Kilnsey born Bill Foster has many fond memories of the show from his childhood in the 1940s, recalling the 'swing boats' and some small wind-up rides. The highlight of the fun fair for Bill however, was the coconut shy which would enable him to win a coveted five pack of Woodbine cigarettes! Another Kilnsey local Anthony Roberts, who has been President of the show four times, also has memories of the fair from this era, recalling "toffee apples in the mud", the hoopla and a shooting gallery where air rifles were used for target practice games.

A more informal aspect of the fun fair were the 'cheap jacks' and 'con men' who would come and set up their stalls and 'games of chance' – something which they'd done since the days of the old Kilnsey Feast. Trevor Robinson, a farmhand who grew up in Upper Wharfedale in the 1930s and 1940s, recalls the colour and variety brought to the show by the cheap jacks. Robinson recalls an array of competitions including throwing a stone at a tree growing out of the crag, seeing how many fifty six pound weights a man could pick up on a shovel, and trying to carry a huge 225 pound wool sack. Ella Pontefract and Marie Hartley, authors of many books about the Yorkshire Dales, wrote in 1938 that the entrance to the showfield was "down an avenue of side shows [where] the cheap jacks spread their toys and jewellery on the ground as they did at the old Kilnsey Feast." In the midst of this scene "two little girls were kneeling on the grass solemnly trying on and discussing the merits of a ring or a wrist-watch." Despite the fact that this unofficial aspect of the show has dwindled over the years, the fun fair continues to thrive, and remains a perennial highlight to young children.

Another popular highlight of the show which also hailed from the days of the old Kilnsey Feast was the 'gala dance' held on the show evening. This was a popular social event in the Dales, and continued as such up until the late 1960s. Many are the memories and stories of dancing in the mud, accidentally ending up in the stream after dark, and of discovering the dents made by cars in the walls all the way back to neighbouring villages the following morning.

Changing farming practices were also reflected in the show's programme. The introduction of tractors to farms around the Dales during the post war era established a new farming skill to be shared and enjoyed, and so the first Tractor Handling Competition entered the show schedule in 1958, with one event for juniors and one for seniors. This was a popular event for many years, particularly for junior entrants, although it gradually declined in the early 2000s, being finally withdrawn in 2011.

As interest in handling the latest brand new tractors for fun waned, that in looking at restored vintage tractors grew, leading to the introduction of the Vintage Tractor Competition and parade in 1995. Similarly other exhibits of Dales farming heritage and nostalgia have also become popular at the show in latter years, such as the hand crafted walking sticks competition, and demonstrations of farming skills such as sheep shearing.

A relatively late entry to the show's ever developing schedule in 2003 was the inclusion of the distinguished Kilnsey Angling Club – the second oldest angling club in the country, established in 1840 – who now have their own riverside marquee from where they present angling demonstrations and host a social event.

Reeling them in: The venerable Kilnsey Angling Club became part of the show in 2003
© Stephen Garnett

Eat, drink and be merry…

The role of food at the show has evolved considerably over the years from its early beginnings as a showcase of home-produced butter, eggs and cheese. These days the Produce marquee includes everything from bread and cakes to wine and quiches. The focus for hungry appetites has always been the 'show luncheon', which grew out of the Feast, where up to a thousand guests would sit down to tea. At the early shows lunch was served at the local inn, The Tennant's Arms, but since 1903 has been hosted in a marquee on the showfield [as seen in the picture on page 18]. For many years invitations to the lunch were restricted to show officials and invited local dignitaries, and up until the 1970s would have been a lengthy affair consisting of several speeches. In recent years the show lunch has become a more accessible social occasion, which all visitors to the show are welcome to take part and enjoy.

The first show advert which contained a reference to a 'Licensed Refreshment Marquee' appeared in 1946. Known colloquially as 'the beer tent', it almost turned into as much of an institution as the show itself. In the days of strict licensing laws, when pubs opened at 12 noon and closed again at 2.40pm, Kilnsey Show's beer tent with its 'all day' licence became a huge and unique draw for day trippers, particularly those from nearby West Yorkshire and East Lancashire, who had local holidays as the same time as the show. From the 1960s to the late 1980s, the show attracted coach loads of visitors, as the prospect of all day drinking coupled with a full schedule of sports, trotting and ring side betting, gave Kilnsey Show all the glitz and glamour of a day at the races.

The flipside of the success of the beer tent was of course the hi-jinks and the scuffles. Local pubs up and down the Dales took to closing their doors on Kilnsey Show day to ensure the inebriated post show crowd didn't 'tip up' and cause problems. With the aim of minimising potential trouble, the beer tent was moved from a prominent position near the main entrance gate, to its current riverside location. These measures certainly didn't deter the informal 'competitions' that took place inside the beer tent, many of which involved grown men shinning up the guy ropes and across the extremely high wooden framework of the marquee. Such antics claimed their fair share of sprains and broken bones over the years – though thankfully nothing too serious.

A typical escapade in the beer tent is recalled from the 1967 show. Officials had cancelled all the horse events in light of the inclement weather and so the beer tent had become particularly thronged, both with its usual drinkers and with people taking shelter from the rain. A particular gentleman in the tent didn't want to venture outside in the rain to empty his bladder so relieved himself in a corner of the tent instead. Someone else not surprisingly took exception to this and words were exchanged. The beer, the crowds and the rain meant that the situation very quickly escalated into a full scale brawl, made memorable to all that witnessed it by the sight of six men in their best suits wrestling around in a foot of mud and water! Changes to licensing and drink driving laws over the last twenty years mean that such stories are now merely a part of the show's rich anecdotal history.

Since the millennium local food and drink has taken a more prominent role at the show, a move which started with the inclusion of the 'Food and Farming for REAL' exhibition in 2000, and which brought with it the show's very popular Farmers' Market and children's area. The food area of the show developed even further in 2007, with the addition of the Cookery Theatre. The growing interest and passion for good food is reflected by the large area now dedicated to local food producers and chefs.

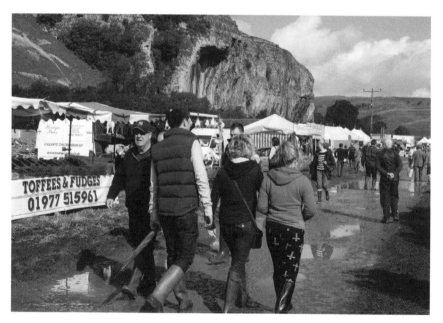

Mud glorious mud: The crowds still turn out in a wet year © Cernan Elias/Alamy

It never rains but it pours...

Kilnsey Show wouldn't be Kilnsey Show without some discussion about the weather. In the run up to show day organisers, exhibitors, competitors and visitors hope for a dry day. Since the earliest years of the show the local paper has always commented on the weather, with the very first show report in 1897 congratulating organisers on having "no cause for complaint" in this regard. The weather has unfortunately rendered some years totally unforgettable, and the year that Kilnsey Show was hit by a hurricane is top of that list.

In 1986 a hurricane which had originated in Florida made its way over the Atlantic Ocean to the UK, bringing heavy deluges and near gale force winds in its wake. They called it 'Charley' and it wreaked havoc – flooding rivers, bringing trees and power lines down and causing at least eleven deaths. The remnants of the hurricane struck Upper Wharfedale the night before Kilnsey Show, its high winds flattening the Horticultural marquee and the rain turning the field into a quagmire. Undeterred, show officials pledged that the show would go on. The River Wharfe which runs adjacent to the showfield was being monitored hourly, and miraculously despite the challenging conditions most of the show classes were completed. Nevertheless just after midday, for the first time in the history of the show, the river burst its banks and the decision was made to evacuate the public from the showfield.

Show officials and stewards dug deep to salvage what they could from the day. Roy Nelson, who's been involved in the show since the 1960s, remembers one of the more comical aspects of the day: "We'd to go to the beer tent before dinner time with a tractor and rescue all the beer because the river was coming over and it would have washed it all away!" Matt Mason also recalls that "After we'd been stood up to our knees in water drinking all afternoon, Roger Ingham said we'd to run the Crag Race as it's been run every year at 4.00pm. So four of us set off and ran it in our wellies. I lost my way and nearly got to Malham [four miles away] before I turned round as the wind was that strong!" The 'official' Crag Race was in fact run three weeks later, such was the determination of show stalwarts that not even a hurricane could stop the famous race from being run.

Stars of the show...

The stars of Kilnsey Show have always been the people – from the unsung heroes who've helped to put the show together, to the hundreds of people who've entered and continue to enter the myriad of classes and events.

Over the years some show regulars have honed their talents and gone on from Kilnsey to achieve greatness in the world beyond, such as former British showjumping champion Harvey Smith, and three times Grand National winner Brian Fletcher, who rode in the flat race 'gallops' at Kilnsey Show prior to winning the Grand National with Red Alligator in 1968, and with the legendary Red Rum in 1973 and 1974.

The trotting, now termed harness racing, has also attracted some of the sports' top drivers and horses over the years too, including Missing Link, the first horse ever to pace a mile on grass in less than two minutes, winning at Kilnsey Show just two years prior to setting this record in 1985.

"The stars of Kilnsey Show have always been the people – from the unsung heroes who've helped to put the show together, to the hundreds of people who've entered the myriad of classes and events"

Kilnsey's iconic Crag Race has always attracted the fell running elite. The biggest fell racing legends to have won the race are Bill Teasdale MBE, a shepherd from Caldbeck in the Lake District who was undeniably the UK's fell racing great of the 1940s, '50s and '60s; and Fred Reeves who to this day is the Grasmere Guides and Burnsall Classic record holder. Other big names include Kenny Stuart who won the World title in 1983, Victoria Wilkinson who won a junior World title, and Mick Hawkins the present Kilnsey record holder and a Commonwealth Games finalist.

Despite the fact that Kilnsey's ever developing schedule of events has always provided entertainment in abundance, the show ring – as well as the air above it – has over latter years added further entertainment and spectacle, with aerobatic displays and birds of prey dominating the skies, alongside gun dogs showcasing their gathering skills back on terra firma.

One of the most memorable spectacles of the show in recent times was a visit from the iconic national hunt racehorse, Cheltenham Gold Cup winner and three times King George VI Chase winner Desert Orchid, who trotted a lap of victory around Kilnsey's show ring in 1999.

The famous Calendar Girls whose W.I. is just five miles from Kilnsey were also in attendance that year, as they have been many other years. The 2003 film *Calendar Girls* features scenes from Kilnsey Show, as does the 2015 musical based on their story.

Stars on parade: The Calendar Girls with Desert Orchid in 1999

Let the music play...

From its inception, a roll call of brass bands have shaped the soundtrack to Kilnsey Show, and in the years before the Second World War a ceremonious pageant headed by the landlord of the Tennant's Arms would have led the band on to the showfield. There have been notable appearances from Kettlewell Brass Band, Skipton Prize Brass Band, Grassington Temperance Brass Band, Kildwick Brass Band, Lofthouse and Middlesmoor Brass Band, Darley Temperance Band, British Oil and Cake Mills Prize Silver Band, Sowerby Bridge Brass Band, Salts Prize Brass Band and Hammonds' Sauce Works Prize Band. This archetypal 'northern sound', mellow as well as melodious, has resonated around the showfield and echoed off the overhanging crag year in year out since the days of the old Kilnsey Feast.

"The melodious sound of brass band music has resonated around the showfield and echoed off the overhanging crag year in year out since the days of the old Kilnsey Feast"

Interspersed between the musical interludes of the brass band, other evocative sounds and voices have also come to form part of the music of Kilnsey Show day. Bill Foster recalls the excitement of discovering that show day had finally arrived, courtesy of being awoken by the show's loud speaker system and the familiar vocal tones of its announcer 'owd' Clegg, crackling and reverberating into life. For many years, local raconteur Ian 'Adge' Douglass has gently entertained the early morning show crowd with his friendly banter, delivered not in Dales dialect but in his unmistakable West Country burr.

As the activities of the morning are completed, new voices provide the soundtrack to the sports and harness racing in the afternoon, commencing with Roger Ingham's humorous and enlightening sports commentaries delivered in his distinctive broad Yorkshire tones, followed by Peter Deighton's flowing north eastern timbre, guiding the crowd through the harness races. All these voices and thousands more – from the stewards, stall keepers, fair hands, bookmakers and the show visitors themselves – blend together to become the chorus of this one remarkable day.

On with the show...

Much like the river that runs beside the showfield, the years have ebbed and flowed as people, events and even the weather have come and gone; and yet the music of the show has played on. A great deal has changed over the last 120 years yet much too has stayed the same. Hemlines have shortened, and the formality of fashion has relaxed – the Edwardian ladies in broad-brimmed hats have given way to jeans and T-shirts – although flat caps and tweed jackets are thankfully still in attendance. To early visitors to the show, our modern means of travel would be beyond comprehension, with concerns about stabling giving way to car parking and traffic jams. Facilities have improved, and choices about what to do, buy, eat or drink have expanded a hundred fold. Yet, quite magically, Kilnsey Show and Sports appears unchanging. The ethos, essence and crucially the sound and music of the day all endure.

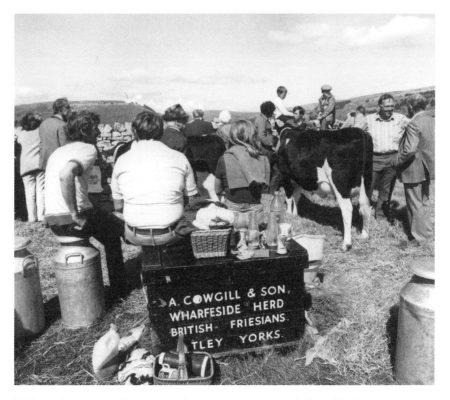

Milking the occasion: Relaxing in the cattle section, 1982 © Steve Haithwaite

2

THE CRAG RACE AND SPORTS

"He won the Crag Race with blood pouring out of his head and into his socks"

A race up and down a hillside is a centuries old pastime, and has been the sporting highlight of innumerable historical feasts, fairs and gatherings across the Dales, the Lake District and Scotland. What distinguishes the Kilnsey Crag Race as one of the most famous and hotly contested fell races of all is its winning combination of awesome challenge and magnificent spectacle. Roger Ingham has been actively involved in Kilnsey Show since 1959, as both a competitor and a helper, and here he shares his memories of the show and its sporting heritage.

The Crag Race is a thrilling spectacle for the crowd at Kilnsey Show. If you think it looks steep from the showfield, then it's twice as bad up there looking down. What makes it special for spectators is that they can see most of the course all the way round. The trouble with a lot of fell races is that runners get too far out of sight, so you just see them coming back in. In this race you can see them slipping and scraping up the scree slopes, which is like running on a shifting treadmill of rocks, then as little dots on skyline, and then the moment when the runners first come off the top is always a sight to behold.

Hawk's eye view: Mick Hawkins en route to the Crag Race record in 1982 (Roger Ingham)

The Crag Race is explosive pace-wise – you need to be in pole position half way up because it's hard to pass on the scree – and it's fearsome coming down! You don't see the runners in the infamous 'chimney' which is a forty foot vertical drop, but you can tell by length of time they're in there that it's like a factory chimney – a sheer descent – and it's certainly had its fair share of casualties over the years.

The legendary Lakeland fell runner Bill Teasdale split his head open in the chimney in 1952, and had to have nineteen stitches, but he still finished and won the race, and I've had two lots of stitches, a broken wrist and grotesque ankle swellings from running the race.

King of the fells: Fell racing legend Bill Teasdale (second left) leads out in 1953 (Ingham)

My involvement with the show started five years after Bill Teasdale split his head open. I've always been passionate about sport and the foundation of my summer sport at primary school, bar listening to athletics and boxing on the wireless, was cricket. I had three 'sport passionate' friends at school, and one of that three was David Jeanes who many years hence would become a Rugby League World Cup winner. 'Jeanesy' from a very young age was going to sports meetings all over the north of England with his dad, who trained athletes. When we got back to school on a Monday, I'd be trying to shove my two penneth' in about my cricket, but Jeanesy would frequently come back with tales about his exploits at these sports meetings.

One name came up frequently, and he was fairly extolling his virtues, and that was Bill Teasdale – the fell running star from up in the Lake District. Just to verify all that he'd been saying about Bill Teasdale, by chance our teacher had brought this slideshow in of where his friend had been touring in the Dales and Lake District over the summer. The teacher's friend had been to Grasmere Sports and Kilnsey Show, and his slides showed, who else, but this great Bill Teasdale – just an odd picture, but there it was: Teasdale when he won the Crag Race in 1952, with blood pouring out of his head and into his socks.

> *"I remember seeing this picture in the paper of the Crag Race going out, and it was Bill Teasdale starring again. I remember saying to my mum: how can they have a race up there?"*

I'd heard about hitch hiking, as I'd seen it in the Beano – so four of us set off hitch hiking the following year in 1953, to try and see Bill Teasdale at a special record challenge race in Burnsall [five miles south of Kilnsey]. The guy who picked us up flapped a bit en route and put us out at Rylstone, so we never got there. But I was still fired up about this Bill Teasdale, and in 1957 I finally hitch hiked up to Kilnsey Show. This was my first intro to Kilnsey Show – and as soon as I went through the main gate I was just taken aback by it all!

Tough at the top: Award-winning picture of the Crag Race © Stephen Garnett

"The Crag Race is explosive pace-wise — you need to be in pole position half way up because it's hard to pass on the scree — and it's fearsome coming down!"

Handicrafts were to the right as they are now, and I enjoyed looking round all the Handicrafts and Produce. Then I wandered down to the main arena, and I was just taken over by all the razzmatazz of the travellers and bookies there, who were doing their own bit of entertaining. There were 'games of chance', and I do remember seeing one of the schedules soon after that said "games of chance not permitted on the field", but of course they were pulling in the crowds and getting them going, and there were a few cheap jacks and con men and all this sort of thing. I hadn't met with Billy Pickering, the Chief Sports Steward back then, but I remember him saying later that the cheap jacks helped to make the show – all these little corners of character and content. There was this one guy who had this whacking big board with lines across – red, blue, green and white. If you got on the white with a dart, it was a thinner line and so you got this exorbitant money prize. "Look I can do it backwards if you like," he would say throwing the dart over his shoulder. He had the crowd all round him and all the puns: "Has anyone here not got any money?" – because you had to pay to go on it; a few would put their hand up: "You with your hand up; turn left and march straight forward!" In other words, 'move out of the way!'

"The cheap jacks helped to make the show – all these little corners of character and content"

There was one of the bookies, with pound notes stuck in his trilby and all the quips. The greatest character of all in the bookies, with a loud and vociferous Scottish bellow, was 'Big Jim' Hepburn from Edinburgh, bawling out his odds in his melodious Scottish accent: "Thoo a one allay" – which meant 'Two to one I will lay!' When the sports started, the bookies went up another decibel.

A prelude to the sports was the showjumping, and I was particularly interested to see a very impressive competitor called Harvey Smith, whom I'd already seen starring at Gargrave Show a year or two earlier. Next came the horse racing, which they called the 'gallops' – it was unbelievable, almost 'circus like', as the track at Kilnsey is big for running at 540 yards – but that's actually quite small for horse racing. So they were leaning round the bends and all that. I was highly impressed, as I don't think Lester Piggott and his contemporaries would have handled that sort of track!

1962 hall of fame: This storm battered quartet won 17 Crag Races between them. Left to right: Reg Harrison, Norman Beck, Bill Teasdale and George Broadhurst (Ingham)

Interspersed in all this horse racing were the running events. The first event was the heats for the 100 Yards Handicap, then the One Mile Handicap, and then the 440 Yards Handicap. I was fair enthralled by the junior Crag Race because Norman Beck, who had grown up with me, won it that year. Then we came to the senior Crag Race, and I saw this great Bill Teasdale for the first time. He did disappoint me in one respect though, as my vision of him was as an athletic powerful sort of guy – but he was actually right craggy and shop-worn looking! Mind you, he'd still another win left in him at Kilnsey, and two or three at Grasmere Sports. That said, I was behind him all the way support-wise. But the new kid on the block, Reg Harrison, beat him and equalled the record of 8.17 minutes, which was a fantastic time even today. They were all running in old fell boots then too, which were far heavier than running shoes today. Also, considering the contours of the course then, it was a tougher race, because the stone wall at the bottom was still built up, and the wall a third of the way was substantially higher than it is now. Reg Harrison come off the top like a rocket when he'd never been round the course in his life, which just took my breath away.

Starter for the sports then was 'owd' Clegg from Ilkley, who I remembered from Skipton Gala. He always added his bit of colour and content: after counting down at the start of a race he'd wind up by shouting "On your way!" The year after, in 1958, I went up on my bike to enter the junior Crag Race. I was a bit sceptical of being good enough to run in the open class, so I thought being from Skipton I could get in with the locals, but they didn't let me. By 1959 I'd met up with Billy Pickering and hooked into his stable for running training a bit, and so he helped me to get in – and after all that, I think I came last!

My involvement as a helper at the show also started in 1959 in that hot balmy summer, marking the track and the 100 yard lanes out with an old football field line marker, along with Norman Beck. It was the night before the show, the midges were biting like hell, it was coming in dark, the marker paint was dried up and we'd run out of water; so we peed into it to finish the job! So that were my intro into helping at Kilnsey Show.

So I was into Kilnsey Show one way or the other, and it soon became a traditional part of my year, like Christmas day, year on year on year. When I left school I worked at a building firm and they gave us the afternoon off for it. It was very much one of the key events in all of Craven and it flourished throughout much of the 1960s. My first prize at Kilnsey Show, for finishing fifth, was in 1960 in the Under 17s Crag Race, and I was third in 1961 when they made it an Under 18s race for one year only. I got my first senior Crag Race prize in 1962 when I was eighteen, and I won 'the mile' twice in 1973 and '74, off the 'back mark' on both occasions.

Very unfortunately for the show the Chief Sports Steward Billy Pickering became ill in late 1963, and he died in '64. We both knew that the committee could have done with lifting the prize money, and odd times if Billy thought another prize was merited he'd shove that in out of his own pocket. He was a very generous giver to the show. Inflation started to kick in a bit in the late 1960s but the prize money remained static at Kilnsey, and at other sports as well.

Race for the line: The sprint final in 1979 (Roger Ingham)

A mounted escort: Young Crag Racers head for the slopes (Roger Ingham)

None faster: Fred Reeves breaks the Crag Race record in 1978 (Roger Ingham)

The problem was you had to decide back then if you were 'amateur' or 'professional'. Prize money was always an attraction for pulling competitors in, but if they were competing for very little, with a massive outlay for themselves in petrol money, then they might very well decide to stop in the amateurs. Money was always an attraction for the 'professionals' that were a bit ambitious, but if you were ambitious in the 'amateurs', you could end up competing for your country. Mine and Billy's argument was that the show should make the prizes worth travelling for.

So the entries dwindled when Billy died, as he'd always had this bit of drive for getting them in. They got very low in the late 1960s – but being passionate about keeping the sports alive, I remember in 1969 I ran in every single event just to help make the numbers up. I ran the 100 Yards – heat and final – One Mile, the 440 Yards, and then the Crag Race – all straight after each other! Ever since first watching it, I had always aspired to win the Crag Race, and if ever there had been a realistic chance of me doing that, that year would have been the one. It was in fact won by a much below par Tommy Sedgwick, destined to soon become a star.

My own chance of winning disappeared even before the 'off', as barely had the 440 Yards finished, and I was still grovelling for breath when the Crag Race field was lined up. The fact that I did eventually manage to prise my way into the prizes reflected more about the poor overall quality of the field, rather than any prowess on my part.

The big triumph for me though was that through contesting every race, especially the track events – including pulling a couple of guys in from the crowd to help make the numbers up – I probably saved the sports from totally going under that year.

Ever since the First World War it had been a tradition, almost year on year, for Kilnsey Crag Race to attract the leading runners from the premier Lakeland classic, the Grasmere Guides Race. However with inflation starting to kick in, and with no corresponding increase in prize money, that previously welcome flow of talent was beginning to evaporate. This was most conspicuous in 1969, 1970 and 1971 by the absence of the Grasmere champion and future fell running legend Fred Reeves.

Salvation thankfully arrived via an ITV television project in 1972, when Reeves finally made his first Kilnsey appearance, although it had more to do with the TV company waving a carrot in his direction than anything the show was offering. Reeves showed his class by winning the race, but it was a heck of a close finish – and the guy breathing down his neck was none other than my mate Norman Beck, whose serious running training had been almost a decade earlier. Long-time committee member and former athlete Billy Foster used this 'nearly embarrassing' result to the show's advantage though, and finally influenced the committee to put the prize money up. A progressive move which paid dividends tenfold. 1972 also saw another top sportsman race at Kilnsey – British professional sprint champion George McNeill from Tranent near Edinburgh – this time as a result of sponsorship from a local business man. Only a month previously the 'flying scot', who had initially lost his amateur status through having played professional football, had just beaten the reigning Olympic Games 200 Metres champion and world record holder, Tommy Smith of the USA, in a sprint challenge series. With McNeil on scratch at Kilnsey, he gave his opponents starts of up to twenty nine yards, but of course he still won – much to the ecstatic appreciation of the crowd.

With a lift in prize money for all of the sporting events in place by 1973, Reeves and Sedgwick continued to return, both upping their game in the years to follow. Reeves the master ascender and Sedgwick renowned for his fearless almost suicidal descents, provided thrilling spectacles year on year throughout the rest of the '70s, with Reeves eventually breaking the record in 1975.

I got onto the show committee somewhere about that time, and I also started helping the show's long time handicapper and starter, Ken McClurg, with the handicapping. He'd been a long time official handicapper and starter at many Yorkshire Dales and South Lakeland sports meetings since the war. I'd noticed that Ken wasn't averse to giving somebody nearly thirty yards in the 100 Yards, which was a third of the way there, but he wouldn't do it pro-rata in 'the mile' – so sometimes on longer distance races there'd be some competitors left out with the washing, as there was when I won 'the mile' off the back mark in 1973. So, Ken started taking a bit more notice of me with the handicapping, and together we helped to make some cracking races in the late 1970s and early 1980s in all the track events.

Hawk mania: Mick Hawkins sprints to a record breaking victory in 1982 (Roger Ingham)

The only downside of it all right through that period was that 'owd' Clegg had died in 1964. Unlike Clegg, his successor didn't give out any background info about the runners. So I kept getting onto the show committee, saying that the crowd needs to know who's in the lead in such as the Crag Race or 'the mile', and they kept saying "why don't you do it?" – but I was still competing keenly then. Interestingly as it all turned out, I was side-lined with an injury in 1980, which resulted in me being stood in the ring feeding information to the public address man whilst the races took place.

Unbeknown to me, my voice could be clearly heard over the microphone – so it was a commentary, but unintentionally! The following year in 1981, after contesting the One Mile Handicap which was one of the earliest races in the schedule, the show Chairman Jim Caygill pushed the microphone into my hand and asked me to cover the rest of the sports – so I finished up commentating in a pair of sweaty shorts for rest of the show! But it seemed to meet with approval from all sides. From 1982 onwards I was doing it properly and the rest as they say is history.

When all the track events were booming in the 1980s and 1990s, the Crag Race used to be the grand finale of a great sporting afternoon. The afternoon had glitz and glamour because everything was building up to a crescendo, and the Crag Race was that crescendo. The sports got too marginalised when all the track events went in early 2000, but now we've got 'the mile' back on, and we are endeavouring to build it back to its glory, and all being well there will hopefully be more track events in the next few years.

56 shows and still going strong: Commentator and former competitor Roger Ingham
© Stephen Garnett

Since 1990 'amateurs' and 'professionals' have been able to race together, which is something I campaigned long and hard for. This means that the Crag Race now draws everyone, from locals having a go to international athletes who want their name forever on the cup. There's also a growing number of women and girls entering, and Kilnsey now offers equal prize money.

In the early years of the show it was mainly local competitors who competed in the Crag Race, but then runners started coming from other dales, such as Tommy 'Pont' Metcalfe from Appersett near Hawes, who won it seven times before the First World War. He was top class and he beat the pre-war Lakeland legend Ernest Dalzell on the odd occasion up in the Lake District too. Truly great runners between the wars were George Woolcock, Ronnie Robinson, Jack James, Ronnie Gilpin and Joseph Conkey, who were all big Lakeland names. By and large the motorbike seemed to be the means of travel for most runners at this time.

After the Second World War, Stan Edmondson was one of the class acts, and obviously the great Bill Teasdale, Reg Harrison, Tommy Garside and not forgetting my stable mate Norman Beck. Then came Fred Reeves and Tommy Sedgwick – Reeves won it six times and Sedgwick won it five. After them Kenny Stuart was the next big name to win Kilnsey. He reinstated with the amateurs and went on to win the World title in Italy soon after winning Kilnsey, which just proves the class that we were getting. Stuart won it twice, in 1980 and '81 and he was the World Champion by 1983. Then there was our local star, Mick Hawkins. Mick came up through the juniors, winning the Under 17s in 1977 and then breaking Dennis Robinson's Under 17s record in 1978 – a record which had stood for nineteen years. The course was tailor made for Mick as it was short and steep, and he could fly coming down. He won the seniors three times, including breaking and setting the current record in 1982 with 7.35 minutes. Shortly after this he reinstated with the amateurs and went on to make the final in the Steeple Chase at the 1986 Commonwealth Games in Auckland.

In 1990 when the race finally became properly 'open' it brought in some of the country's top amateurs – not least of all Ian Holmes from Haworth, who'd won every big fell race everywhere before he came to Kilnsey. He'd won the Ben Nevis Race, the Three Peaks Race and the race up Mount Kinabalu in Borneo, where he holds the record. Stephen Hawkins, who started at Kilnsey with his brother Mick, returned after winning the British title in the amateurs. When the race became open Mick also came back and won it again from Andy Peace who was another class act runner – very close and thrilling race that was, as 'Peacey' was in front of Mick coming down the last bit. Then came Rob Hope from Wheelton in the Lancashire Pennines, who is another class act runner, and who broke Teasdale's record number of wins, with a staggering nine Crag Race victories in the early 2000s. The most recent local to win it was Ted Mason in 2011. Simon Bailey, the seven times England Champion, is our current reigning champion and he's won it three times now. He's a sheep farmer from down in Cheshire, which is a nice blend for the show because it was often shepherds winning it in the early years.

Whoever comes in first gets an ovation like an Olympic champion coming up the home straight – and if it's an exciting battle to the wire then the commentator will be going up another crescendo with it! Two of the best show-downs I can remember as commentator were between John Atkinson and Steve Carr in 1987 and Mick Hawkins and Andy Peace in 1995 – but of course there have been others, including the Reeves-Sedgwick battles which thrilled the crowds in the years when I was competing. Great classics and a bit more besides!

Athletics coach and former all round sportsman Roger Ingham, who received an MBE for his services to sport in 2007, became involved with Kilnsey Show in 1959, graduating to the sports committee in the 1960s and the show committee in the early 1970s. Dubbed Craven's 'Mr Sport', for the past thirty five years Roger's distinctive Yorkshire accent, lively personality and encyclopaedic knowledge of fell running have enabled him to win many plaudits as the commentator at several high profile sporting events – not least Kilnsey Show.

Local hero: Appletreewick-born Ted Mason leads out on his way to victory in 2011
© Stephen Garnett

3

SHEEP

"He could judge anything from budgies to elephants and get it right"

It's hard to tell the story of Kilnsey and its show without giving centre stage to sheep. Sheep have been the lifeblood of Upper Wharfedale for more than 700 years, ever since the monks of Fountains Abbey reared vast flocks on the fells, making their fortune from trading wool across Europe. Until the 1960s annual sheep sales were still held under the shadow of the crag, with farmers bringing their sheep from miles around. This heritage is a core part of Kilnsey Show, and Chief Steward and local farmer Matt Mason tells the behind-the-scenes story of how today's show continues this venerable tradition.

I've done every show in my lifetime as my dad was a sheep steward back in the 1950s and '60s, so we always went. My first memory of the show is from the early 1960s when I was just seven or eight. It was a wet show, and I remember it like yesterday. We had parked our Vauxhall Victor over near the river, and because it was wet we were sat inside with the windscreen wipers on so we could watch the trotting, which in those days was a mixture of horses with riders, and horses with sulkies, which are like two-wheeled carts. A horse fell in front of us, and it was bleeding out of its nose, the jockey got back on and took it round again, but then it fell again and died.

True Dalesman: Local farmer Matt Mason has Kilnsey Show in his blood
© Stephen Garnett

A majestic setting for Kilnsey Show's sheep section © Dales Countryside Museum

As a kid you just remember stuff like that. Following on from that, because we'd had the windscreen wipers on, when we wanted to go home the car wouldn't start because the battery was flat. My brother got a load of his mates from the Young Farmers' Club to push it up the river banking to run it off, which didn't work, and so someone towed us off with a Land Rover. Now when you're seven that is fun, and you don't forget it!

My earliest memories of getting involved and helping at the show are through the Young Farmers' Club. Since the late 1960s the Young Farmers have helped to put the show up. I've been involved with the Young Farmers since the 1970s, and got involved with the show then.

By the 1980s I'd moved onto the sheep side of things, firstly stewarding sheep and then progressing to Chief Steward in 2000. The days prior to the show can be stressful and I lose a bit of sleep wondering if we've got things right, and if the weather is going to be okay; but on the show day I always enjoy it. In my lifetime the numbers of sheep have grown immensely, we are up to 600 entries in the sheep section now. To say once of a day there was just Swaledales, Dalesbreds and Mashams – we now have Mules, Suffolks, Texels, Lonks, Gritstones, Beltexs, Charollais and Blue Faced Leicesters showing. Fat lambs have come on as well, which we now call 'prime lambs' as it's more politically correct! The sheep pens used to be at the main gate where the luncheon tent is now, but when the show expanded in the mid 1980s they moved into another field at the north side, but even so we are already getting short of space again.

> *"The days prior to the show can be stressful and I lose a bit of sleep wondering if we've got things right, and if the weather is going to be okay; but on show day I always enjoy it"*

In the past there would have been just three judges; now we are into 'teens' of judges. Our judges come from all over the north of England, we've even had one or two out of Scotland, and we once had a judge from Cornwall. We also use judges out of Wharfedale, but we don't want to ask people if we think they're going to show their own sheep, as we don't want to put anybody off from showing. The main thing is we get the numbers and quality of sheep there, as we want to put on a show. You get good shows of sheep by picking the right judges as well. If people respect who you've chosen they'll think, "I'll bring some sheep because he's going to get it right." It's how the show originated: "I've got the best whatever" – "Well let's have a judge and sort it out."

On show day I don't see other parts of the show. We are there at 7.00am helping people pen up. My wife usually makes a big stack of bacon and egg sandwiches which we wind through. We start judging about 9.30am. Usually we finish before lunch, by 12.30pm at the latest, and then we have lunch with all the judges. We then come back for the Supreme Sheep in Show

competition at 2.00pm. When this finishes we'll have a look round a few cattle, watch the fell races, and waste a bit of money on the horses. There's a lot of Kilnsey Show that I've not seen for years, but I'm not bothered because I really enjoy what I do.

We've been having the inter-breed Supreme Sheep in Show competition for nearly twenty years now. It's a thing that's sort of grown into all shows over the last twenty or thirty years, although it's a strange thing to do, as how do you compare a Beltex with a Swaledale? They are totally different animals. How it works is that the winner of each individual breed section comes back for a final 'play off'. We judge it on a points system now, and all the different judges award points to each sheep, although they don't give any points to the one they originally judged, so they can't be biased to their own breed. The overall winner of this section wins the title of Supreme Sheep in Show. In 2015 the overall champion was a Charollais. The National Farmers' Union gave the cup that we have for this competition, and originally we had just one judge. Now picking a judge to do that was quite difficult. The late Tom Robinson senior from Slaidburn was a good one that I can remember, as he could judge anything from budgies to elephants, and he was capable to do it, and get it right.

"My earliest memories of getting involved and helping at the show are through the Young Farmers' Club, who've always helped to put the show up"

If you are judging any livestock, the thing to look for first is that it's got to be able to walk – it's got to have some stance and some presence and some carcass. Then you work into what you call the 'finer points' of the various breeds. With Swaledales, you want a good contrast with the white and the black on the nose; and the white should appear silver – if it's white, it's dull – it's got to be silver to contrast with the black. You want it in the right places as well: silver around the eyes and on the end of the nose, silver at the front of the legs and black behind, and a bit of silver on its back hocks. Any animal, whether it be a bull or anything, has got to have its conformation and a bit of style about it.

Serious debate as local farmers confer © Colin Priestley

For the generation that farmed before us, if you rented a hill farm in the Dales then your wool paid your rent. Now the wool's a complete by-product. From the very first show to the 1960s, wool was considered a very important part of any sheep, and the judges would put great emphasis on the type and quality of wool, and many a time there would have been classes for the sheep with the best fleece. Nowadays farmers don't care if there's a bit of black in the Swaledale wool or brown in the Mule wool, because it's such a low value relative to the rest of the sheep. I remember the farmer next door to us, when he clipped his tups he used to weigh the fleece, and when he took them to market he would say, "This clip is so many pounds of wool," and it was a selling point. Nobody would dream of doing that now.

The show should reflect the sheep industry in general, in particular the breeds that are relevant to the local area, and Kilnsey Show does that brilliantly. It accommodates the modern breeds and some imported breeds, but most importantly the traditional breeds of the north of England that are currently in decline. Showcasing our native local breeds at Kilnsey Show is one way of helping to maintain these breeds within the future of Dales' farming.

Matt Mason is a second generation sheep farmer from Appletreewick, who has been actively involved in helping at the show since he was a teenager in the 1960s. For the last fifteen years Matt has been the Chief Steward of the sheep section, during which time the section has grown enormously in both numbers and prestige. His son Ted won the Crag Race in 2011.

Kilnsey sheep sale in the 1950s © NYCC Unnetie digital collection BU08423

4

THE A-Z OF SHEEP

"The funny thing is that they won't judge it, but they'll still be on the showfield watching"

The huge sheep section today gives visitors the chance to admire the best of breeds, from Dalesbreds to Zwartbles. Local farmer and long-time sheep steward Richard Stockdale talks about the importance of continuing to showcase a wide range of sheep breeds to the general public at the show.

I've done the commentary for the inter-breed Supreme Sheep in Show for the last fifteen years or so. To me part of purpose of the show now is educating the general public. We had fourteen different breeds of sheep at this year's show, which meant that we had fourteen winners from the individual breed classes lined up for the competition. As stewards we know 'what's what' on our side of the fence, but a lot of people on the other side don't, which is why we started the commentary. I explain what breed each sheep is, give a bit of the history of the breed, the purpose of that breed, where it comes from, and the type of land it prefers.

When you get more general public at the show, and less people involved in farming, then you need to incorporate in your education bit, which is a great thing because generally people are becoming more and more distanced from what they eat.

'How've you been?': Old friends catch up over a pen of Masham sheep © Steve Haithwaite

Well turned out: Judges all hatted up in 1906 (Ben McKenzie)

Best in show: Charles Marwood with the Supreme Sheep in 2015 © Stephen Garnett

The popular breeds evolve as well – Suffolks are a traditional British breed of sheep, yet in 2015 for the second year we didn't have any at the show. Twenty years ago most of the sheep at the show would have been Suffolks – they would have been Suffolk lambs going to produce your prime lambs for your butchers' market and your butchers' shops. But things evolve, and so the Texels have taken over, the Beltex have taken over, and the Charollais, because they produce a carcass with the conformation and fat cover which is required for today's export market – which is where the larger percentage of the British lamb crop now goes. So the Suffolks have fallen by the wayside. We are going to replace the Suffolk class with an Any Other Pure Breed class. It's nearly come full circle in a way, as there is currently a resurgence of some of the older breeds. We are hoping for Shetlands, White Faced Woodlands and a few others at future shows.

The most prevalent breed at the moment is the Texel, and for the cross-bred ewe which prime lambs are bred from, it's the Mule. There are various sorts of Mule, but up here in Wharfedale we traditionally have the North of England Mule, which is the Swaledale ewe crossed with the Blue Faced Leicester ram. Mules make good mothers and they generally produce more than one good sized lamb. The North of England Mule goes on to be crossed to produce lambs for the supermarkets and export market. The North of England Mule is probably the Mule which is most common across right across the country, from Cornwall to the top of Scotland.

For the North of England Mule breeders, of any show they most want to win, it's Kilnsey. It's a little bit to do with timing, as it's just prior to the main autumn sheep sales and they are just starting to get their lambs ready for the sales. It's become noted that if you win at Kilnsey then you've got the best Mules. Because of this, people come to watch the Mules show from all over. Buses come from Wales and Scotland to watch. It's a selling point in the sale rings across the north of England if a particular animal is related to one that won at Kilnsey Show.

We've had quite a few judges turn down the job of judging on the Mules, as it's a bit unnerving due to the size and quality of the class. The funny thing is that they won't judge it, but they'll still be on the showfield watching.

Breeds started to evolve in the 1800s during the agricultural revolution, and it was a man called Robert Bakewell who pioneered it. If there was something a bit different from down that end of the valley, farmers would cross it with something a bit different from the next valley, and so a new breed would start to evolve. The aim behind it was to produce better quality or quantity of meat. Scientists do it now; farmers did it then.

Once of a day a hardy hill breed with horns was called a 'Scotch Ewe' or a 'Scottish Blackface'. Kendal Roughs, Dalesbred, Swaledales – they were all 'Scotch Ewes'. With regard to the Swaledale and Dalesbred, they've both gone their separate ways now and are getting more distinctly different as time goes by, but originally they were deemed to be one and the same breed. The Dalesbred has changed the least, and is the more recognisable sheep from its early origins, whereas the Swaledale has changed beyond recognition, the most predominant difference being that they have been bred to have a lot less wool.

In 1919 the Swaledale and Dalesbred Association separated. The Dalesbred Sheep Association held their first meeting as a separate breed society at Buckden around this date. The meetings for Swaledale sheep were held further north in Swaledale. Two of the notable founder members of the Swaledale Sheep Breeders Association from Upper Wharfedale were H.K. Demaine from Fold House, Barden and Frank Laycock from Bridge House, Burnsall, who was in fact my great great uncle.

In the future our aim at Kilnsey Show must be to put on a show of sheep that's not just of interest to farmers, which is very important, but to continue to educate the general public about breeds, their uses, and how they affect and protect our rural environment.

Richard Stockdale is a third generation cattle and sheep farmer. Richard became involved in the show in the late 1970s. A sheep steward for twenty five years, Richard conducts the Supreme Sheep in Show commentary, as well as running the Young Farmers' Sheep Judging Competition from his farm in Burnsall.

A showcase of rural life © Yorkshire Dales National Park Authority (YDNPA)

5

HEAVY HORSES

"There isn't so many of us left that's actually worked a horse"

Horses were once as ubiquitous in the Dales as cars today. Homes and businesses would all have kept horses as the means of transporting people and goods; for farming they were an indispensable part of the routine jobs of ploughing and haymaking. Horses have been integral to Kilnsey Show, ever since a challenge to determine the best local foal led to the first show in 1897. The horse classes flourished throughout the twentieth century until mechanisation within farming led to their demise in the mid-1950s. George Emmott describes these changes as well as his role in helping horses make a comeback to the show in 1977.

There isn't so many of us left that's actually worked a horse. We did everything with horses, right up until I was eighteen. When we were mowing, my father would get up and go and mow while me and my mother milked. He'd probably go out about 5.00am while it was still cold, so that the horse didn't get too hot and too tired. He'd just mow so much, then he'd fetch the horse back to be fed. We'd go out then, and what he'd mown the day before we'd turn it with a rake, by hand. Then after dinner we'd shake it out, by hand, and then all three of us would start and make some rows. We'd make two rows and then me and my father would start loading it. We'd get the horse out again, and I'd fork it up to him, and so together we would cart up all this hay.

Two's company: George Emmott and his young Shires in 1985 (Roger Ingham)

After a few years we got two horses, and what they called a 'side delivery' that turned the hay. So we had a horse that could mow, and a horse that could turn it and shake it. This machine could also row it up, which made a heck of a difference to the time it took, and how much you could get done. Everybody else had gone onto tractors by the mid 1950s, little Massey Fergusons and such like. My father was the last man in our district to have horses. We finally got a tractor in 1958 when I was eighteen, but my father never drove it.

When me and Gladys started going out, Gladys's dad had horses. So after we'd finished our hay time I went and helped him with his horses and mowing for a year or two. Me and Gladys married and got Currerwood Farm in 1962 when I was twenty three, and then Gladys's dad used to fetch his horse down to help me mow all the grass here. So we'd horses involved right up to that time.

It's funny what changes we've seen, from mowing with a horse, to picking it up with these foragers like they do now. Once we'd got going nicely at Currerwood, I bought a tractor and a mowing machine and a trailer, all on the same day at Kilnsey Show – that would have been about 1968. It was a David Brown 880 with a mounted mower on the back. It was a heck of an upgrade from a horse! A few years after this, a drum mower came out, it had four little drums, and by heck that could mow. We had a bigger tractor then, and we got this new drum mower on, and I set off and mowed the field in about two hours. The old landlord from the Manor next door came to the gate when I'd finished and said, "I've never ever seen 'owt like that in my life!" So what he'd think today when they come in and out in half an hour, all finished and wrapped up?

I also got friendly with a neighbour down the road from our farm that kept Shire horses. One day, in the early 1970s sometime, he asked me, "Were I doing 'owt special tomorrow?" I said, "No not really," so he said, "Well I've bought a horse, the other side of Ilkley." He was a right character of

Plaits, ribbons and a first prize rosette in 2015 © Stephen Garnett

a fellow. He said, "Don't come in your muck, come dressed up." So there we were coming out of the yard and turning to go to Ilkley, when he said, "Go the Keighley way." Anyway we finally get to where we're going, which was Winterton by the Humber Bridge! He'd bought this horse, which was being shown there that day. After it had won the Champion in Show, we set off back home with it. Next day he rung me up and said, "This mare's in service, can we take it tonight to West Houghton, wide of Manchester?" So off we went. Just as we got there, there was a man fetching a yearling out of a box, which I quite fancied the look of, so I asked him if he'd sell it to me. He said to me, "I've three mares to foal down in that field, and if one of them has a filly foal, I'll see you get it." So we went back three weeks later to pick up my neighbour's horse, and one of these mares had had three filly foals – so I bought the yearling filly I'd already seen, which was a grey one, and a black filly foal with four white legs. I'd always said as soon as I could afford a horse I'd have one you see. So that's how I started with my Shires.

So we fetched these foals home and we started showing them the following year. In Lancashire at that time there were shows every Saturday; starting with Barrowford, then Nelson, Burnley, Norden and Bamford, Bolton, Bury, Great Harwood, Great Ecclestone, Morecambe and Lancaster and Goosnargh and Longridge.

We used to go to all of those shows besides all the Yorkshire shows. In the beginning we used to do about twenty-three or twenty-four shows a year, all through the summer. It's a shame, but a lot of them have finished now. We had five local shows here starting with Gargrave, then Malham, Kilnsey, Keighley and Pateley – all within a little space of time.

At first when we started going to these shows, Kilnsey in particular, it was a lot of fun. It was all farmers that were showing in the 1970s and 1980s, and in those days after you'd finished showing, whether you'd won or lost there'd be a bit of 'craic'. We'd all go nearly straight into the beer tent when we'd finished, and there'd be a bit of banter about winning and who should have won, and then after ten minutes we'd all be friends again. It was before the breathalyser and such, and it was a lot of fun. As times gone on there's been some folk come into it who aren't farmers and they've tried to make showing Shires and heavy horses a business. They've spoilt it a bit because they've made it all about winning – they wouldn't go to a show to take second place.

Kilnsey Show actually started with horses in the late 1800s, and looking at a couple of early catalogues I can see they used to have some decent classes then. They wouldn't be show beasts like they are now, they were working horses and they would have gone back to work after the show. About fifteen to sixteen hands they were, which is what you call a 'vanner' and isn't so big – so they would most likely be Dales fell ponies. What they did have in those early days was more ridden types of heavy horses, which are actually coming back in at some shows. When they brought heavy horses back to Kilnsey Show in 1977, I helped to sort the classes out with Jim Caygill, and we've shown pretty much every year since. When Jim was President he said I'd been one of stalwarts of showing at the show.

Keeping Shires and heavy horses has changed over the years. Those older men, they would never have bought a horse with four white legs like I did. The saying was: "Four dark legs buy it, one white leg try it, two might be a chance, but if it's three leave it alone." They reckoned white legs were soft. If you've a horse with black legs, it'll have black hard feet, but these with white legs have white soft feet.

A winning trot in the heavy horse competition © Stephen Garnett

They judge early at Kilnsey, and at one time it used to take you ages to get there if you didn't set off before the traffic. So we always get up about 4.00am, wash the horses and away. This one year, 1986 it was, it was siling down and so I said, "We're not going." Gladys kept saying, "We have to go, Jeff Dibb's President and if we don't go he'll be upset." So we carried on washing them and set off. We were somewhere near Kilnsey when we saw one of our horse friends coming back, so I said "Look, he's not stopped" but Gladys said, "We're still going." So we got there and got all the horses ready, but it never stopped raining. The horse area was in the corner of the field near the beer tent then. Anyway they judged these horses, and I don't know whether we won or we didn't, but as soon as we got judged everyone was into their wagons and getting towed off the field. We were just coming across the field when the river burst its banks, and the water started coming over as fast as we were getting pulled off the field – it followed us off! We got back here, unloaded, and we were back in bed by 3.00pm. It was a fair day was that one.

Taste of history: The Tetley Shire horses pulling a dray in the late 1980s (Roger Ingham)

It's always been a full day out, has Kilnsey. We've won in many years, but one that stands out is the centenary year in 1997, when we won the Champion Horse in Show. That was one of best years we've had at Kilnsey.

I also used to go up to Kilnsey Show before we had horses. They closed all the pubs, so you couldn't go in any pubs on the way up to Kilnsey. We'd a mate then that ran the beer tent at the show. He had it down in that bottom corner by the river where they have it now, and he used to bring a tanker of beer and park it up against the wall, and connect it up to his beer pumps. All he did all day was take money out of the till and take it to the bank which had a stand on the showfield. Then after Kilnsey Show him and his wife and family used to go to Malta for a month with the profit. He was a character!

Nearly thirty years since, the Shire Horse Society asked me to become one of their accredited judges. I had to judge at six shows with another judge and then I'd to go in front of the society's men and give my reasons why I'd placed the horses as I had. I passed, but some of the other lads on the course couldn't give their reasons; you see I'd been in the Young Farmers so I was used to it. Another thing was that you'd to know how to do 'turn-outs' as well, which is when a horse is yoked up to a dray or a cart. There's all sorts of chains and such like to fit on, and every turn-out is different depending on what vehicle it is. Well these lads had no idea, but I'd been brought up with it. In the early years of Kilnsey Show there were classes for a horse and turn-out, whereas nowadays they just tend to have the Shires with a dray as an attraction.

I've judged all over the country since then, even at the Shire Horse of the Year Championship at the Horse of the Year Show in 2007. I've only judged at Kilnsey the once though, as usually I'm showing.

There's a saying that I think about when I'm judging: "Legs and feet and feather; tops may come, but bottoms never." It means, if the top's not so good on a horse, you can feed it and make it better; but if a horse's legs are no good to start with, then they never will be. These men that have come into showing, say that a horse should be like a beauty queen, but I don't just agree with that to a certain extent.

Horses have been integral to Kilnsey Show, ever since a challenge to determine the best local foal led to the first show in 1897

Judging the heavy horses © Stephen Garnett

It's always been said that you should be able to put a barrow between a horse's front legs and just the wheel between its back ones. But now they've bred them a lot narrower at the front and I don't like that, because when they were working they needed some width and some strength, but they've lost a lot of that. They've bred them for this fanciness and lost strength I think. When I judge, I judge on what I like, and some of these men that's just in the job don't like that sometimes; but I tell them why. They say we're breeding show horses now, not work horses – but the whole idea of showing horses is about maintaining the Shire horse breed.

When you're judging a Shire, they want a good foot; there's some breeding them flat, but they want to be round like a bell. Then the joints above the feather at the bottom of the leg, the ankle joints, they don't want to be bulky. You want a bend in the leg, they don't want to be too straight, and then a flat bone up to the hocks. They want a big bright head, a good neck, a good back, and a good back end on them. You want all that with some good movement; you've to walk them and trot them, and they've to be able to use their hocks and everything. There's a fair lot goes into it to judge them.

If you're showing you've to make them look right too, but this old mate of mine used to say, "We're judging horses – not ribbons!" But it's part of it all, on show morning you wash them down, then you put their ribbons in. We've always had our good friend Bob Whiteoak come and help us on show days. He wrote a letter to me forty years ago when he was a teenager asking to come and help, and he's been doing it ever since. In the early 1900s, the horses might have been decorated up a bit but not as much. They've been doing ribbons for over a hundred years though, as the Shire Horse Society has been going a hundred years, and they've old photos of horses with ribbons in.

Since we started keeping horses we will have bred a foal every year, and some years we've had as many as three. So we'll have bred nearly a hundred foals over the last forty years. We've shown all over, and won all over, and they've been really good happy days, and we've made a lot of friends. We've had a marvellous time with them, we really have. The pinnacle of showing was qualifying for the Shire Horse of Year Show twice in 1997 and 1999 with Hillmoor Deborah. We won Show Champion at Kilnsey three years on the trot with her as well.

Six of the best: Heavy horse men watch the action (George Emmott)

Winning that crystal rose bowl in 1997 at the centenary show was one of the best days that we've ever had – it's up there with Horse of the Year. There were a lot of folk who'd gone to win it that day, but we won it. They were bidding me a lot of money for it – I think they got up to £500 afterwards in the beer tent – they were all wanting it!

We've seen big changes in our lifetime, more than others would see; from horses working at farms and mills and such like, to horses virtually disappearing in the 1950s and 1960s when tractors and trucks became popular. I remember in the '50s, there were only seven senior stallions left in the whole country. It's important that we continue to protect these traditional breeds and show them off at shows like Kilnsey.

For over forty years George Emmott, a cattle and sheep farmer from Steeton, has been breeding Shire horses and showing them at events throughout the UK. George helped Kilnsey Show to re-establish the heavy horse section in 1977, and has shown at the event virtually every year since. George has qualified for the Horse of the Year Show twice, and was invited to judge the competition a few years later.

6

CATTLE

"My grandfather used to spend most of spring and summer trying to find the one cow that might be right for the day"

Cattle have always played an important role in the economy of the Dales. During the eighteenth century Scottish drovers gathered for huge cattle fairs on Malham Moor, and the valley once boasted over twenty dairies, so it's no surprise that butter and cheese were keenly fought classes at early Kilnsey Shows. Things started to change with the introduction of milk quotas in the 1970s, compounded by the devastating impact of Foot and Mouth in 2001 – now many farmers have left dairy farming altogether to breed beef cattle. The Carlisle family have a long tradition of farming cattle in the area, and here fourth generation farmer and Chief Steward John Carlisle discusses the changes.

My first memories of Kilnsey Show are as a very small boy, as we always used to show cattle at the show. Both my great grandad, my grandad and to a lesser extent my father were all tremendous show people – they enjoyed showing. We used to show cattle at Gargrave Show, but Kilnsey was always the one more local to us, and the one that we really wanted to do well in.

My churn for the seat: John Carlisle (standing) and brother Robin in 1962
(Kathleen Carlisle)

In those days we had dairy cattle, and we used to have a lot of cows and heifers that we reared on and then sold newly-calved in the local markets. So around August to September time we always had newly-calved beasts, and our ambition was to have one on the best form it could possibly be for Kilnsey Show. The blue ribbon event in those days was the 'newly-calved heifer' and 'newly-calved cow' classes and there was a great deal of competition to win. However there was a very short window for showing in such classes, as in the 'newly-calved' classes they generally tended to be shown within a week or ten days of calving, whereas now a cow shown 'in milk' can often have been calved two or three months, giving a longer period where that animal can be shown. In those days many of our cattle were going on to be sold to people in Lancashire, Cheshire or local dairy farms, and as the show was the showcase for that it was crucial to hit upon one being exactly right. My grandfather used to spend most of spring and summer trying to find the one cow that might be right for the day, hoping that it would calve at the right time.

Although a few noted showmen from outside the area came to Kilnsey, most of the people that showed in those days were local to the Dales, and there was tremendous competition – there were the Lamberts, Fosters, Dibbs, Listers, Carlisles, Caygills and a few others. Up until the 1970s or '80s it was more local oriented and a matter of local pride; wanting to show the community what fine animals you had – whereas now the competitions attract more regional exhibitors. We still have as many cattle at Kilnsey as we ever had, but now they come from further afield.

"Most of the people that showed at Kilnsey in those days were local to the Dales, and there was tremendous competition"

Around the 1980s farming in the Dales changed significantly. Traditionally there used to be large amounts of heifers reared on hill farms and small dairy farms, and they would be sold off at the auction marts to supplement their farm's income. But dairy farming became more intensive during the 1980s with larger herds and economies of scale, and so the dairy cows on smaller farms went by the wayside, particularly with the introduction of milk quotas.

Kilnsey-born show President William Roberts with an Ayrshire in the late 1950s

Class 26

No.   2

"*The setting at Kilnsey Show is absolutely brilliant and we have one of the finest shows of beef cattle anywhere in the north of England*"

The Supreme Dairy Champion 2015 © Stephen Garnett

Chewing the cud: A Shorthorn awaits the judges c1935

John Carlisle's grandfather Dawes with a dairy cow c1940 (Kathleen Carlisle)

In the very early days of the show Dairy Shorthorns were the breed you'd see, then in the 1960s and 1970s Friesians from Holland became the pre-eminent dairy breed. In the 1980s Holsteins came in from America and they started to be crossed with them; so the breed evolved into a Holstein Friesian, which is taller and gives a lot more milk for a longer period of time; at least ten months. This was a big change to dairy farming and meant that there were significantly less cattle summered in the Dales, since the old-fashioned dairy cow used to only milk for six or seven months, then it would be dry for about five months of the year, and turned out onto the pastures in the high Dales.

By the late 1980s most of the people who came to show cattle had pedigree herds, so pedigree cattle classes were introduced to sit alongside the local and commercial dairy cow classes. By that time many of the locals who used to show had given up; my family showed dairy cattle at Kilnsey for the last time in 1986. The main prizes came to be dominated by people who had large pedigree herds. A pedigree animal is one that is registered with the Breed Society, like the Kennel Club for dogs, so you can trace an animal's lineage back. Pedigree dairy cattle are kept to both produce milk and to further the genetic improvement of the breed, whereas commercial animals are mainly kept to produce milk for the supermarket shelves.

There were just a small amount of beef cattle at the show in the 1970s, but unlike today's beef cattle that are halter-trained, and that have been round several shows, some of the ones then tended to be more like wild animals that were rounded up and put into six foot high pens to be examined by the judge from a distance. They certainly weren't walked round the show ring as now.

By the 1990s the numbers of dairy cattle being shown had reduced even more, which was a trend seen all over, and so the show had become predominantly a show of beef cattle. So new classes were introduced, not just for commercial beef animals, but for the pedigrees too. We had Charolais, Simmentals, Limousins and one or two more. Depending on the numbers of people showing we've altered these classes over the years. The beef classes that we've got at present are Commercial Beef, Limousin, British Blue and Any Other Pure Native Breed, which includes Blondes and Parthenais. We've also got quite a few classes for Highland cattle, which have been established at the show for quite a long time and have been very popular with the general public.

We are trying to increase numbers in our Any Other Pure Native Breed class as well. There have been quite a few British native breeds put onto the hills of late because of various government schemes: there are Beef Shorthorns, Belted Galloways, Luing cattle, Angus's – although Angus's have always been in this area, as have Herefords; and we are trying to encourage more of those to come to the show at present. So the show continues to evolve.

For the casual observer looking at the show, they would probably think that Kilnsey Show is just the same as ever it was, with the cattle section in the same place and so on. But if you look through the catalogues for the last thirty or forty years, you will see that it has been evolving all the time, with new livestock classes and new events constantly being added.

Most of the people that show today tend to come from a wider area and have a 'show team' of cattle which will go round a large amount of shows during the summer months. They will go to some of the local shows and also much further afield, up into Cumbria and Northumberland. One of our local show people however, John Stephenson at Bordley, is really pre-eminent in his field, rearing excellent British Blue cattle and commercial beef cattle. As well as being successful at Kilnsey, he is also extremely successful at a regional level as he has some of the best cattle in the north of England.

Another thing that's changed is the bureaucracy, as the people who tend to show now need a government approved isolation unit for showing, and they will bring their animals in and out of that for the shows. Without the licence and the isolation unit, it would mean that by just showing at one show you would be unable to trade cattle or sheep for the next six days, which is a restriction that came into force after the Foot and Mouth crisis in 2001. Kilnsey Show falls not only at a busy time for showing but also at a busy time for trading livestock. We had one family that we tried to persuade to come to Kilnsey in recent years who had some dairy cattle, but they decided to take them to Gargrave and Malham shows first which then meant that they couldn't do any trade for two whole weeks. If they'd come to Kilnsey Show as well that would have been another week where they wouldn't have been able to go and sell at the local livestock auction.

Blonde ambition: Kate McNeill and her prize-winning Blonde Aquitaine in 2015
© Stephen Garnett

We always encourage locals to exhibit at the show, but it is difficult to try and compete with people that show cattle week in and week out. If you were going to bring a few animals to Kilnsey, in addition to the issues surrounding the movement of livestock, it would take weeks and months of halter training to get them just exactly right to cope with the show ring. It's testament to Kilnsey's profile and prestige that despite all the work involved in showing cattle we still get in the region of one hundred cattle shown by upwards of thirty farmers year on year.

Kilnsey is on the surface a traditional show. Today the show has the Angling demonstration and marquee, Farmers' Market, children's area and Cookery Theatre. Yet none of these were there twenty years ago, so we've continually had to adapt and change, whilst keeping the show day seeming outwardly much the same.

Our focus is as a conventional rural event, and unlike some shows we have kept on the route of it being mainly a traditional Dales show with livestock. We want it to be a show where serious farmers can come and look at extremely good cattle. The setting is absolutely brilliant; the backdrop of the crag really does help. We have one of the finest shows of beef cattle anywhere in the north of England at present, the sheep show is exceptional too, and although many shows have fell races, they don't have a spectacular fell race like Kilnsey; it's short, it's very very steep – it really is a highlight. Kilnsey Show really is one of the most picturesque and unique shows in the whole country.

John Carlisle is the fourth generation of his family to farm sheep and cattle at Coxon's Farm in Cracoe. John's family have been at Cracoe since 1894, and his great grandfather Leonard won first prize for his bullocks at the second Kilnsey Show in 1898. John has been actively involved in the show since he was a child, has shown both cattle and sheep, and for the last ten years has held the position of Chief Cattle Steward.

Champions: Crag Race legend Bill Teasdale with a prize-winning cow in 1955 (Ingham)

Class 32 No. 1

7

HORSE SPORTS

"They were called 'flapping' meetings in them days and Kilnsey was the biggest one"

Kilnsey Show used to have a full programme of horse sports, with flat racing, pony hurdles and showjumping; today only the Hunter classes and harness racing remain. Changes to regulations made it untenable for the show to continue offering all the horse sports, however the legacy of these events lives on as world class jockeys and riders such as Brian Fletcher, three times Grand National winner, and Harvey Smith, celebrated international showjumper, honed their early talents on Kilnsey's turf. Harvey Smith recalls his first introduction to Kilnsey Show.

When I was a lad, for my summer holidays I used to go up to Tennant Gill Farm on Malham Moor, which Mason Hodgson owned. He had one fell pony which he did shepherding with, called Lassie, and who he rode at all the local gallops. The first time I ever went to Kilnsey Show was in 1949, when I was given the privilege of riding Lassie in a pony hurdle race; I was just twelve or thirteen – and so it all progressed on from there. When I was at Kilnsey Show I remember watching the horses, the trotters, and the gallopers. I remember Dennis Smith who was a leading flat race trainer later on in life; he had a great big grey horse called Master Richard, and he used to race that at Kilnsey.

Leaping into the spotlight: Future Grand National winning trainer Sue Smith on Silver Mount in 1988 (Roger Ingham)

In them days just after the war, all the shows around held flapping meetings where they had the gallopers, the trotters, and the show combined. At Kilnsey they had the pony races, and then the 13.2 hands, the 14.2 hands and then the open racing. The horses were used to the ring: they put pegs in and the horses went round the pegs. They were called 'flapping' meetings in them days and Kilnsey was the biggest one.

After that I got into showjumping and so I was away on the circuit doing that. George Thackery, who had horses with me, got the showjumping going at Kilnsey Show, which is when I went back to Kilnsey. George also did the Great Yorkshire Show and he used to build show jumps at Otley and all the shows round here. When I started jumping there was an open class and a novice class, and they used to put on a 'consolation' which was a race for those that hadn't qualified for the final.

"The old version of the show used to be all country sports and country goings on – the galloping, the pony racing, the showjumping, the hunters. It was all that which made Kilnsey Show"

The showjumping classes that Kilnsey put on weren't as important as the ones at the horse shows, so we'd take the young horses, school them there, and get them ready for the bigger scene. It was same all over Yorkshire with the local shows; they were the training ground. We used to win regular away.

They used to get quite a good gathering at one time, thirty or thirty five years ago, when they were attracting better horses, but then the show downgraded the horse side of things and made it more localised somehow, instead of pulling in the better ones. The old version of the show used to be where it was all country sports and country goings on – the galloping, the pony racing, the showjumping, the hunters. It was all that, that made Kilnsey Show.

All clear: A clear round on a clear day © Stephen Garnett

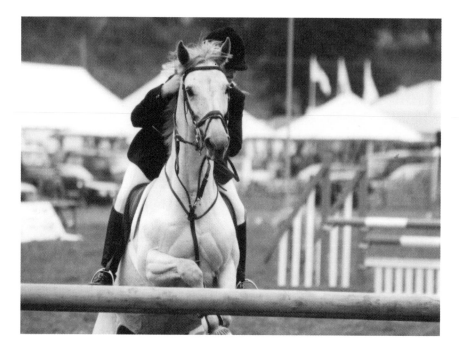

Kilnsey wasn't like going to a horse show – it was a day out. When the show-jumping had finished, there was the sports and the fell race and everything. If you want a unique day out go to Kilnsey Show. I still go there, any time I get chance to go, I still go. We land in about 2.30pm, when the sport is coming on and the trotting's coming on, and have a wander around. We spend a lot of time up the Dales, because we love the Dales, but Kilnsey Show is the one.

Harvey Smith is a former top British show jumping champion, who competed in the Nations Cup over a hundred times, as well as representing Britain in two Olympic Games. Harvey competed on and off for forty years at Kilnsey Show, initially in the pony hurdles and later in the Open Show Jumping. Since the 1990s Harvey and his wife Sue have trained racehorses including Aurora's Encore, the winner of the Grand National in 2013.

Top: **Showjumping at Kilnsey;** Right: **Joy Robson in the pony gallops in 1949**

"*When we were coming up to the post the cheers were just amazing, as I won!*"

"One Christmas morning when I was eight years old I came downstairs to find a pony in the kitchen! This was my first horse and she was a Shetland pony called Silver. She was very small but she did give me confidence, and so the following year my grandad gave me another pony, Blossom, who we got started in the racing.

I first attended Kilnsey Show in 1949 when I was twelve years old. Galloping was on the schedule along with the trotting then. My pony at that time was thirteen hands and called Mighty Fine. My pony was the smallest in the race – the One Mile Pony Gallop. When we were coming up to the post the cheers were just amazing, as I won! That was my first Kilnsey Show, and I have hardly ever missed going since. The last big win we had at Kilnsey was in 2005 with Tom's the Man in the Open Handicap Harness Race. Harness racing used to happen all over once of a day, but now Kilnsey Show is the only one keeping it going in the Yorkshire Dales which I applaud, as it is such a thrilling sport to watch…"

Joy Robson is a horse breeder and trainer from County Durham.

8

HARNESS RACING

"This is chariot racing – it's Ben Hur!"

The spectacle and excitement of trotting, now termed harness racing, has been a deep-rooted Dales passion since the mid eighteenth century. Trotting at Kilnsey actually pre-dates the show, being an advertised feature of the old Kilnsey Feast as far back as 1884, and probably even earlier. Originally what is now termed a 'sulky' would have just been a farmer's cart or trap, and the horses were more likely to have been fell ponies than any particular racing breed. Trotting returned to the show schedule in 1927 and has remained a highlight ever since, due to the spectacle of the sharp track and the top horses and drivers it attracts. Leading harness racing commentator Peter Deighton uncovers this traditional Yorkshire Dales sport.

My first introduction to harness racing was in 1954 at Hipswell, Hollyhill and Hudswell, which was a grass track meeting near Richmond. I'd gone to watch some motorbike racing there and unexpectedly some harness racing came on afterwards, which rather whetted my appetite – so I started going to harness race meetings a lot after that.

In those days harness racing was largely based in the Dales, as that's what it used to be – the sport of the Dales people. Gargrave Show used to hold races, Clitheroe used to hold them, Cross Hills did, also Hellifield held a meeting a little before my time.

In the thick of the action: Marjorie Parrington at Kilnsey in the 1980s (Roger Ingham)

Betting on a grand day out: The bookmakers ('Big Jim' Hepburn, left) in 1982 (Ingham)

The premier meetings in those days were the bank holiday Whitsuntide meetings at Appleby, and they also had a big trotting meeting in June to coincide with the Appleby Horse Fair. There was a very popular meeting at Hawes, and also Bainbridge, Grinton in Swaledale and Low Row in Swaledale. I used to go to all these meetings, purely as a spectator.

Then in 1972 I went to a grass track meeting at Kilburn, famous for the White Horse and Robert Thompson the wood carver. There I was at Kilburn, and the horses were going round the track and there was nothing happening, no information or anything. In the end I went down to the centre of the track and said, "Have you no commentator?" and they said "No we haven't." I'd never commentated in my life, but I took up the mike, and it all fell into place! I quickly became the official Eden Valley Trotting Association commentator, as it was called then, commentating at all the grass track events across the north of England. I had a commentating colleague in the early days, a gentleman called Maurice Hartley, but he passed away which left me as the only commentator in the area, and it was this that brought me to Kilnsey Show, which I first attended and commentated at in 1974.

In the 1800s and the early 1900s the trotting races across the Dales, in particular at shows like Kilnsey, would have been mainly between local farmers who would all have kept horses back then – there wasn't any formal racing as such. It wouldn't have been racing with any pure-bred type of horses that had any speed either, just 'Jack has a horse' and 'Bill has a horse', and so they would get together to have a race. These early trotting races would have been a type of 'flapping meeting', which means there wouldn't have been any rigid rules governing the sport, like we have today.

It has always been referred to as 'trotting', but the horses are actually 'pacers' in Great Britain. This is why at Kilnsey Show I say to the crowd, "Welcome to the trotting; but this isn't trotting it's harness racing!" Trotting is an umbrella term, but proper trotting is free legged, which is few and far between in this country, although more common in Europe, particularly in France and Malta. Pacing is when the horses have the hopples on, which are a type of harness, and which keep their legs in a trotting gait. The hopples are adjustable to a horse's particular gait or length of stride, and prevent it from breaking into a gallop. What is interesting though is that when the horses are born – the Standardbred that is, which is the breed of horse used for trotting and pacing – the foals pace automatically, as it's a natural gait to them. The hopples simply keep them in that gait, so that when they strike forward they can't go too far.

Icing on the cake: Vincent Wareing winning on My Birthday in 1976 (Roger Ingham)

The spectacle and excitement of harness racing has been a deep-rooted Dales passion since the mid eighteenth century – today Kilnsey Show helps to keep it alive

Harness Racing pulling in the crowds in the late 1980s (Roger Ingham)

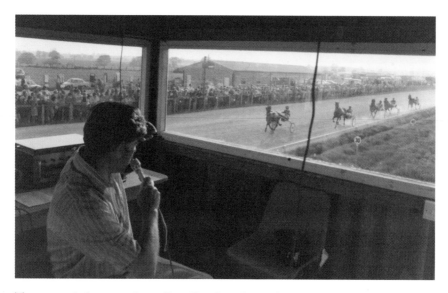

The man with the microphone: Peter Deighton brings home another harness race

The prestige meeting in harness racing is the famous Musselburgh Pace at Edinburgh, on the Musselburgh Racecourse. There's a charter dating back to the 1890s which allows harness racing to take place there once a year, and so it's our biggest festival. I started commentating at Musselburgh in 1975 and I worked for them for twenty seven years. It is a fantastic venue with a proper race track and a very big crowd. I was also the first man to commentate at Wolverhampton, which is the all-weather track where they have thoroughbred racing now, although they still have the odd harness race there. I also worked at Doncaster Racecourse when some French trotters came over, and we had a big pace there. In France their thoroughbred racing is integrated with trotting, so they'll have a trotting race and then they might have four thoroughbred races, and then finish with a trotting race. The British Harness Racing Club had envisaged and hoped for that to happen over here, which would have helped to raise the profile of harness racing nationally, but unfortunately the Jockey Club don't seem to want to work with us to any great extent. The result is that harness racing has just never quite taken off in this country. That's the beauty of Kilnsey Show though; the fact that we can have upwards of ten thousand people there, and probably fifty percent have never seen harness racing or know anything about it. Consequently the crowd are thrilled by it all, and are very appreciative, which is the thing I love.

I always break down the sport for the crowds at Kilnsey; I talk about the breed of the horse, and explain that this is 'trotting' but these are 'pacers'. I explain about the hopples, tell them that the jockey's sat in a sulky, or the driver – we don't refer to them as a jockey – is sat in the sulky, which is a lightweight cart with two wheels. These days drivers also wear a skull cap and back protection. I also point out that the wheels of the sulky are like bike wheels. Going back to the 1970s, they actually had open spokes and horses could get their feet caught, so the British Harness Racing Club addressed that and now we have plastic discs on the sulky wheels. Astonishing really that forty years ago they would have raced wearing flat caps, and with open sulky wheels! But thankfully we never had any serious accidents at Kilnsey Show.

Since 1969 the trotting world has been controlled by the British Harness Racing Club. Everybody who works for them and is involved in harness racing – such as the horse owners, the trainers and the drivers – is licensed, and every horse that races has to have a chip in its neck which is scanned after every race. Horses are dope tested too, as and when required, similar to the way the Jockey Club operates.

Another rule applies to the horses themselves, as they've got to qualify to be able to race. Any horse in the country has got to pace or trot a mile within a specific time, before it can race at a racetrack or a show. On the hard tracks at York a horse has to pace a mile in approximately 2 minutes 15 seconds, although on grass a slower time is acceptable, which is somewhere in the region of 2 minutes 22 seconds. Once a horse has done that time and qualified it is then certified to race in what we call 'maiden races', which are over the distance of one mile. If they win a 'maiden race' they go into a 'novice company', and from there they can progress into the open handicaps. Today there is a lot of discussion about handicapping horses, but the way we handicap them at present is on a 'monies won' system. When a horse has won the total of £700, it will move from 'go' to one second, which is the equivalent of a ten yard pull. If its winnings have amounted to £1400 it would have a two second handicap, and a twenty yard pull, and so on. Kilnsey Show usually has two novice races and then three to four open handicaps followed by the final, which is ideal for the show. It is such a thrilling sport, and at Kilnsey with its sharp track it is quite a spectacle.

Mud and glory: Pam Haythornthwaite after winning the harness racing final in 1998
(Roger Ingham)

We used to get some of the top horses at Kilnsey, but over the last fifteen years or so, as horses have become faster, the owners have tended not to send their 'speed merchants' to race at Kilnsey, because of the tight corners on the track.

Kilnsey still gets the top drivers though, and I always make sure the crowd knows this – I'll say, "He's a professional driver this man, because he won at Musselburgh." We get Mick Lord, Alan Haythornthwaite, Andrew Cairns and 'Rocker' Laidler, as well as the top women drivers, such as Pam Haythornthwaite, Vicki Gill and Clare Bousefield, which is just fantastic for the show crowd.

In the 1970s, a horse called Turn of the Tide won the Musselburgh Pace, which is the 'Derby' of harness racing. Not only that, Turn of the Tide won Musselburgh at three years old, which was the first time any three year old had done so. Then the following year it raced and won at Kilnsey. So we had a top horse winning the blue ribbon of harness racing at Musselburgh, and then racing at Kilnsey Show.

Up until the 1980s no horse had paced the mile in two minutes. Horses were winning in two minutes and one second at York, but the magic 'two-minute mile' never came. Eventually however, a horse called Missing Link owned by Alan Tattersall from Hellifield, broke the two-minute barrier, pacing a mile in 1.59.09 on August 29th 1987. Two years prior to that it had raced and won a heat at Kilnsey Show, going on to come second in the final. So that horse, the first horse to break the two-minute mile, raced at Kilnsey Show.

The fact that I've been commentating for forty years means I don't really need to do too much preparation before show day. Each jockey has his own colours – Mick Lord drives in a light blue, Alan Haythornthwaite drives in red and yellow, and so on. So consequently there might be four horses in a race, but three are familiar to me, so I've only got to research one of them. I always look at their past month's racing and jot down key wins and performance to try and give the public in the crowd some relevant information.

The pick-up truck that people might recall seeing racing round the ring before a race starts is actually the 'mobile start', which is something they do at all the national race meetings. How it works is that the truck has a boom on which takes four horses maximum for the mobile start. After their warm up I say, "This field's now in motion", and then the truck will come onto the track and gradually build up speed, as it does so the horses and their drivers will all take up their positions – they might be on 'go', or trailing ten yards, or whatever. The man on the back of the truck checks their distances and will let them know if they aren't correct. As they pass the starting post the truck pulls away and off the track. A mile and quarter at Kilnsey is four laps of the track, and a mile for the maiden and novice races is three laps.

One thing I've always found frustrating at many race meetings is the time keeping, so it's important to me at Kilnsey Show, particularly with the show crowd of several thousand, not to have people hanging about. I keep the crowd informed if there is a delay, but my aim is to race on time, as per the race card. We start racing around four thirty and finish around seven to seven thirty, and the general public who haven't come specifically for the harness racing, tend to start drifting away after the second race. That's another great thing about the harness racing as it helps to filter off the crowd, and prevent ten thousand people from trying to leave the showground all at once.

> *"The intimacy and friendliness of it is what makes Kilnsey Show so special. I love the reaction I get from the crowd – everyone is clapping like mad, which is something you just don't get at a normal race meeting"*

The intimacy and friendliness of it is what makes Kilnsey Show so special. I love the reaction I get from the crowd, which is why I like to explain everything to them and get them involved. They've come for that day out, and suddenly they're thinking, "This is chariot racing – it's Ben Hur!" And everyone is clapping like mad, which is something you just don't get at a normal race meeting. I truly enjoy Kilnsey and I want to promote it, as I have done for forty years, and I hope it goes on for another four hundred years!

Peter Deighton has been a commentator for the British Harness Racing Club and the Eden Valley Harness Racing Association for over forty years, and his distinctive tones have been ringing out across the showground at Kilnsey since 1974. Now in his seventies Peter still commentates regularly at race meetings throughout Yorkshire and Derbyshire.

The grand finale: Harness racing brings Kilnsey Show to a fitting close each year
(Roger Ingham)

Class No. 9

Class B3 No. 4

9

TRADITION AND CHANGE

"When the announcement came that a car was under water, it was time to abandon the show..."

The 1980s and 1990s were a boom time for Kilnsey Show, with television coverage helping to attract crowds of almost 20,000 people. Yet despite its popularity, it was important that it retained the ethos of a traditional agricultural show, a place to meet up with family and friends. Local farmer Jim Caygill was Chairman of the show for almost two decades, and during that time he was charged with maintaining traditions and ensuring the event continued to grow and evolve. Heavy horses, a mainstay of early shows, were reintroduced after an absence of several decades, along with new attractions in the show ring. As Jim reveals, he faced everything from Hurricane Charley to the show's centenary celebrations.

My family have been involved with Kilnsey Show for as long as anyone can remember. My grandfather was born in 1858 and my father in 1903, and my father was taken as a boy in the early 1900s, which means he must have been to one of the earliest Kilnsey Shows. My family were in Lancashire then, and they used the show to meet up with their relatives who farmed in the Dales. It was a family friendly show, so it was a case of "I'll see you next year", that being the only means of contact they had from one year to the next. This, of course, is what the show was built around – meeting family and meeting friends.

In it for the long haul: Former show President and long-running Chairman Jim Caygill

My earliest memories of the show would be from the 1940s: I can vividly remember toffee apples and mud. To me as a young boy the show was massive, and the crowds were simply enormous, as we weren't used to those numbers of people and that type of event. I also remember seeing the racing in the ring and the fell race; I was amazed and enthralled by it all. I thought, "I'd like to run up there", which my son did, and now my grandsons are going to run the Crag Race.

It was ironic when I came to the Dales forty eight years ago that I actually became involved in the show, after visiting it for so many years. I was Chief Horse Steward from 1978 and then Vice Chairman in 1980 when Harry Plews was Chairman. When Harry unfortunately became ill he said "I'll stand down Jim", but I said, "You're Chairman and that's how you will remain." I took over the role in 1981, but officially didn't become Chairman until 1982. I continued as Chairman until 1998 and then I was invited to be show President for two years, which I was delighted to accept.

My first year helping at the show was in 1978, a memorable year in which we were literally engulfed with people: eighteen or nineteen thousand came, and so everything failed in terms of catering and facilities that year. As Vice Chairman and subsequently as Chairman I wanted to make sure that didn't happen again! So we put in some new trackways in the early 1980s. We put a hard track off the main road into the main entrance to the showfield, and another in off Conistone Bridge at the other end of the showfield. They've been a saviour and the foundation of keeping the show going, otherwise there would have been many years when it wouldn't have happened.

This is how it evolved in the 1980s – the show grew rapidly and the infrastructure grew as well. After a while cattle became more valuable, so I introduced covered accommodation for them, which was very well received by the exhibitors as it wasn't too common at the time. This led to us having 160 entries in the dairy and beef cattle classes. We introduced the Highland Cattle, and there would be twenty or thirty of them. We also introduced the Piedmontese Cattle as an attraction, as the beef from the Piedmontese is very low in cholesterol. We also had ostriches one year as an attraction, and then birds of prey and gundog displays, which we've continued to have to this day.

We were always looking for new things with the sheep classes too – new breeds, extra breeds. Consequently that grew to be one of largest sheep sections of any show. It became the show to win for Mules – and it still is.

We were constantly looking for new events that would interest people and that were very much connected with the Dales. Of course there's nothing more connected with the Dales than shepherd's crooks and walking sticks, so we thought it would be an excellent idea to introduce these classes, which we did in 1980. They've been a boon in actual fact, as people find them incredibly interesting, and so they've gone on ever since. There's always been those who've made crooks, and would spend their evenings creating them with sheep's horns and that sort of thing. Once of a day it would have been another way for shepherds and farmers to earn something extra. The sticks we get these days are works of art. Kilnsey is well known for having these classes and they are well supported.

Carved to perfection: Hand-carved crooks and sticks being inspected by Bob Cannon
© Stephen Garnett

The heavy horses had faded and gone out of existence at the show with tractors taking over in the 1940s and '50s. But I knew that horses were how the show had started in 1897, with a challenge to determine who had the best foal from the travelling stallion! So I was quite resolved that we should reintroduce them. We introduced classes for the heavy horses and the Dales ponies, a smaller horse suitable for the Dales terrain. They came back in numbers and still continue. These classes start at 9.00am in the morning and go on until lunchtime in part of the show ring, which means we have some attractions in the main ring from early morning. We also at one time had the Show Jumping, then we introduced the Hunters as an extra attraction, which has also grown to become a very important part of the show.

We had to move the horses from one side of the field to the other after the happenings of 1978 with the 18,000 people attending. Originally all the equine attractions were held near the cattle, but that became inappropriate with the numbers we were getting, which is why we put the hard track in from Conistone Bridge, so all the heavy lorries and horse transportation could come along that road, keeping the horses separate.

After that year with the huge numbers we piped water to the field and introduced flushing toilets, which was definitely a big step forward. We also managed to secure the purchase of a ninety nine year lease on the showfield from the Roberts family who own the field and surrounding land. I felt that was a great thing to know that Kilnsey Show will always remain. Kilnsey Show wouldn't be Kilnsey Show if it wasn't in that field, with the back drop of the crag – but now that's all sorted for many years to come.

Then we come rather unfortunately to Hurricane Charley in 1986. I'd got up at 5.00am and it was raining and raining and raining. I went up to the showfield and I was monitoring the river; I was putting a piece of wood a foot above the river on the banking, and then monitoring how long that stayed put. I went through four pieces of wood, which meant it had risen between three and four feet in about five hours. I remember the tannoy messages, "Will the owner of 'such and such' a car return to their vehicle as the water is rising." Then the last call was, "The car is now under water." I'll never forget when that last announcement came, I just thought, "It's time to abandon," which we did at 12.30pm.

Heavy going: A muddy year brings out the bulldog spirit © Stephen Garnett

Hurricane Charley was a truly horrendous day, although it was credit to everyone concerned, all the stewards and everyone, that we completed the judging. We appreciated those who brought their animals and exhibits, and all the stewards who worked so hard to keep it going. There was a relaxed atmosphere after it was cancelled, and a few of them ran the fell race to make sure it was run, just for fun of course. That day was the greatest challenge in terms of completing the show.

My family showed sheep and cattle throughout the 1980s during my tenure as Chairman. Over the years we won many prizes, but my goodness the competition was strong! In those days, show day was like 'the morning after the night before'; it took a day or two to get over it. It built up to a crescendo, but because I wanted things to go right, and because I was fairly pernickety in that respect, that was what created the pressure. Showing during those years as Chairman meant life was hectic and it was quite a commitment for the family. We used to trailer the sheep and lorry the cattle.

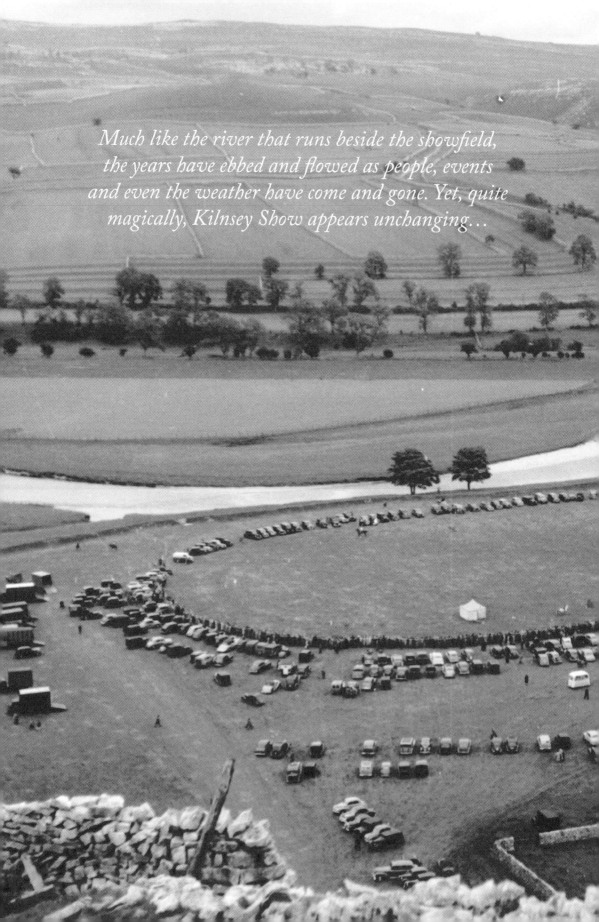

*Much like the river that runs beside the showfield,
the years have ebbed and flowed as people, events
and even the weather have come and gone. Yet, quite
magically, Kilnsey Show appears unchanging…*

Kilnsey showfield in the early 1950s © NYCC Unnetie digital collection BU08443

Good retrieve: A working gundog display in the show ring © Stephen Garnett

We were showing in most classes with two or three in each. We probably took twelve to fourteen cattle and maybe half a dozen sheep. So we'd be up at 4.00am to get the routine jobs done, and then I always wanted the lorry on the field by 8.00am so we had time to prepare the animals to show them at their best. There was just one tap so everyone would be queuing up with their buckets to get this water – it was a pantomime of the highest order!

There was such strong competition as there were so many farms up the Dales in those days. I can recall a story I was told, although I can't mention any names, but this man had this particular beast that looked like it could win the show. Mysteriously a calf got out the night before the show and suckled this cow – just one side, which of course rendered it not fit to show!

The show really did mushroom from the 1980s to 2000 in terms of its facilities and infrastructure. I coined the phrase that Kilnsey "is a show that never changes, but never stops changing". People know of Kilnsey Show as a traditional Dales show, but we've always been moving on, with classes and with entertainment. We had the mail coach that used to go from York to London one year, and when I was President in 1999 we had Desert Orchid there, the famous Cheltenham Gold Cup winner. I always attempted to have something of interest relative to the show and to the history of the show.

I finally stepped down from being Chairman in 1998, after the centenary show. That was a show to remember. The great thing about the centenary show was the dinner, which was held on the Sunday prior to the show. We thought if we got 200 there we would have a good night, but in the end we had 600 there, with 120 on the waiting list. We had Robin Dunlop who was former President of the Royal Highland Show and a very good speaker. We also had Peter Maloney, who had won Speaker of the Year four times in this country. He was absolutely mind boggling, as he held the audience on the edge of their seats for the whole time with his stories and anecdotes. As a finale we had the '60s pop group The Bachelors. People said they'd never ever had a night like it in the dale.

As Chairman, the work goes on all year round, on the telephone, encouraging people to enter in the cattle, horse and sheep sections. Every week I would allocate nights to Kilnsey, because that was the only way to improve it, to pick up ideas, and to move forward with what we were doing. I went to other shows for networking, for viewing and so on. All that was for the success of the show. I was always looking for something new to keep it interesting within the constraints that we worked within. We are not a fair; we are a show. So that's why we work very hard to ensure we have livestock, the different breeds, always ensuring it is the show to win. It was a constant challenge to improve the show year on year, making it something that people would want to visit.

> *"We are not a fair; we are a show, so we work very hard to ensure we have livestock, the different breeds, always ensuring it is the show to win. It's a constant challenge to improve year on year, creating something that people want to visit"*

My proud moments are looking back at how Kilnsey Show built up over those years. I knew what I wanted to improve – such as the attractions, the facilities, the penning. Nowadays I'm just involved in organising the harness racing. I liaise with the harness racing people and go to the Eden Valley meetings. It's all about networking, keeping contact, making contact and understanding people.

Kilnsey Show finishes on a high with the Crag Race and the harness racing – where other shows end in the afternoon, Kilnsey works up to a finale. And let's not forget that we have two of the best commentators in Roger Ingham and Peter Deighton, who bring the day to a crescendo. There are many attractions in the show, but then we move onto the foot racing which Roger is a past master at, and then onto the harness racing with Peter. A lot of people come just for the harness racing later in the day, so after the fell races the crowds filter off gently and slowly which avoids any bottle necks, and you are just left with people interested in the harness racing. That's why it is Kilnsey Show *and* Sports.

The boom years for the show were between 1980 and 2000 after some initial television coverage, however things are more challenging these days, as there are fewer farmers. There's also the time factor to consider as well – with three times as many animals to farm and less staff, what comes first? So you've got to look at things in that realistic way, and you've got to be aware of the changing scene. In the UK there used to be about 20,000 milk producers, now there's about 8,000. And of course there's so many other attractions, and people are more mobile nowadays. Once it wasn't easy to travel and so people only travelled to certain places, but now the world is your oyster. So we've got to be aware of that and try and hopefully stay one step ahead.

My overall achievement was seeing the show grow under my leadership. Change wasn't on a whim and fancy – it was for the short term and the long term. However the real secret to the success of the show is the people who give their time and commitment to it. There are so many who do something in some small or large way that makes the show tick; people that you never see, who steward and work in other ways to keep things moving.

Jim Caygill, a retired sheep and cattle farmer from Rylstone, has been Kilnsey Show's longest standing Chairman to date, at the helm during the show's boom years throughout the 1980s and 1990s. Jim still plays an active part in the show as a member of the Management Committee and as Chief Steward of the harness racing.

Show day specials: Community police share a moment with an alpaca © Stephen Garnett

10

DRYSTONE WALLING

"Wallers are a special breed – their working lives have changed very little since drystone walls were first built"

For centuries drystone walls have helped to punctuate the pastures, moorlands and rugged fells of Upper Wharfedale, becoming a much-loved part of the Dales landscape. Many of the walls around Kilnsey have been standing more than two hundred years, crafted with stones hewn from craggy outcrops and from beneath the soils. The show has been promoting these distinctive walls since 1939. Here local farmer and Chief Steward of the Dry Stone Walling Chris Nelson reveals the mastery of this traditional Dales craft.

Over the years farming has evolved tremendously: tractors have replaced horses, electricity's come, and quad bikes have replaced walking – but building drystone walls has remained virtually the same. The only difference is that drystone wallers now have a vehicle to get to their walling, and a pair of gloves to wear when they're working. They're out in nearly all weathers and I have a great respect and admiration for anyone who earns a living from walling. It's a tremendous job. I am very interested in walling and I like walling, but I just do it when the weather's fine; I can pick my day, and if I think it's a bit wet or a bit cold I find something else to do. Whereas the professional wallers have to be working whenever they can be, whatever the weather.

Master builder: Eight-time winner David Caton on form in the late 1980s (Ingham)

One upon two, two upon one: Ronnie Egglestone (right) winning in 1955 (Philip Dolphin)

The purpose of the competition at Kilnsey Show is to promote drystone walling. We are in an area of drystone walls and it's very appropriate that it should be on the schedule at Kilnsey, because there's examples of walls all around. Walls are not only used for splitting fields and enclosing animals, they are also important as a shelter for animals in bad weather.

Stone for the walls will have come out of quarries a bit, a lot will have been clearance stones which were collected when they originally cleared the meadows, and out on the tops where there's very little soil they would have pickaxed them out of the ground or off outcrops of rock. In limestone areas there's often a plentiful supply of stone just a few inches below the surface.

Kilnsey is considered a difficult competition to compete in because of the nature of the stone, which is limestone, and which is harder to wall with than sandstone or millstone grit. You can have good limestone and bad millstone grit, but generally it isn't regarded as particularly good limestone at Kilnsey. It's said "If you can wall at Kilnsey, you can wall anywhere", and so the competition has always attracted the best people, and is regarded to be a tough competition.

The rules for the competition at Kilnsey Show are basically the same as when the competition first started in 1939. We haven't put any extra prizes in for a good foundation, or a good 'first lift', or a good 'set of throughs', or a good 'second lift', or a good top, because one person might say, "Well I know so and so's good at 'topping', so I'm going to put some of my top stones in the bottom so I can get a prize there." There's none of that, we just have a prize for the best overall wall from start to finish, as it's always been.

Nowadays there's lots of competitions around that have special prizes for different things. I recently went to a competition not very far from here, and there were twenty four prizes on offer for the likes of: oldest person, youngest person, person who'd travelled furthest, you name it – it was just ridiculous! That took the glory away from the winner somewhat. People will have gone away from that competition and they wouldn't really know who'd won what. There were twenty three competitors and twenty four prizes up for grabs.

The way I got involved with the Dry Stone Walling Competition was that I was asked to judge it in the 1980s, and then I went back the following year and started stewarding, becoming Chief Steward in 1989. There are two more stewards who work with me: John Tiplady, who's been helping quite a long while, and Roger Gibson from Arncliffe, who took over from Chris Benson when he retired a few years ago. We get ready the day before, find out how many's coming, and then get the 'stints' measured out. These days the stints are seven and half feet wide, as opposed to nine feet which is what they used to be. That is one of the things that has changed, and because we've reduced the length of the stints, we've also reduced the timings of the competition.

The competitors work on their own stint of wall, which they've to dismantle first. The rules of the competition are that the foundation course has to be 2ft 9in wide, and the wall about 5ft high. We're not fussy if there isn't enough stone to get it to 5ft, we're not bothered to within an inch or two. There must be two rows of 'through stones', and each competitor must consider their neighbour and fit a stone to tie in with them and their stint of wall – in other words, they must agree with each other. There's just a string for the bottom and a string for the top as a guide, and the only tools allowed are a pick for rigging out the foundations, and a shovel for shovelling a bit of soil away. The competitors' positions are balloted for at 9.00am, and all work must be completed by 4.30pm.

"If you can wall at Kilnsey you can wall anywhere, and so the competition has always attracted the best people, and is regarded to be a tough competition"

We try to get as many judges from the people who've walled in the competition in the past. It wants to be somebody who the wallers will respect. We think about it quite a bit, and just at the moment we have two or three in mind for the next two to three years. It's important to have just one judge, as two judges doesn't really work. You get a compromise and that's not fair on the wallers. If one person judges it, they can say why they made a particular decision.

Different judges have different criteria they'll be looking for. I go for a strong job and it needs to be straight. It's what they call the 'batter' – the wall starts at 2ft 9in at the bottom and comes in to about a foot wide at the top, and that is your batter – the degree to how much the wall tapers in. The sides of the wall want to be straight up on the diagonal, with no bends or kinks. I like straight lines and I like a tight job, very tight and firm, with no gaps and nicks in between. A lot of people say that joints should be crossed, so that you have one stone upon two stones, and two stones upon one. Well, ideally they should be, but to me it isn't a big fault if the stones are firm and tight.

Plenty to go at: The drystone walling competition in the 1980s

They wall two sides and then put a 'through stone' right through from one side to the other every so often, which binds the sides together. The more through stones a wall has, the stronger it will be. Then there is the fillings to go in between and it's important they get the middle of the wall packed tight. The top goes on and that holds it together again. Top stones go across the top and in my opinion they want to be set on the wall perpendicular, so that every stone carries its own weight. The weight wants to go straight down through the wall, rather than leaning on its neighbour. It's a lot easier to top with them leaning on each other; with my way you have to spend a bit more time, but in my opinion it's a better way, as it makes the wall stronger.

The judge will walk in amongst the competitors and check how they're building and filling the wall. The judge can get criticised sometimes but it's very seldom a judge is wrong. You can't see what they can see when you're spectating.

The cup for the competition was first presented in 1940. It's the Henderson Silver Challenge Trophy, which was kindly given by W. Beckett Henderson, a local landowner and former five-time show President. David Caton from Cowan Bridge will have won it the most times – he's won it eight times in all. The juniors win the Yorkshire Dales National Park Shield – they've sponsored the junior competition since they first provided the shield in 1985. That's been won the most times by Edward Waller from Killington, who's won it five times in all. The junior age is under twenty one on show day, so Edward will have been quite young the first time he won it. He's also won the seniors a time or two as well. We get around eight seniors entering and two juniors, although we have had a lot more. We never push a junior to wall, we never pester them because Kilnsey is a daunting place to go and wall, with everybody looking on.

The general public come to watch the walling competition. They will watch it in the morning, come back mid-morning, come back early afternoon, and then again when the prizes are being given out after 4.30pm. People come and go to see how things are progressing. They don't stand there watching it all day, they just come and go. Wallers that have walled in the past will always be watching.

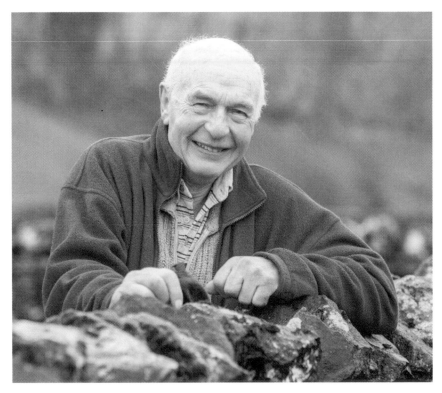

Nelson's column: Chris Nelson knows what keeps a good wall standing
© Stephen Garnett

They are a special breed are wallers: they go out walling and their working lives have changed very little since drystone walls were first built. They're building walls virtually the same now as they did a couple of hundred years ago. Everybody else gets into a centrally heated tractor or Land Rover, and there's a machine to spread the muck, and a machine to milk the cows nowadays; but a waller's job has carried on in the same way for centuries. Well-built walls will outlive the waller who built them, which says most about how tremendous they are, and why they are a very important part of the show.

Chris Nelson's family have farmed cattle and sheep at Bordley since 1947. From childhood Chris has been interested in drystone walling, even helping his father to 'put the fillings in' a wall at the age of four. Chris has been involved in the Dry Stone Walling Competition for over thirty years and has been Chief Steward since 1989.

11

SHEEP SHEARING AND DRYSTONE WALLING

"The top shearers are some of the fittest people you'll ever meet"

The legacy and tradition of shearing sheep at Kilnsey dates back 750 years to the monks of Fountains Abbey, who gathered their immense flocks at Kilnsey every mid-summer for washing and shearing. Like walling, sheep shearing remains relatively unchanged by the passage of time, although most shearers nowadays favour machine shears over traditional shears. Professional waller and shearer Roger Charnley shares his passion for both of these time honoured Dales crafts.

I started walling with my dad at nine or ten years old, when we lived in Dentdale. We used go to the Young Farmers and do the drystone walling competitions, and at that time my cousin Kevin Bateman was winning a lot of the competitions. The most memorable competition I saw him win was at the Moorcock Show when I was thirteen, when he got presented with a cup by Prince Charles. We then moved over to Raisgill near Buckden in 1992 and I joined the Upper Wharfedale Young Farmers which got me involved in setting up Kilnsey Show. My cousin Kevin had won the Henderson Challenge Trophy at Kilnsey in 1990, '91 and '92, and watching him spurred me on. I entered most years from 1993 onwards, and kept getting thirds and fourths. I found it hard, because no one wanted to teach you anything in case you beat them. In drystone walling people will teach you only so much, but in a competition it's a little bit different, as there are little 'tricks of the trade' you can do to make it easier and help you to win.

Short back and sides: Shearer Adam Berry demonstrating his art © Stephen Garnett

In 2002 I thought I was going to have my best chance of winning. It got to dinner time and there was a previous winner, Jimmy Sayer from Buckden, watching and he said to me, "If you keep going like that, you'll win." So I was confident but then I found it very hard work in the afternoon, and was struggling like mad. That day my cousin Kevin Bateman was judging, and in the afternoon he said to me, "You'll not win today", but he wouldn't tell me why. Anyway, I ended up learning more that day than I ever have in any walling competition. My cousin eventually told me the reason why I'd not won: it was because I'd started to talk to people in the afternoon, I'd got too relaxed and I'd lost concentration. It's hard when it's a local show and you know a lot of people. Each show you've to learn new things, and that day I learnt about not losing focus. The last few years have been quite hard as well, because we've got small children now and so they want to come and join in!

So I had a break from it for a while, but then I thought I'm going to have to try and win this competition by the time I'm forty. I started back in 2010 and I came second; in 2011 I came second as well. Then in 2013 I got there and I won it, and I won it again in 2014 and in 2015 – so I can retire now! In 2013 I did the hat-trick and won at the Malham, Kilnsey and Pateley shows. I was delighted because I wanted to win the competition at Kilnsey by the time I was forty and I did. Chris Nelson who runs the walling competition said I had to come back and regain my title, and then I thought, "Aw well, I'll try and win it for the third time." I'd have been nearly in tears if I'd have lost it that last time. It's very hard because it's a judged thing and sometimes it boils down to a personal opinion.

This is one of the biggest walling trophies there is in the country, and it's one of the hardest ones to win, because the stone at Kilnsey is limestone, which is one of the most difficult stones to wall with. People come from Wales, Cumbria, Lancashire and all over to try and win. It made me really satisfied, as there's only four other people who've won it three times in a row. I've made a living out of walling, and I've got quite a few jobs from the show. If you haven't a lot of work on, the walling competition's a good shop window.

I've been sheep shearing for quite a lot of years as well, so when I started getting a bit frustrated with the walling competition, I decided to start the Sheep Shearing Demonstration, with Phil Hargreaves and Richard Caton.

Top stones: Roger Charnley wins the walling trophy for the third time © Stephen Garnett

The very first year in 2004 Philip and Richard sheared and I commentated. I remember asking where to go and site the demonstration, and we got told to go right down to the bottom of the field, as no one would be interested in watching sheep shearing. So I thought, "I'll show them!" I remember that first year, there was about 150 people watching. We did it in the same format for a couple of years, with me and Richard Caton taking it in turns commentating. We used to include little tricks to make it funny, like telling the audience that the shearer was going to shear a sheep blind folded and get them all revved up – but then put the blindfold on the sheep! We once got a lad out of the audience and invited him to have a go – he was a banker, but actually he could shear. In 2006 Natalie Crisp came to help us and in 2008 we were joined by Joy Armstrong. Female shearers have brought us a lot of publicity.

For the last couple of years we've also been helped by other local people, in particular Mike Martindale and Adam Berry, who's won the British Shearer title for the last few years on the trot. In 2014 we decided to change it and introduce a 'speed shear' competition. The idea is to shear one lamb as fast as you can. It works quite well, so that's become part of the show. We still do two or three demonstrations throughout the day, and then in the late afternoon we do the competition. Our competition's like a 100 metre sprint, where the shearer will shear one lamb in less than a minute, whereas in most shearing competitions they will shear twenty sheep in about fifteen minutes.

We always try to inform the public about how to take the wool off a sheep with the shears, and explain how hard a job it is, as it is hard to keep a sheep settled. We explain about the special clothes that you wear: moccasins on your feet, which stop you slipping, and mean you can get close to the sheep and control the sheep; and special trousers which have two layers on the front to stop the grease from the natural lanolin giving you grease boils on your legs. We use about thirty of local farmer James Lambert's sheep to do the demonstrations, and we use Mark Falshaw's lambs because they're actually farmed on the showfield. It's a long process to learn how to shear a sheep, and I was lucky enough to go to New Zealand to learn when I was younger. I've also won a lot of competitions over the years, progressing to open grade, which is the top grade of shearer where you compete with shearers from all over the world. If you can learn to hold a sheep right you've mastered it. When you're working as a shearer you'll start by shearing fifty sheep a day, but as you become experienced you are aiming to get up to shearing 300 a day. Those top shearers are some of the fittest people you'll ever meet!

Roger Charnley is a professional sheep shearer and drystone waller who works throughout the Dales. Moving to Wharfedale in 1992 prompted Roger to join the Upper Wharfedale Young Farmers, who in turn introduced Roger to Kilnsey Show. Since then Roger has competed in the Dry Stone Walling Competition fourteen times, winning a hat trick of titles in 2013-15, as well as starting the Sheep Shearing Demonstration in 2004.

Traditional sheep shearing on what was known as a 'stock' or 'cratch' (Maureen Heseltine)

12

SHEEPDOG HANDLING

"When you run your dog and everyone you know is sat on straw bales watching it can be quite nerve-wracking"

To the Dales shepherd, a good sheepdog has always been worth its weight in gold. Even in the age of quad bikes it would be nigh on impossible to gather flocks from the remote valleys and fells without one. Not surprisingly, skilful working sheepdogs are in high demand and can fetch as much as £10,000 at auction. The Kilnsey Sheep Dog Trials Competition is one of the oldest elements of the show, entering the schedule in 1899. Sheep farmer and sheepdog breeder Carol Mellin added her name to this illustrious trophy in 2005, and here describes what it takes to win this prominent competition.

When I came to Moor Lodge Farm in 1991 I hadn't ever owned a sheep dog. I'd always watched *One Man and his Dog* on the television, and had tried to work out how they could get them to go left and right, but I'd never had anybody to show me. It was like something inside me waiting to come out. I absolutely love my dogs – I love breeding them, I love trialling them and I'm also lucky enough to say that I do okay with it all.

'One Man and His Dog' Kilnsey-style in 1982 © Steve Haithwaite

When I came up here my late husband Albert introduced me to the sheep and to the sheepdogs and started teaching me, and that's now been passed onto our son Philip.

I always remember the first time I went to Kilnsey Show, as it was so unlike any other sheepdog trial that I'd been to. Normally when you are at a sheepdog trial you just have people there who are running dogs, you very rarely get the public watching so you haven't got so much pressure on you. But when you run your dog at Kilnsey Show for the very first time, everyone you know is sat behind the fence on straw bales watching you. If you haven't been running dogs long that can be quite nerve-wracking. As you gain confidence, and if you have a good dog, which I was lucky to have, you change from being really nervous to actually thinking, "Right, these people watching will be expecting a decent run off me!" If you can pull that off and have a good run then there's no better feeling in the world. I've been lucky really as I've had some decent dogs to run at Kilnsey. I won with Maisie at Kilnsey Show in 2005, a run which helped me to qualify for the English National Sheep Dog Trial. I was also asked to judge the following year for the 'doubles' [pair of working dogs or bitches] competition.

"If you can pull it off and have a good run then there's no better feeling in the world"

The Kilnsey Show 'doubles' competition – now that is a memory! I remember as I gained confidence in my dogs I fancied having a go at the 'doubles', so I entered a sheepdog trial at Harden Moss to run with a pair of dogs. Over the two days I ended up third out of six or seven runners. The funny thing was that both my dogs were on the same commands, but I'd thought "Well it doesn't matter what happens at Harden Moss as it's so laid back." So I had a bit of fun there and then when I came third I thought, "I'll take these dogs to Kilnsey." I took the self-same dogs to Kilnsey, but this time it did not go well, and I just wanted the ground to open up and swallow me. I was so embarrassed, as I'd forgotten that everybody who knew me would be there watching. As I stood there struggling with two dogs who were on the same whistle, I just thought to myself that I will never ever do this again!

Better than any quad bike! © Stephen Garnett

Now that I've been going so many years to Kilnsey Show, I've started to learn what the routine is. For me I try and avoid running my dogs when the Crag Race is on, as all you can hear is Roger Ingham's voice bouncing off the rocks, whilst your dogs are trying to hear your whistles at the other end of the field. If you've a dog that can easily get wound up that is not the time to run. I don't like to go really early and get run and finished – I like to try and build myself up. I like to feel the atmosphere of the people coming to watch.

The 'singles' or single dog trial is out of a total of ninety points, with so many points for each section. You start off with your 'outrun', which is when you send your dog from your feet, either left or right. They go out either hand and come in quietly behind the sheep at the bottom of the field. For that there is twenty points. You might lose points off that if your dog was to come in and you had to stop it, and 'blow it' back out again. If it stops short of its sheep without you stopping it you can lose points there. If it 'over-flanks' and goes past the sheep without you asking it to then you'll lose points there. If it approaches the sheep really 'crawling' and you've to ask it to keep going, then you'll lose points for that too.

Nearly there: The sheep inch towards the pen (Roger Ingham)

There is then ten points for what they call the 'lift', which is when you start to bring the sheep down the field towards you. If they don't come in a straight line and quietly, you'll have points deducted off that ten. If they go off at an angle, points will be deducted there. If your dog comes in too tight on the sheep they will probably lurch forward, which shows he's been too close, so you would lose a lot of points there. He wants to bring them down really quietly, and just get a nice quiet lift.

They always say that the success of a trial depends on the lift. If you have a quiet lift the sheep will invariably keep quiet for the rest of the trial. If you have a lift where your dog has come in really tight and upset the sheep, then you'll need to try and quieten them down, which can be easier said than done.

After the lift you've then got twenty points for your 'fetch', which is when you bring the sheep in a straight line from where you picked them up to your feet. There will also be a couple of hurdles, such as two small wooden gates, for them to negotiate. Were they to miss the gates, or not come through the centre of them, there would be so many points deducted for that. There will also be points deducted for what they call 'line deviations' – if you can imagine a straight line from the sheep to your feet, the idea is that they've not to come off that line.

You then turn the sheep either left or right, depending on how the course has been set up, around the back of your feet, before you start on what is called the 'driving element'. This is in three sections with two sets of two hurdles to negotiate, and there's ten points for each section – a total of thirty points. Again you've got to keep your lines dead straight, and when the sheep go through the hurdles they've to take nice tight turns. Then you bring the sheep down the last part of your driving element towards the pen, and finally there's ten points for the pen. If they come down past the pen and go behind it you lose points. If you open the gate and they walk straight in, you lose no points. If you spend a long time trying to get them in the pen, and you do finally get them in, then you might end up with just one point.

The whole trial is judged out of ninety points, and the time element will vary from seven to nine minutes, depending on the judge on the day and what type of sheep are being used. If it's Mules, which will go round nice and quietly, the trial will most likely last between eight and nine minutes. If it's Swaledales, which will fly round, it might be just six minutes.

Kilnsey gets around fifty to sixty people entering the trials. The location, with the crag behind it, creates a really unique atmosphere. It's not like an ordinary trial, as you get lots of people meeting up with old friends which makes it feel really relaxed. I've always regarded Kilnsey as my favourite show. The input you get from the public builds your confidence up, and when you go to run at Kilnsey, you known darn well that there will be people sat there that literally haven't got a clue about how to run dogs, so you can always guarantee that whether you fail miserably or whether you do well you'll be applauded.

I'm probably like a lot of the other farmers and people who run their dogs at Kilnsey, as I use my dogs for work at home. I never ever keep a dog just for trialling; they've got to work first. My dogs gain experience at lambing time, and they gain experience when they go out on the moors. I don't let my dogs get away with anything at home, because I know I'll pay for it down the line if I do. When I go to a trial it's like a work environment in a way, because I'm asking them to go out and pick the sheep up and bring them back to me, so I can eventually pen them up – which is basically what I do at home. So I don't do any special preparation, as I know that my dogs are hopefully trained well enough to do what's required of them.

I don't keep all my 500 sheep together; they are kept in 'packets'. So if I have a hundred sheep on a particular side of the moor, I go out with my better dogs to gather the moor. I don't take a young dog on the moor, I go with a dog that has a lot of experience, that will turn back when I ask it, that will work at a distance away from me, will listen to what I say and can work off its own initiative. The beauty about Moor Lodge Farm is that I've got meadow land, pasture land and moorland – which means that I've got something that suits each particular dog, and I've got the opportunities to make a young dog better.

I use the traditional commands of 'come by' [to the left], 'away' [to the right], 'lie down' and 'walk on' initially when I'm training my dogs, but then I add whistles, so eventually I don't have to say the commands. If you're working your dog far away you don't want to be shouting and bawling, and the whistle carries much further anyway. Often you'll find that your dogs react better to a simple whistle command rather than a voice command, because you can use such a soft tone and work them a lot quieter, which looks and sounds better.

I am lucky enough to live in an area which I'd call the 'hot spot' of the sheep dog trialling world. Top trialling families, such as the Croppers and the Longtons, all congregate at Kilnsey. If you win at Kilnsey Show you're doing well because you have your top people there. That puts a lot of pressure on, but it's a good pressure. You'll find at a trial that some people are chatting and they don't watch the sheep, and they don't watch the runs; but I always study the sheep and I always study the good people. My thinking is that if they're constantly in the tickets and getting the results, they must be doing something right.

Front row seats: A knowledgeable crowd watches the sheepdogs

Woman's best friend: Carol Mellin with her prize-winning dog Maisie © Newsquest

You'll get your type of people that will say, "But they had good sheep, they were lucky!" That's not true though: good handlers can make bad sheep look good; like Jim Cropper, who's won Kilnsey three times – he can make bad sheep look good. So I watch him and I study him and his ways. You never get to learn how he trains them – he always keeps that to himself – but I watch how he runs at trials and how he handles his sheep. Jim has a saying that "You must always run on your sheep like they're going to lamb tomorrow." In other words, treat them very quietly and very carefully, and I've always tried to adopt that policy myself if I've had a particular dog that I can run quietly, which I could with Maisie. So by watching Jim and constantly seeing how he does things I hope it's made me into a better handler. You've not to be overwhelmed by the fact that there are people running at Kilnsey who've had sheepdogs in generations of their family, but you've got to try and learn to be equally as good as them, and then better on the day.

At the end of the day though sheepdog trialling has got to be fun. You should go to the pole wanting to win, wanting to do your best, wanting to prove that your dog is good. But if you lose, if something goes wrong, it doesn't matter. If my dog runs and I don't get in the tickets it doesn't matter, as long as I'm happy with my dog. If my dog does something wrong, I take it home and correct it.

And do I class sheepdog trialling as a hobby? No. Do I class it as a sport? No. I think that we do the trialling to enhance the quality of the working sheepdog. I am one of the most competitive people around, and when I go to that pole I go to win, but I also go to feel the adrenaline and to feel the atmosphere. I love Kilnsey Show, it's the best show and I just love to run there. And if I win? Then it's even better!

Carol Mellin is a sheep farmer and sheepdog breeder from Oakworth near Haworth, who has been trialling sheepdogs since 1991 and training dogs since 1993. She won the Sheep Dog Trials at Kilnsey in 2005, and judged the event the following year. Carol has qualified for the English National Sheep Dog Trial on seven occasions.

The sheepdog trial at Kilnsey in the 1950s © NYCC Unnetie digital collection BU08444

13

VINTAGE TRACTORS

*"There's a tractor from Halifax – the only
one in England – it's in its original state,
and it runs like a sewing machine"*

*The tractor is a highly adaptable and capable machine, which over
the twentieth century has brought about a revolution in farming
methods and efficiency. In its earliest incarnation it was simply an
engine for pulling and hauling, but over time it has evolved into
the backbone of the modern farm. The tractor has a legacy which
spans over a hundred years, and here vintage tractor restorer Geoff
Dunn, who set up the Vintage Tractor Competition at Kilnsey
Show, provides a unique insight into some of the history behind
these mechanical horses.*

We used to live at Starbotton in Upper Wharfedale and I started going to
Kilnsey Show when I was seven years old, with our friends the Listers in
their old livestock wagon. I was that small then, they'd stand me inside a
milk kit and put me in with the cows in the wagon, so that I could get in for
nothing. I was right enough though, as they didn't put the lid on!

I'd never seen show cattle and sheep before Kilnsey. Watching them
cleaning them all up was very interesting, as I'd never seen anything like
it. Even the trotting at night – I'd never seen anything like that, and it just

Harking back to a bygone era: Ian Waddington with his 1942 Standard Fordson tractor
© Stephen Garnett

sticks in the back of your mind for the rest of your life. They used to have me carrying and fetching water to clean the cows up, and I'd to help to comb them out as much as I could.

After a few years I saw my friends selling catalogues and sports programmes, and they were getting paid for doing it. I thought, "I want to be in on this!" So I did that for quite a number of years. Get there, get my name down and go out to where they were selling programmes in the car parks. Then I was asked if I would go up onto the top of Kilnsey Crag for the fell race and stamp the runner's hands. They used to give me ten shillings for that. There was none of this modern technology then, so we used to go up and stamp their hands to make sure they'd been to the top and round the post, before they ran back down.

"I'd never seen show cattle and sheep before Kilnsey. Even the trotting at night – I'd never seen anything like that, and it just sticks in the back of your mind for the rest of your life"

I was a young lad when tractors were starting to become more popular, but I can vaguely remember odd farms still having horses. My father was a 'horse man' on a farm, and I can remember when I was three years old, we lived on the outskirts of Leeds then, and we'd go out on a horse and trap delivering milk with a can and measures. Then when I was four I can remember in hay-time I used to sit on the horse's neck, because the width of the horse was too wide for my little legs. I'd just sit on top of the horse all day long, holding its mane, while my dad was mowing grass or turning it, or whatever he used to do.

Just before I was five we moved to Starbotton and my dad went to work for the Closes who farmed there. Mr Close had a pony, and he was the boss, and he used to ride round on that pony all day. He lived on that pony. For a few years my dad mowed the grass with some horses, but then they got an old tractor and so the poor horses had to give up. The late 1940s and early 1950s was the change-over time really from horses to tractors.

Making Tracks: A 1947 Oliver Cletrac with John Harry Greenwood © Stephen Garnett

I started driving tractors aged eleven or twelve and got the bug. Tractor Handling? I thought to myself, "I want to be having a do at that!" So for quite a number of years I did the Tractor Handling at Kilnsey Show, and kept getting first, second or third. I was doing alright – and then I won it for maybe about five years on the trot. It's backing and reversing through posts on a time schedule, and if you touched a post it was so many points off. The winner was the one who did it in the quickest time with a clear round. You'd draw through some circles, and then you'd to back through a different way, and finally you'd to back into the parking place, and that was it. I did the junior Tractor Handling and then as I got older I did the senior Tractor Handling. I was very interested in it all, and as I grew up and got into my late teens, me and my friend Lister Walmsley, we both decided to give a cup for the Tractor Handling – one for the juniors and one for the seniors.

Massey Ferguson, David Brown, International, John Deere – they all used to come with brand new tractors to the show. We'd take it in turns asking one of them each year if we could have a new tractor for the Tractor Handling Competition; it needed to be brand new, the latest thing. They always used to give us a tractor and a trailer for the day. When we started we were inundated with kids wanting to go on the tractors – but the only way they could get on one was to enter!

As I got a bit older, I got a vintage wagon and some old tractors. So when I went to Kilnsey Show I'd take my old tractor, a 1945 E27N Fordson Major, and I'd park it down at the bottom on the river banking, near to where the beer tent is. I did that for a year or two, then I took my old wagon, a 1960 Ford eight wheeler. After a few years of this the show asked me to do a bit of a section. So I started and I fetched a few tractors, only three or four tractors at first, and initially they were all mine. Then I asked some Dales farmers that I know to bring some of their vintage tractors that they still use, and so it got bigger and bigger. Soon I asked if we could have a better pitch because we were running out of room. Where we are today, by the Farmers' Market, it's marvellous because we can get forty tractors in. So I started asking a lot more of my friends from all over the country to come along. I say, "Fetch your tractor to Kilnsey Show and we'll show it."

Red hot favourite: A 1952 David Brown tractor still in its original 'working clothes'
© Stephen Garnett

Ever since we moved to the current place I've done the commentary and everything, organised it all for them, and made sure that all the tractor lads get a plaque each year as a memento. We are limited to forty tractors and we got thirty eight in 2015, which was some sight!

The tractor lads love Kilnsey Show, as they get the chance to ride round the show ring and for everybody to see their tractors. That is a unique thing at Kilnsey Show, being able to show your tractors off to everybody, so people can see how they run and what they sound like. I do a bit of a commentary and I tell everyone what's coming round, and how old they are, and who they belong to. It's gone from just me and one tractor in 1995, to forty tractors going round the ring as a major event. People come from all across Yorkshire with their tractors. It's a good meeting, particularly as there's some tractor lads that I only see once a year at the show.

The excitement for me about vintage tractors is doing them up. It's hard work, and it costs a lot of money. As I say in my commentary, "We're here again with our old scrap, our heaps of old iron." That's a joke though, because they're like brand new – newer than new – which they are, and worth a lot of money. So I talk about things like that on the commentary, and we always get a standing ovation which is brilliant.

There's a tractor that's been twice to Kilnsey Show – it's the only one in England, and it comes from Halifax. It hasn't been done up – it's in its original state, and it runs like a sewing machine. It's still in what I call its 'working clothes'. We give a cup at Kilnsey Show for the most original tractor. It doesn't matter what make, it's just to be one that's never been touched. This one is a 1956 McCormick International Farmall Super FCD Rowcrop. It was imported from France in 2012, and it's the only one I've ever seen with lifting arms at the back.

My oldest tractor is a 1933 Fordson N. I've also got the first petrol 'Fergie' [Massey Ferguson] which came to the Boothman brothers in Linton in the early 1940s with the mowing machine on the back for £300. I've also got the first diesel tractor that went up into Littondale. It was delivered onto the green at Arncliffe and I've got all the paperwork for it.

Early pulling power: A Standard Fordson petrol engine © Stephen Garnett

Simpler days: Dashboard of a 1952 David Brown Super Cropmaster © Stephen Garnett

Living history: Geoff Dunn on his restored 1962 Massey Ferguson 65 © Robin Moule

I've got an Allis B, which is like an orange sausage, and it has a mid-mountain mower on between the front wheel and the back wheel. I bought that one because when I left school at fifteen I worked on a farm, and that is what I did farming with, what I really learnt to drive on.

Massey Fergusons – of which I've quite a few – are getting to be worth quite a lot of money: between £1,000 and £3,000 before renovation, and £6,000 and £7,000 after. I've got the Massey 'Fergie' 35 and the Massey 'Fergie' 135, which are classed by Ferguson Heritage and The Ferguson Club as the top two Massey Ferguson tractors in the country. These are two tractors that I've done up from scrap.

The little Massey 'Fergie' 135, I paid £65 for it, scrap. Six months before Foot and Mouth I was running five livestock wagons. Foot and Mouth came and I was at a total standstill, nothing to do, so I thought, "Well I'm going to rebuild that tractor." I rebuilt it nut and bolt. All original parts. I've had parts for it come from all over world. You can get parts for tractors nowadays which are reproduction, but they aren't the same. All tractor parts if they're original are stamped with the manufacturer's logo. Every part that's on those tractors has got the Massey 'Fergie' logo on, and that's what makes those tractors what they are. You can do a tractor up for little money, using reproduction parts, but that isn't the same, not for me anyway. If I do it, it's got to be right.

I've just done up a yellow and grey Massey 'Fergie' 65. The Oversbys of Grassington bought one brand new in 1962 when I worked for them. I was just seventeen. I remember it coming into the yard with a loader on, and then I went snow digging up into the Yorkshire Dales on it, and I didn't come back for six weeks. So I've found one identical to it and done it up like new. It took me three years to do it because I was looking for the original parts. The two back tyres for it came from South Carolina; there's only four left in world that size, and that tractor has two of them. I fetched it to Kilnsey Show in 2015. That was its first time out, and it was very popular.

It's the nostalgia that everyone likes. The first Tractor Handling Competition was held at the show in 1958, but the Vintage Tractor Competition means people can still enjoy watching tractors from that era at Kilnsey Show today.

Geoff Dunn has been a livestock transporter for the Yorkshire Dales for over thirty years. He has been to every Kilnsey Show since he was seven years old, and has been actively involved in the show since he was a teenager. Geoff stewarded the Tractor Handling Competition throughout the 1970s and 1980s, and as a lifelong vintage tractor restorer he then started the popular Vintage Tractor Competition and parade in 1995, and still runs it to this day.

14

SHOW LIFE

"Shampoo the cattle, groom them out,
back comb them, fluff their tails
– and then they're ready to go!"

From its modest beginnings Kilnsey Show has become a significant
organisational challenge, requiring months of preparation. Ensuring
that the needs and requirements of the show's 10,000 plus visitors,
thousands of cars, dozens of marquees and hundreds of animals are all
accommodated is a mammoth task, undertaken by a committee headed
up by local farmer and current Chairman Robert Lambert. Here
Robert talks about his time showing cattle, why the Chairmanship is
a role he is committed to, and highlights some of the future challenges
for Kilnsey Show.

My first recollection of Kilnsey Show is when our family moved here, to
Conistone-with-Kilnsey, in 1958 when I was just seven years old – and
I've been to every show, every year, since then. As a child it just seemed
so big, with the fun fair, toffee apples and whatever, everywhere you went.
My favourite thing was the grand parade of cattle round the ring, which
was always a spectacle. Unfortunately they don't do that anymore; it was
stopped in the 1990s on health and safety grounds. The problem was getting
the cow or bull from the cattle rings, through the crowd into the main ring.
Nothing ever happened, but it was stopped just in case it did. The cattle
parade in their own steel fenced ring at the side now.

Robert Lambert winning 'Best Local Heifer-in-calf' in 1971

Harker & Son of Grassington selling hardware in 1935

Changing tastes: The trade stand area today

My first proper involvement in Kilnsey Show began when I was allowed to start showing cattle, which was into the late 1960s, and which brought excitement as well as dread. When you go to show cattle you don't just turn up with them and walk them round. You spend probably the month before practising to halter lead them, with a rope around their heads. They drag you around for the first week, and then it's a fight of equal strength for the second week, and eventually by the third week you'll get them to walk calmly on the lead. Obviously if you just turned up at the show with a 'wild animal' on a rope you wouldn't be able to hold it; it would just set off and create havoc amongst the crowd – so they must always be halter trained. The day before you go to the show you shampoo them, wash them down, and get them into something like a reasonable order. On the show morning it used to be an extremely early start, about 5.00am, and we'd get our routine jobs done, which in our case was milking, and then we'd be across at the showfield somewhere between 7.00am and 7.30am. In the early days we took milk kits full of hot water, which would be cold by the time we got there, and then we'd start the whole process again: shampoo the cattle, wash them with cold water, wait until it dried, groom them out, back comb them, fluff their tails, and then they were ready to go!

On show day we'd take part in various cattle classes, hoping to win something. It was never ever about the money, still isn't I don't think – it was the prestige of doing it. We only ever had one big win as I recall, it just used to be seconds and thirds – but to win, that was a heck of a feeling! It was a smashing feeling for the whole day. We've a photograph of that one on display; the Upper Wharfedale Challenge Cup for the Best Local Heifer-in-calf.

By the early 1980s we'd more or less given up showing. I was given the job of helping to sort out the car parking initially, then the admissions on the gate, and I went on to become in charge of all that. So for about twenty years I was in charge of car parking, vehicle and pedestrian access, and admissions, which was some logistical exercise. In the good old days we were probably talking about five or six thousand cars, parked over three fields. Parking didn't used to be free, but the reason we brought in free car parks was because there was that much traffic queuing down the dale trying to get to the show. The Police were saying that there were queues back to Rylstone, seven miles away, so we had to do something to try and get the cars off the road, and quick – so we made the decision that the outlying car parks would be free.

I became a Vice Chairman to Ronnie Metcalfe as Chairman in 1999. The previous Chairman to Ronnie was Jim Caygill, who'd done seventeen years. Unfortunately a few years after I was appointed Ronnie was taken ill, and so I was suddenly thrown in at the deep end as Chairman. That was 2003, and I've been Chairman ever since. The role involves a heck of a lot: sorting out the caterers, sorting out the tent firms, and planning everything from the livestock entries to the horticultural classes. All year round there's meetings with different committees and sub committees, deciding on what to have in the main ring as well as other attractions, such as the sheep shearing contest. There's also meetings in Appleby to attend with the harness racing boys. In the run up to the show I'm on that field for ten days solid – farming actually goes on hold for ten days!

The show organisers are responsible for all the wear and tear on the field; so if we have a wet year it can cost the show anything between £10,000 and £15,000 to get the field right again – which is why we can't afford too many of those! Probably the greatest achievement in my time as Chairman is the development of the hard tracks on the showfield. In 2011 we managed to get agreement that we could extend the ones which were put in in the 1980s, and we extended them again in 2013. The difference now is that we will never need to cancel a show, and we will never need to stop vehicles from coming onto the showfield, because we can handle a wet day. This is probably one of the biggest achievements.

We also seem to spend our life putting drainage in. We are always digging holes somewhere, wherever there's a wet bit. Back in 2006 the river bank started eroding and sorting that out was a huge job. We put in a lot of rock; probably 3,000 tonnes of rock we put in under that river. It is a huge commitment, but the job of Chairman means everything. I'm devoted to the show; you have to be devoted to it. My proud moments are just seeing that field improve: the drainage, the road, what used to be wet spots – now dry – fantastic! And to look down the valley and see the traffic flowing in, with no traffic jams. It's things like this that do it for me. It's gone from being a laid back relaxed show to more of a logistical exercise, but when everything goes right it's great.

The most idyllic car park in the country? The showfield in 1982 (Roger Ingham)

Setting the showfield up starts about ten days prior to the show day. There's a team of chief stewards, probably ten or fifteen of us, who go along with all of the Upper Wharfedale Young Farmers. They do a heck of a lot of it, and have done since I can remember. They write down their hours, and then the show pays them a lump sum which goes back to the Young Farmers' Club, to help them run it for the year. So we've two weekends setting up, plus the Bank Holiday Monday, and then we have a weekend taking it down. The amazing thing is everyone knows their own job. People just turn up – you don't tell them what to do, they just all disappear off and do their own thing: the Daggetts turn up with a trailer with a post knocker on and whatever else, and it all just comes together, just like that.

> *"The amazing thing is everyone knows their own job. People just turn up – you don't tell them what to do, they all disappear off and do their own thing – and it all comes together"*

Nowadays your average show is somewhere between nine and eleven thousand admissions. When I first started it was somewhere between fourteen and seventeen thousand. The problem is there's that much choice – mum and dad say, "Are we going to Kilnsey Show or Alton Towers?" There's a lot of choice and a lot of competition which there never used to be and which is why I'm dead keen that Kilnsey Show has to stop as a proper agricultural show, because it'll lose its identity if it doesn't. A lot of shows have fallen by the wayside, and others have become far too commercial. You need a slight commercial element there because there's people who are coming looking for that, so you have to have those sort of trade stands. Over the last few years we've tried to vet our trade stands very carefully so we get an even mix and match. You don't want all riding gear, but you don't want all novelty kids toys or whatever either. It's the same with the food now – we are working more to try and cut out a lot of the hamburger stands and get more locally produced food on the field, and that's where the Farmers' Market comes in. It's hitting that happy medium though, as you've still got to cater for the other end of the spectrum, as there will still be those who want to buy a burger.

Armchair viewers: A grandstand view of the show ring © Stephen Garnett

Forty winks: A young farmer's life can be hard © Stephen Garnett

The Farmers' Market started in 2000, but then we enhanced that whole area and put a cookery theatre in and called it 'Food and Farming for REAL'. We also had a display tent featuring various organisations such as Yorkshire Water, Country Landowners' Association, the National Farmers' Union as well as local food outlets doing demonstrations, and various local farmers talking about their jobs as guardians of the hills. We set up the REAL Committee, and we were trying to put the message out about what hill farming provides. Basically everybody's water in the country comes out of the hills, and hill farmers are the guardians of that. All the breeding stock for lower down in the country is all bred in the hills too.

There were five of us on the committee, and we went down to London to Number 10 and to the House of Commons and lobbied. We were trying to promote it, as the government were talking about taking the subsidies out of the hills. We were trying to say that the input that hill farming was putting in was far greater than what hill farmers were actually taking out. We'd a meeting with five MPs from the shadow cabinet: Jim Pace who became Agricultural Minister, William Hague and a few others, and then we used the show as the base to promote it all. Christine Ryder, Stephen Crabtree, Alistair Davy who founded Yorkshire Dales Farmers' Markets, and Mike Keeble,who used to do the commentary at the Great Yorkshire Show, were all part of it.

We've still got the Cookery Theatre and the children's tent but the display tent has gone. The REAL Committee disbanded a few years ago, but its legacy at the show has continued to evolve. The idea is that we have the Farmers' Market there so people can go in and buy locally grown or locally made produce, or locally reared meat and fish, and then go over to the cookery theatre and find out how to cook it. It's about showing people the range and quality of food that's being produced on the show's doorstep. It takes the concept of hill farming full circle.

Being Chairman is a year round job but we have a great team of unpaid stewards who put so many hours into making Kilnsey Show the success that it is. The biggest challenge for the running of the show in the future will be maintaining that steady influx of people willing to help, as we're already struggling getting young people who want to come and do the job of stewards, or become committee members. What I'm trying to do now is bring in young ones as junior stewards, at thirteen or fourteen years old – before they've learnt what a pub is, or what the opposite sex is! So if we get them then, then hopefully we've got them for the rest of their lives.

Robert Lambert is a cattle and sheep farmer from Conistone-with-Kilnsey whose family have farmed in the upper Dales since 1958. Robert has been actively involved in the show since the late 1960s, being appointed Vice Chairman in 1999 and Chairman in 2003.

15

LOCAL FOOD AND PRODUCE

"Shows like Kilnsey have really helped to put Yorkshire and its local produce on the map in a massive way"

The fertile valleys of the Yorkshire Dales are rich in produce, from lamb and beef to game and fish. From the outset Kilnsey Show has endeavoured to reflect this – from its early Produce section showcasing locally made butter, cheese and eggs, to the more recent Farmers' Market and Cookery Theatre. The success of this aspect of the show, coupled with the current enthusiasm for high quality local food, means that the Cookery Theatre continues to attract some of the best chefs from across the region. Local farmer's daughter Stephanie Moon, now a very recognisable figure on the Yorkshire food scene, shares her experiences of the show and her passion for its local produce.

I've some great memories of doing the Cookery Theatre at Kilnsey. In 2013 I did the *Great British Menu* on BBC2, and following that I was asked to do a programme on BBC1 for daytime TV, which was a great thing for me. Rather awkwardly this programme was due to be filmed the day after Kilnsey Show, so I thought, "I'll do Kilnsey Show and then I'll set off and drive straight to London to do this TV programme." When you're doing these cookery demonstrations at shows like Kilnsey you have boxes of stuff to bring, as you have to bring your own pots, pans and utensils, and then you have a large cool bag with all your food in too.

Stephanie Moon showcasing the best of Kilnsey's local produce © Welcome to Yorkshire

It's always a bit of a trek to get to the Cookery Theatre at Kilnsey Show, as where you park and where you demo are about two fields apart. Anyway, this particular year it was a really hot day and I was walking with all these boxes of kit, and my arms were groaning. As I walked past the Upper Wharfedale Fell Rescue, there was this guy called Stewart, whom I knew on the stand, who came running over and said, "Steph, let me help you!" So he took these boxes from me and carried them to the Cookery Theatre, which was quite a distance away. I could have hugged him, he was such a great help.

I did my cookery demonstration and then I set off to drive to London. The programme being filmed was called *Chefs: Put Your Menu Where Your Mouth Is*, and I was up against a Michelin-starred chef called Galton Blackiston, who's well known in the chef world. I remember feeling a little bit out of my depth being on TV and competing against Galton, and then the programme makers came and asked me to nominate a charity for the show. My mind went blank – I couldn't think of anything except Stewart helping me out the day before at Kilnsey Show, and the Upper Wharfedale Fell Rescue, so I nominated them! They took us around all these markets in London and we had to buy our food and then we had to pitch a menu. I remember my menu: it was salmon, and the salmon dish I did was very similar to the trout dish I'd done the day before at Kilnsey Show, so I pretty much did the same dish as it was all still fresh in my mind. I also did a lamb dish, and some kind of chocolate and lemon dish for dessert. The concept was all about how much money you could make taking into consideration all the costings and any food waste. Anyway, the astonishing thing was that I won, as more people chose my menu, and it was the most cost effective. So consequently I made about £900, which they announced on the programme was all going to the Upper Wharfedale Fell Rescue. Stewart had saved my life that day, because I was worried and rushing, and so it just felt so well deserved for them.

When I was at school I felt pretty unremarkable and didn't have much confidence in myself. I remember buying a book, *How to Get a Job Without an O' Level*, because that's how much I thought I was going to get my O' Levels. School was great, but I wasn't overly academic, although miraculously I did end up getting four O' Levels by the skin of my teeth. Shortly after I left school I went for an interview and I got a YTS [Youth Training Scheme] job

Prime crop: Prize-winning leeks in the Horticulture marquee © Stephen Garnett

at the local pub. In a stroke of fate my cookery teacher, who must be credited with her help in my career, rang up my parents and said that she thought I should go to college.

My parents therefore took me to Craven College for an interview. The college had forty places on the catering course at the time, and I was the forty first student that they took on, so I was in – but it was a close call! Getting in that tight meant I just went for it, and I loved it. I took to the course like a duck to water; it just felt right for me.

I did the course for two years and then in the second year there was this competition where they chose one student to go to London to work at The Dorchester hotel. Unbelievably, they picked me! I was as shocked as everybody else, because again confidence still wasn't a strong thing for me. Before I went down to London my tutors said, "Get in early, work late, go in on your day off, ask all the questions, and get that job!" And lucky for me I managed to do just that. Tosside to London was quite a big step, as where my parents live and farm we were half a mile from the nearest neighbour, and suddenly there I was living and working in London at eighteen years old. I was fourth Commis Chef, lowest of the low, peeling potatoes and picking spinach and that kind of thing, but I really made the most of it. I'd been there just over a year when Anton Mosimann, who was the Executive Chef at the time, left to open his own club. The Dorchester then closed for refurbishment and they made everybody redundant, which for most people was horrific, but for me at nineteen it presented a great opportunity.

From this point on I've pretty much travelled the world with my job; I worked in Switzerland and then I worked in Germany, in Munich. From Germany I went back to The Dorchester after it re-opened, working in the pastry department when Paul Hollywood was Head Baker. I then emigrated to Australia to work in Sydney for a year at The Park Hyatt, which is the boomerang shaped hotel just next to the Sydney Harbour Bridge. I was working there when I won a gold medal in the prestigious Salon Culinaire competition. From there I went to the Hayman Island in the Barrier Reef, which is a very small island, about seven miles wide by three miles long. All there is, is the hotel on the island and around 460 people working there, doing everything from purifying water to cooking – all this for about 380 guests!

Ready Steady Cook! Stephanie puts on a show in the Cookery Theatre © Charlotte Gayle

After that I came back to the UK, finally moving back to the Dales in 2007, to The Coniston Hotel, which was under construction at the time. This was a great job for me, as I was very ready for coming home. Somewhat aptly this was the year that Kilnsey Show introduced their Cookery Theatre, and so I got involved with that right at the very beginning, and since then it has gone from strength to strength.

Initially the Cookery Theatre was in a little section of the Farmers' Market marquee, then it had its own marquee, and now we're in the 'Circus of Food' cookery theatre. This is a kind of demonstration trailer and audience tent, which opens up to create this cookery theatre with cameras and a big TV screen so that the audience can view close ups of the cooking being demonstrated. It also has its own one hundred seater marquee which keeps everything together; it's just this really practical demonstration space. There is also a large marquee next door to this which is the Farmers' Market Food Village; this is where all the local shops and producers are, such as Bracken Hill, Sawley Kitchen and Kilnsey Park. In the space to the side of the cookery theatre there are other chefs and producers, like the Guyrope Gourmet, Chris Wildman and his hog roast, and other things like that. So the whole area is just this total foodie heaven.

Some of the local chefs I've worked with who've done cookery demonstrations at Kilnsey Show are: Chris Oakden from The Coniston Hotel, John Rudden from Grassington House Hotel, Jason Wardill at Keelham Kitchen and Bruce Elsworth from The Angel at Hetton. Bruce and I actually did a 'Ready Steady Cook' at Kilnsey Show one year as well. We were given produce from the stalls there – so I had trout and he had lamb. Kilnsey Park, who are right next door to the show, are very proactive and supportive so they'd given some trout and we'd also got some vegetables from one of the growers, and meat and Yorkshire Chorizo from Chris Wildman at Town End Farm Shop. Mark Dale, who owns the 'Circus of Food,' also gave us some pigeons. We then had just twenty minutes to create our menus. I remember whispering to Bruce, "How many dishes are you going to do?" and he replied, "I'll do two, or I might do three…" So then I was like, "Alright!" thinking, "Oh crikey!" because I didn't want to do any less or any more than he did. We had a great laugh though, pinching each other's ingredients and things like that. Fair play to Bruce though, as when he'd finished the 'Ready Steady Cook' demonstration he went and ran the Crag Race! I'm there walking home with all my pots and pans while he's running up the crag with some of the country's best fell runners. I think he came fifth as well.

These days people's interest in food has gone beyond mere interest into an absolute passion. Certainly in the Dales, people love local food and have always supported their own producers, but over the last ten years or so the level of interest and people's thirst for knowledge about food has sky rocketed. Everyone has an opinion about food, and people's opinions really count now. People want to know: Who's produced these sausages? Which farm is this from? Is this a local cheese?

When I come to the show I bring along some basic ingredients, but the food I cook with for the main part of my demonstration will be local to Kilnsey. I always do a starter or main using Kilnsey rainbow trout, as everything they do at Kilnsey Park is really good. A lot of trout that you can buy is very earthy, whereas at Kilnsey the rain comes down off the hills and goes into the ponds, so you've never got that dirty churned up trout taste – it's always very clean and fresh tasting.

Taste of the Dales: Local producers display their wares © Stephen Garnett

Other good local producers are Jacksons of Cracoe, who are very good farmers and butchers, Thomas the Bakers, Voakes Pies and Bleikers Smokehouse. These days people are thinking: if it's not local, what are you doing? Who's this joker up on stage? You've got to use the local produce as it's expected – they want to know where it's from and they want to taste it.

Something like trout can be a hard sell if people aren't used to eating fish. Most people generally eat cod, haddock or salmon, but not many will have tried trout, because the bones tend to put them off. But if you show people how to take the bones out easily, which is one of the first things I do, as I take the whole fish, then fillet it, prep it, and cook it – so it's done quick – it transforms their perceptions of it. Usually a cookery demonstration is half an hour – so when I do mine, I do a starter, a main and dessert in half an hour, which is quite a task – but I think it's nice to show a full menu through from start to finish.

I think food is one of those things that, if you love what you do, it shows when you're cooking. The chefs who are at Kilnsey Show are what I'd call 'regulars' on the food circuit – they know how to demonstrate, and they're not shy about standing in front of three people or a hundred people. Sometimes when you do a cookery demonstration there might just be two or three people watching, but you must still give your best demonstration as you don't know who those people are.

This smoked trout has come just a few metres from the Kilnsey Park lakes and smokehouse
© Kilnsey Park Estate/Joan Ransley

I once did a Farmers' Market and there were about six people watching, and it was raining and cold, and it was in this little gazebo, with a little camping gas stove and a bowl of cold water to wash my hands in. However it turned out to be a great success, as I got six days of filming for Asda's website as a result of someone who'd seen me there. Every time I've done cookery demonstrations at Kilnsey Show it's always been busy. A lot of my demonstrations are around lunch time which is great because the area's at its busiest then, with people going to the Farmers' Market looking for something to eat.

As an agricultural show, Kilnsey is up there as one of the biggest shows that there is. Kilnsey Show has a very strong history in supporting local farmers, and also supporting the local chefs that support them. The people that Kilnsey Show pick to do the demonstrations are all locals, and I think that's how it should be. The audiences that we get are all wanting to know where we've brought the food from: Where's that from? Can I buy that here? I think the concept is working well if people are asking those questions.

Food has already come such a long way, but now local producers are taking things to the next stage with new products and better products. People are not sitting back, they are striving for it, and it's shows like Kilnsey, and events like the Tour de France visiting Yorkshire in 2014, which have really helped to put Yorkshire and its local produce on the map in a massive way. Kilnsey Show is quite a long drive for me now, but I love coming to it as it's always felt like the closest show to home, and I just love using all the wonderful local produce that is on offer at Kilnsey, which to be honest, is about as good as it gets!

Stephanie Moon was brought up on her parents' hill farm at Tosside near Settle, and following her training has worked with some of the world's top chefs in some of world's finest restaurants and hotels, winning numerous accolades and awards along the way. Stephanie currently runs her own consultancy business and has demonstrated at every Kilnsey Show Cookery Theatre since it started in 2007.

16

BEHIND THE SCENES

"One year I forgot to notify the taxman and two very tall and muscular gentlemen appeared in the Secretary's Tent"

One of the most important roles within any show is the Secretary, who coordinates everything from applying for the gambling and alcohol licences, to booking the portaloos – as well as being advocate, diplomat and general all round 'firefighter' on actual show day. Kilnsey Show has been fortunate in attracting and retaining many dedicated secretaries over the years, including Wendy Riley who served the show from 1976 to 1988. Here Wendy recalls some memorable highlights from her career with the show.

My involvement with Kilnsey Show started in 1976 when I took over as Secretary after the death of Robert Carradice. The only correspondence I could find was a letter from 'Claphams of Bedale' about tentage for the show which simply said, "Thank you for your enquiry, the matter is being dealt with" – which rather stumped me! However with the help of committee member Bill Foster I was able to piece together all the numerous strands of putting on a show. Bill was also able to enlighten me about the safety-pin requirement for the runners' numbers and advised me not to be too economical with the strings for the show jumpers and the cattle class numbers – too short and they wouldn't meet to fasten.

Cutting a dash: Show President Walter Walker in 1988 (Roger Ingham)

Besides the tentage, the catering, the ice cream rights and the bookies' stands, the other major requirement was toilets, which for many a year had been a trench behind a wall for the men, and canvas cubicles with seats on buckets for the ladies. Of course, today's volume of visitors and their expectations of hygiene now requires a more sophisticated arrangement.

Going back to the bookies, it's a Revenue requirement that the authorities are notified that there is a betting meeting at Kilnsey Show for the harness races and sports. Having inadvertently omitted to notify them of it one year, two very tall and muscular gentlemen appeared in the Secretary's Tent demanding to know why not. It was agreed that they would come back to discuss the matter the day after the show – which they duly did, opening the conversation with, "Anything you say may be taken down as evidence…" This of course implied a potential court appearance, but having admitted my omission – putting it down to forgetfulness rather than any intent to defraud HM Customs – they let me off with rapped knuckles. However they weren't prepared to take notification of the following year's betting meeting as "it was too far ahead for them to remember", so after they said that I did feel vindicated.

Another main duty of mine was to take entries for all the showing classes and prepare schedules and programmes. To an outsider, show schedule committee meetings could possibly sound quite tedious, the majority of the classes being the same each year, but the reasoning and decision on whether to have four or six shortbread biscuits in a class, or whether a particular project was more suitable for the 'under 7s' or the '8 to 11s' could take some time to resolve.

Selecting judges was another consideration which one year caused the show a little embarrassment. I was given the name of a cattle judge with just his village name. Unfortunately, I invited the brother of said gentleman – same initial, same village, but different address – and a subsequent conversation between a committee member and the intended judge looking forward to him accepting the appointment of course caused confusion. The brother did an excellent job and it meant we didn't have to look for a cattle judge the following year!

Sweet sounds: The Lofthouse & Middlesmoor brass band in action © Craven Herald

Take a bow: The winning Shire horse and foal leave the ring © YDNPA

There is a strict rule of not accepting entries after a deadline to enable the catalogues to be printed. One show day however a gentleman arrived asking "Where do I put me marra'?" When informed we didn't take entries on the day, he was somewhat miffed that he'd come all the way from Halifax for nothing, and no, he did not want putting on a list to send him a schedule next year. I don't recall whether his marrow would have been a winning one or not.

The weather on show day plays a major part in its success – sunshine is always preferred – but wet or fine the show goes on. Memories of Hurricane Charley with marquees falling down and hanging onto Mr President's tent in the pouring rain, being driven round the ring in an open carriage in glorious sunshine, meeting the iconic Desert Orchid in 1999, being filmed for television programmes and interviewed for radio programmes – all stay with me.

My abiding emotions are remembering the anticipation at 7.00am of looking down the rows of trade stands, the enjoyment of seeing all the crowds and familiar faces, the pleasure of hearing the cheering on of the Crag Race runners and the running commentary for the harness racing; and then, looking down the showfield again at the end of the day and feeling the contentment and satisfaction of contributing to such a special Dales event. Come the next day it all started again – meetings to organise, tenders to be got, minutes to write, schedules to prepare, ready for the next August Bank Holiday Tuesday – and mustn't forget to notify Customs & Excise!

Wendy Riley has attended the show since childhood, her father Fred Clayton being a Vice President and steward for many years. When the position of Secretary was advertised Wendy applied and was appointed, fulfilling the role for twelve years. Today Wendy remains a Vice President and member of the Produce Committee.

These chaps know their onions: A local grower awaits the judge's verdict in 2015
© Stephen Garnett

EPILOGUE

That night in the darkness we stood and looked back at the show ground from Conistone Bridge. The side shows were lit up, and their gaudy awnings made splashes of colour in the night. Their lights shone onto the tents and marquees, so that they seemed to glow from inside. There was a dance in one of them, and the strains of music wafted across to us. The lights faintly lit the crag behind, making it a white, mysterious background which grew plainer as we looked. It all seemed bizarre and unreal in that setting, and yet not alien, because it was so obviously temporary. It was like an eastern caravan halting in the limestone country.

Extract from *Wharfedale* by Ella Pontefract and Marie Hartley (1938)

Pontefract and Hartley's book is a huge inspiration to anyone seeking to understand and learn about the history and culture of the Yorkshire Dales. We have included some of Marie Hartley's lovely woodcut illustrations throughout our book.

SOURCES

(in chronological order)

Lancaster Gazette (September 11th 1869)

Chronicles and Stories of the Craven Dales by A. H. Dixon (1881)

Craven Herald and Pioneer – various editions from 1884 to current date

Picturesque Fell Land by Edmund Bogg (1904)

Two Thousand Miles in Wharfedale by Edmund Bogg (1904)

Wharfedale by Ella Pontefract and Marie Hartley (1938)

The Dalesman (April 1940)

Working with the Curlew by Trevor Robinson (2003)

ACKNOWLEDGEMENTS

With thanks to:

Ken Blakey, Lisa Bullough, Kathleen Carlisle, John Chapman, The Dales Countryside Museum, Ian Daggett, Michael Daggett, Philip Dolphin, Bill Foster, Charlotte Gayle, Wendy Gibson, Penny Hart Woods, Maureen Heseltine, Kathy Lambert, Ben McKenzie, Matt Metcalfe, Robin Moule, Roy Nelson, North Yorkshire County Record Office, Colin Priestley, Anthony Roberts, Lady Alexandra Roche, Skipton Library, Skipton Old Pictures, Alan Stockdale, John Townend and Dave Woodhead.

An especial thank you to David Joy (whose publishing expertise and insight has helped to make this book a reality), Stephen Garnett (who has been unstinting with his time and his beautiful photographs), Roger Ingham (a walking encyclopaedia of show anecdotes and memories) and the Craven Herald & Pioneer.

Plus all the unpaid helpers at the show without whom there would be no show … And all the contributors to this book without whom there would be no book.

We gratefully acknowledge the financial support of the Yorkshire Dales National Park's Sustainable Development Fund.

YORKSHIRE DALES
National Park Authority
Sustainable Development Fund

ABOUT THE AUTHORS

Victoria Benn lives and works in the Yorkshire Dales and is best known for her lifestyle feature writing published across several regional publications. Victoria has a strong family connection to Kilnsey Show through both her parents, in particular her father who has helped to run the sports there since 1959. *Studs & Crooks* is her first book.

Jamie Roberts' family have farmed the land at Kilnsey for four generations. Jamie has a strong interest in preserving Dales culture and history. He was previously Director of the National Trust on the remote island of Saint Helena and helped to save the world's rarest tree from extinction. Today he runs Kilnsey Park Estate.

Top: **Victoria aged three seated on her Grandad's knee at Kilnsey Show in 1973**
Bottom: **Jamie with Matt Metcalfe, Kilnsey's oldest living resident** © Stephen Garnett

THE SHOW IN PICTURES

Left page (clockwise from top left): A scene from the hurricane year of 1986; A one pint measure for measuring milk out of a churn; Young boy with a Holstein Friesian calf; A show catalogue from 1913; Teasdale is finally beaten and a new Crag Race record is set by Keith Clements in 1954 (Yorkshire Post and Leeds Mercury); Happy times in the sheep section © YDNPA; This plate is one of the only known relics of the original Kilnsey Feast – also known as Kilnsey Gala

Right page: Life-long horseman George Emmott with a prize winning pair in the late 1980s

Left page: Ian Waddington on his vintage tractor © Stephen Garnett

Right page (clockwise from top left): Young crag racers begin the climb © Stephen Garnett; First show report from September 10th 1897 (Craven Herald); Jim Spencer and Tommy win the working horse class in 1954; Dalesbred ram sizes up the opposition © Stephen Garnett; Victoria Wilkinson, future World Mountain Running Champion, having won the Girls Under 14 Crag Race in 1990 © Dave Woodhead

UPPER WHARFEDALE AGRI-CULTURAL SOCIETY.

SHOW AT KILNSEY.

The newly formed Upper Wharfedale Agricultural Society promoted their first annual show on Tuesday at Kilnsey. There was a certain element of novelty in the venture, and there were not a few who, when the idea was mooted, were somewhat sceptical of the result. However, the committee, who were fortunate in having for their secretary and treasurer a gentleman of Mr G. E. Clayton's calibre, determined to proceed with the undertaking, and it must be admitted that they achieved a gratifying success. So far as the stock was concerned there was every reason for congratulation, and it will not be overstepping the bounds of prudence if we predict for what has already come to be popularly known as Kilnsey Show, an increasing measure of success and a much enlarged sphere of operations next year. It is admitted that a good show of this character has inherent possibilities

Left page (clockwise from top left): Sharing a good joke © Stephen Garnett; PC 'George' Rose from Skipton on traffic duty in the late 1960s (Wendy Gibson); Lambs awaiting judging; Fred Reeves and *Emmerdale Farm's* Frazer Hines (aka Joe Sugden) in 1975; Runners descending the infamous 'chimney' © Dave Woodhead; The traditional bowler hat originally worn by the show's judges; The fun fair in the earliest days of the show c1900 (Ben McKenzie)

Right page: Ornately carved walking sticks © Stephen Garnett

The Strange Origin of Kilnsey Show by M'DUKE MILLER

Nothing short of a war can stop Kilnsey Show, which is a great event in the Dalesman's calendar. Whether or not the Show will be held this year is now under discussion, and a meeting of the Show Committee is to be held in June to make a final decision. In this article our contributor tells the story of its strange beginnings.

Morning Star is the apple of Mick's eye and it follows that his thoughts travel more that once to his precious charge in his more expansive mements when dominoes have given place to song, recitation and step-dance. The bar parlour rings to the applause of these men who know how to enjoy the simple pleasures of life and they join with gusto in rousing choruses.

"The wood lies low in the valley O" is among the favourites and the company revel in its repetition as each chorus produces an added phrase until the final line takes one from the yolk in the egg by easy yet vociferous stages to the nest on the twig and back to the wood that lies low in the valley O.

Mr. "Willie" Robinson, of Kettlewell

Left page: The showfield watches as the runners ascend in 1978 (Roger Ingham)

Right page (clockwise from top left): A Swaledale tup; Front cover of *Dalesman* magazine September 1982; Young girl leading a calf; Traditional fell running boots – lighter running shoes became available in the late 1960s; A muddy year brings a touch of Glastonbury to Kilnsey; An article about the origins of the show appeared in *Dalesman* in 1940; Traditional sheep shears

Left page (clockwise from top left): Competitors awaiting the sheep judge © Stephen Garnett; Traditional sheep shearing moccasins provide extra grip to prevent the shearer from slipping; The 440 Yards in the late 1960s; 1950s trotting in a trilby hat before the sport became more regulated; A harness racer's silk cap

Right page An old-timer enjoys the show © Stephen Garnett

GLOSSARY

BACK MARK – in a handicapped race the 'back mark' refers to starting from 'scratch' or the position furthest back in the line-up; whereas other runners may have a starting point of five, ten, or fifty yards / metres etc

BATTER – the degree of taper in a drystone wall

BAY HORSE – brown horse

BOOKIES – colloquial term for book makers and 'turf accountants'

CAN AND MEASURES – the term refers to measuring milk out of a milk churn with pint and half pint measures into a householder's own jugs before the introduction of bottled milk

CHEAP JACK – unauthorised trader who sets up a stall or game amongst the crowd

COLT – young male horse

CONFORMATION – the shape and structure of an animal

CONSOLATION RACE – a race for those horses that didn't qualify for the final

FEATHER – the long hair on the legs of most breeds of heavy horse

FILLY – young female horse

FLAPPING MEETING – unregistered or unauthorised horse race

FORAGER – a farm implement that harvests forage plants to make silage (also known as a forage harvester, silage harvester or chopper)

GALLOPS – flat horse racing

HALTER TRAINED – the practice of training cattle to walk calmly and safely on a rope

HANDS – the unit of measurement used to measure the height of horses in most English-speaking countries. It was originally based on the breadth of a human hand, and one 'hand' equates to 101.6mm. It may be abbreviated to "h" or "hh" e.g. 13.2 hands – thirteen-two hands high

HEIFER – a cow that has not yet borne a calf, or has only borne one calf

HOCKS – the upper part of a sheep's or horse's hind legs

HOPPLES – a harness which keeps the legs of a horse in a trotting gait

IN SERVICE – when a mare is at her most fertile

PRIME LAMB – lamb that is sold for its meat

QUOITS – a traditional Yorkshire Dales game which involves the throwing of rings over a spike

RIGGING OUT – digging out (for instance the foundation of a wall)

SCOTCH EWE – traditionally the name given to all the hardy hill breeds of (female) sheep

STANDARDBRED – the particular breed of horse most suited to the sport of harness racing

STINT – the length of drystone wall to be built

SULKY – lightweight two-wheeled cart used in harness racing

SUMMERING – the practice of turning cattle out onto the pastures in the high Dales in summertime

THE FETCH – when a sheepdog brings the sheep to the handler's feet

THE LIFT – when the sheepdog starts to bring the sheep down the field towards the handler

THE OUTRUN – when a handler sends their dog out from their feet to circle round behind a flock of sheep

THROUGH STONES – long stones which stretch across the two sides of a drystone wall, helping to tie them together

TUP – male sheep, or ram

TURN-OUT – refers to the harness that a horse wears to allow it to pull various horse drawn vehicles, such as a dray, cart, wagon or plough

VANNER – a heavy horse which is less than 16.2 hands in height

YEARLING – year old horse

CRAG RACE WINNERS – MEN

1897 William 'Bill' Simpson from Buckden

1898 Jim Stubbs from Grassington

1899 Jim Stubbs from Grassington

1900 Jim Stubbs from Grassington

1901 Jim Stubbs from Grassington

1902 Robert Spencer from Appletreewick

1903 Robert Spencer from Appletreewick

1904 Kavanagh from Killinghall, Harrogate

1905 Kavanagh from Killinghall, Harrogate

1906 Billy Stubbs from Grassington

1907 Tommy 'Pont' Metcalfe from Appersett, Hawes

1908 Tommy 'Pont' Metcalfe from Appersett, Hawes

1909 Tommy 'Pont' Metcalfe from Appersett, Hawes (record set of 6-01 – straight to a point on the skyline and back down again)

1910 Tommy 'Pont' Metcalfe from Appersett, Hawes

Replay needed: A photo finish of the sprint in 1955 (Roger Ingham)

1911 Tommy 'Pont' Metcalfe from Appersett, Hawes

1912 H. Shires from Threshfield

1913 Robert 'Bob' Thomas from Accrington

1914 - 1918 Show not held

1919 Will White from Carleton in Craven (unconfirmed)

1920 George Woolcock (1st time race run on similar course to today, however Woolcock fell and received a bad head injury)

1921 Gilbert Reynard from Kilnsey (race re-routed across river and up Conistone Pie this year due to previous year's injury)

1922 Arthur 'Ant' Metcalfe from Appersett, Hawes

1923 Arthur 'Ant' Metcalfe from Appersett, Hawes

1924 Arthur 'Ant' Metcalfe from Appersett, Hawes (race now following its current course)

1925 Jack Thornburn from Braithwaite, Keswick

1926 Ronnie Robinson from Finsthwaite, Newby Bridge

1927 Ronnie Robinson from Finsthwaite, Newby Bridge

1928 Jack Thornburn from Braithwaite, Keswick

1929 Jack Thornburn from Braithwaite, Keswick

1930 Ronnie Robinson from Finsthwaite, Newby Bridge

1931 Ronnie Robinson from Finsthwaite, Newby Bridge

1932 Ronnie Gilpin from Braithwaite, Keswick

1933 Billy Conkey, from Lorton, Keswick

1934 Ronnie Robinson from Finsthwaite, Newby Bridge

1935 Wilson Huck from Scotforth, Lancaster

1936 R. W. Andrews from Ross-on-Wye

1937 Ronnie Gilpin from Braithwaite, Keswick

1938 Johnny Dawson from Ambleside

1939 - 1944 Show not held

1945 Jimmy Staveley from High Bentham

1946 Alan Hodgson from Shap Fell

1947 Stan Edmondson from Borrowdale

1948 Stan Edmondson from Borrowdale

1949 Bill Teasdale from Caldbeck

1950 Bill Teasdale from Caldbeck

1951 Bill Teasdale from Caldbeck

1952 Bill Teasdale from Caldbeck

1953 Bill Teasdale from Caldbeck

1954 Keith Clements from Kendal – new record set 8-17 (just by inches from Teasdale)

1955 Bill Teasdale from Caldbeck

1956 Keith Clements from Kendal

1957 Reg Harrison from Oxenpark, Ulverston – equalled record

1958 Bill Teasdale from Caldbeck

1959 Tony Denby from Lowgill

1960 Reg Harrison from Oxenpark, Ulverston

1961 Reg Harrison from Oxenpark, Ulverston

1962 George Broadhurst from Flookburgh

1963 Norman Beck from Skipton

1964 Norman Beck from Skipton

1965 Norman Beck from Skipton

1966 Tommy Garside from Hawkshead

1967 Reg Harrison from Oxenpark, Ulverston

1968 Reg Harrison from Oxenpark, Ulverston (the last winner in 'old fashioned' fell boots)

1969 Tommy Sedgwick from New Hutton, Kendal (the last race when all the walls were at full height and fenced on top)

1970 Tommy Sedgwick from New Hutton, Kendal

1971 Tommy Sedgwick from New Hutton, Kendal

1972 Fred Reeves from Coniston

1973 Tommy Sedgwick from New Hutton, Kendal

1974 Fred Reeves from Coniston

1975 Fred Reeves from Coniston – record set of 8-11

1976 Fred Reeves from Coniston – record set of 8-3.2

1977 Tommy Sedgwick from New Hutton, Kendal

1978 Fred Reeves from Coniston – record set of 8-1.7

1979 Fred Reeves from Coniston

1980 Kenny Stuart from Threlkeld, Keswick

1981 Kenny Stuart from Threlkeld, Keswick – record set of 7-46.5

1982 Mick Hawkins of Grassington – current record of 7-35.8

1983 Mick Hawkins from Grassington

1984 Mick Hawkins from Grassington

1985 Steven Hawkins from Grassington

1986 Steven Hawkins from Grassington

1987 John Atkinson from Ireleth, Broughton in Furness

1988 John Atkinson from Ireleth, Broughton in Furness

1989 John Atkinson from Ireleth, Broughton in Furness

1990 John Atkinson from Ireleth, Broughton in Furness

1991 John Atkinson from Ireleth, Broughton in Furness

1992 Robert Hudson from Malham

1993 Alfie Atkinson from Riddlesden, Keighley

1994 Ian Holmes from Haworth

1995 Mick Hawkins from Grassington

1996 Alfie Atkinson from Riddlesden, Keighley

1997 Steven Hawkins from Grassington

1998 Ian Holmes from Haworth

1999 Ian Holmes from Haworth

2000 Ian Holmes from Haworth

2001 Show not held because of Foot and Mouth

2002 Rob Hope from Wheelton, Chorley

2003 Rob Hope from Wheelton, Chorley

2004 Ian Holmes from Haworth

2005 Rob Hope from Wheelton, Chorley

2006 Rob Hope from Wheelton, Chorley

2007 Rob Hope from Wheelton, Chorley

2008 Rob Hope from Wheelton, Chorley

2009 Rob Hope from Wheelton, Chorley

2010 Rob Hope from Wheelton, Chorley

2011 Ted Mason from Appletreewick

2012 Rob Hope from Wheelton, Chorley

2013 Simon Bailey from near Macclesfield

2014 Simon Bailey from near Macclesfield

2015 Simon Bailey from near Macclesfield

A classic battle: John Atkinson narrowly beating Steve Carr in 1987 (Roger Ingham)

"Whoever comes in first gets an ovation like an Olympic champion — and if it's an exciting battle to the wire the commentator will go up another crescendo!"

Mick Hawkins quickly takes the lead in the 1982 Crag Race (Roger Ingham)

CRAG RACE WINNERS – WOMEN

1984 Fiona Thompson from Cowling

1985 - 1987 No women ran

1988 Kirstin Bailey from Keighley

1989 Fiona Thompson from Cowling

1990 Kirstin Bailey from Keighley

1991 Theresa Stanforth from Barnoldswick

1992 Tamara Hird from Silsden

1993 Kirstin Bailey from Keighley

1994 Kirsty Lowther from Gargrave

1995 Helen Sedgwick from Burton in Lonsdale

1996 Jean Shotter from north Leeds

1997 Karen Slater from Kelbrook

1998 Karen Slater from Kelbrook

1999 Karen Slater from Kelbrook

2000 Jo Prowse from Ilkley

2001 Show not held

2002 Kirstin Bailey from Keighley

2003 Kirstin Bailey from Keighley

2004 Helen Sedgwick from Burton in Lonsdale

2005 Helen Sedgwick from Burton in Lonsdale

2006 Kirstin Bailey from Keighley

2007 Lisa Lacon from Holmfirth

2008 Lisa Lacon from Holmfirth

2009 Helen Ilsley from Ilkley

2010 Gill Myers from Wharfe Valley

2011 Gill Myers from Wharfe Valley

2012 Lucy Needham from Saltaire

2013 Caroline Lambert from Wetherby

2014 Caroline Lambert from Wetherby

2015 Caroline Lambert from Wetherby

1990 Ladies champion Kirstin Bailey in the infamous 'chimney' © Dave Woodhead

SHOW PRESIDENTS

1897 Mr James Hammond

1898 Mr James Hammond

1899 Lieut. Colonel H. P. Dawson

1900 Lieut. Colonel H. P. Dawson

1901 Mr C. A. L. Swale

1902 Captain R. F. Roundell

1903 Mr Clement Holdsworth

1904 Mr Clement Holdsworth

1905 Mr Ottiswell Robinson

1906 Mr W. A. Procter

1907 Captain R. F. Roundell

1908 Mr James Hammond

1909 The Duke of Devonshire

1910 The Rev. Trevor Basil Woodd

1911 Mr G. E. Clayton

1912 Mr G. B. Holdsworth

1913 Lieut. Colonel H. P. Dawson

1914 - 1918 Show not held

1919 Sir J. C. Horsfall

1920 Sir Ellis Denby

1921 Sir Ellis Denby

1922 Colonel R. F. Roundell MP

1923 Sir Ellis Denby

1924 Mr Ottiswell Robinson

1925 Mr Bird

1926 Mr G. B. Holdsworth

1927 Mr James Roberts

1928 Mr James Roberts

1929 Mr G. B. Holdsworth

1930 Mr G. B. Holdsworth

1931 Mr William Roberts

1932 Mr William Roberts

1933 Mr T. W. Irving

1934 Mr T. W. Irving

1935 Mr William Roberts

1936 Mr William Roberts

1937 Mr William Roberts

1938 Mr W. Beckett Henderson

1939 Mr W. Beckett Henderson

1940 - 1944 Show not held

1945 Capt. W. Beckett Henderson

1946 Capt. W. Beckett Henderson

1947 Mr William Roberts

1948 Lieut. Col. George Butcher

1949 Mr William Holdsworth

1950 Major J. T. Bairstow

1951 Mr M. W. Dalton

1952 Mr William Roberts

1953 Mr William Roberts

1954 Mr William Roberts

1955 Mr William Holdsworth

1956 Mr James Procter

Dennis Robinson setting the Under 17 Crag Race record in 1959 © Colin Priestley

1957 Mr James Procter

1958 Mr William Roberts

1959 Mr William Roberts

1960 Mr William Roberts

1961 Major M. W. V. Hammond Maude

1962 Mr Stephen Butcher

1963 Mr Stephen Butcher

1964 Mr Stephen Butcher

1965 Mr W. Beckett Henderson

1966 Mr Anthony Roberts

1967 Mr Anthony Roberts

1968 Mr Ronald Bray

1969 Mr Ronald Bray

1970 Mr James Procter

1971 Mr James Procter

1972 Mr Peter Roberts

1973 Mr Peter Roberts

1974 Mr Charlie Kitching

1975 Mr Charlie Kitching

1976 Mr Dawes Carlisle

1977 Mr Dawes Carlisle

1978 Mr John Bainbridge

1979 Mr John Bainbridge

1980 Mr Bernard Close

1981 Mr Bernard Close

1982 Mr Anthony Roberts

1983 Mr Anthony Roberts

1984 Mr William Mason

1985 Mr William Mason

1986 Mr Jeff Dibb

1987 Mr Jeff Dibb

1988 Mr Walter Walker

1989 Mr Walter Walker

1990 Mr Jim Falshaw

1991 Mr Jim Falshaw

1992 Mr Anthony Dean Sr.

1993 Mr Anthony Dean Sr.

1994 Mr Jimmy Lambert

1995 Mr Jimmy Lambert

1996 Mr Alan Huck

1997 Mr Alan Huck

1998 Mr Jim Caygill

1999 Mr Jim Caygill

2000 Mr Russell Carlisle

2001 Show not held

2002 Mr Russell Carlisle

2003 Mr Bill Foster

2004 Mr Bill Foster

2005 Mrs Pat Metcalfe

2006 Mrs Pat Metcalfe

2007 Mr Jerry Stockdale

2008 Mr Jerry Stockdale

2009 Mr Donald Carlisle

2010 Mrs Sheila Foster

2011 Mrs Sheila Foster

2012 Mr Malcolm Dibb

2013 Mr Malcolm Dibb

2014 Mr Donald Sunderland

2015 Mr Donald Sunderland

2016 Mrs Dorothy Dean

Anthony Roberts presents the Crag Race cup to Mick Hawkins in 1983 (Roger Ingham)

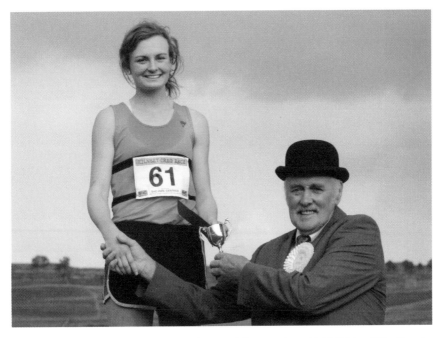

Malcolm Dibb presents Caroline Lambert with her trophy in 2013 © Dave Woodhead

Front cover: **Mick Hawkins en route to the Crag Race record in 1982** (Roger Ingham)
Back cover: **Sheep shearing at Kilnsey Show** © Stephen Garnett